THE PORTRAIT AND THE COLONIAL IMAGINARY
Photography between France and Africa, 1900-1939

Simon Dell

The Portrait and the Colonial Imaginary

Photography between France and Africa
1900–1939

Leuven University Press

ISBN 978 94 6270 215 8
D / 2020/ 1869 / 4
NUR: 694
Design: DOGMA
Cover illustration: Élie Allégret, 'Pastors Kuo, Ekollo and Modi Din, Cameroon', c. 1918–1920, photographic print, Défap, Service protestant de mission, Paris.

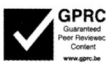

GPRC
Guaranteed
Peer Reviewed
Content
www.gprc.be

Contents

Illustrations

Acknowledgements

This rather short book was written over rather a long period of time. Therefore I am particularly grateful to my colleagues in the Department of Art History and World Art Studies at UEA for their continued encouragement and example: Jo Clarke, Jack Hartnell, Ferdinand de Jong, Ed Krčma, Sarah Monks, Dan Rycroft, and Nick Warr. I am also grateful to Veerle De Laet and the team of Leuven University Press.

Thanks also to: Aristoteles Barcelos-Neto, Sam Bibby, Elizabeth de Bièvre, Max Carocci, Neil Cox, Ella Margrethe Fyrstenberg Thomsen, Alexandra Galitzine-Loumpet, Sarah Garland, Sandy Heslop, Pat Hewitt, David Hopkins, Christian Joschke, Claire-Lise Lombard, Helen Lunnon, John Mack, John Mitchell, John Onians, Matthieu Rivallin, Anke Shürer-Ries, Hugo Thøfner, Carolyn Trench, and Bronwen Wilson.

Finally, I owe particular debts to Nick, Deborah, Ruth, Gabriel and Sarah, to Anne, Richard, Charlotte and Lucas, and to Ruth and Charlie. This book is for Margit and Ruth.

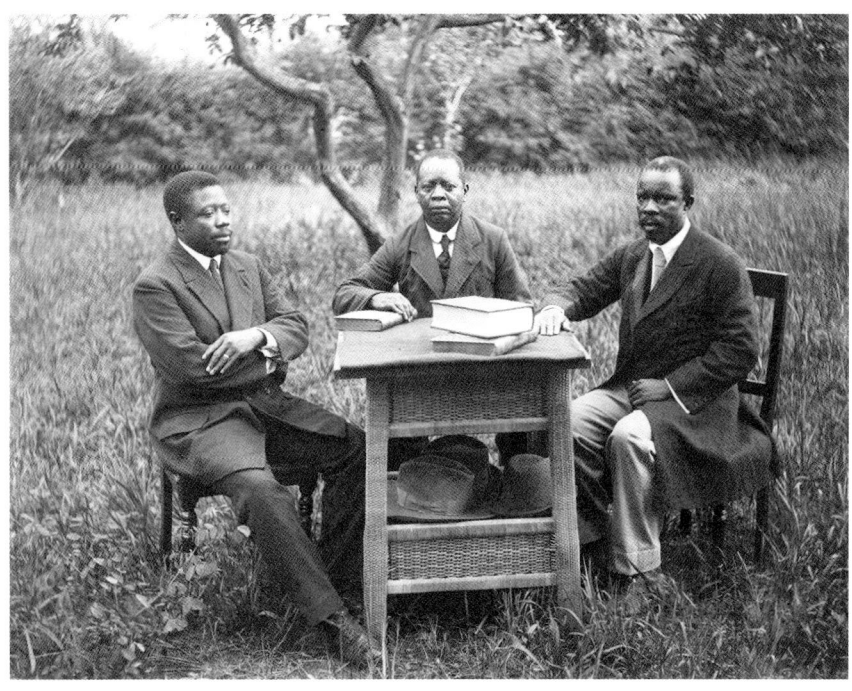

Figure 0.1. Élie Allégret, 'Pastors Kuo, Ekollo and Modi Din, Cameroon', photographic print, c. 1918–1919.

Introduction

In May 1919 the Protestant missionary Élie Allégret fell to meditating on his duties to God and the French state. In a confidential report to the committee of the
Société des Missions Évangéliques de Paris, he set down his thoughts on French
colonial policy and the role of the missionary. Writing in Fumban, Cameroon,
Allégret noted that "colonial policy has become much more liberal; today, one
acknowledges the rights of natives in their homelands; one would like to give
them a role in the administration".[1] However, he also felt obliged to register that
secular programmes of education had failed to equip the "natives for such roles.
Whilst the educated inhabitants of the French colonies may have abandoned
their former cults, they have embraced only the 'most confused sense (...) of the
Rights of Man'."[2] And so he continues: "one searches in vain for men capable
of collaborating in the moral and economic development of the country. As one
administrator said to me: 'Your role is to give us men, only you can do it'".[3] It is
not surprising that Allégret should wish to record these comments for the benefit of his superiors. His task as a missionary was to convert, to bring indigenous
populations to Christ. If, in fulfilling that task, he would also help to form a
cohort of educated "natives" who could and would collaborate with the colonial
administrators, then he was only demonstrating the obvious and manifold benefits of his mission.

From Allégret's point of view, members of the educated cohort were exemplary, and, as a consequence, they became eligible for portrayal. Certainly, this
was the case for three of his friends, the Pastors Kuo, Ekollo and Modi Din, who
posed so that Allégret could take their photograph, probably either in 1918 or
1919 [Fig. 0.1]. In this image, the three men are neatly dressed and seated around
a small table; they have removed their hats for the photograph and stored them
on the shelf beneath the table. This formality might seem somewhat at odds with
the outdoor setting, which is not even a lawn but an unmown meadow. However,
the incongruity is perhaps part of the point.

How then is one to understand such an image? How does it represent the
educated cohort of men? Pastors such as these were usually appointed to their
offices after a long devotional journey and at the end of a lengthy process of formation, as implied by the books on the table, the largest of which is probably a
Bible. Thus one precedent for the composition of the pastors' portrait would be

the group portrait of scholars, the image showing the learned gathered to debate. Yet in such images books tend to lie open whilst in this photograph the books are closed and so are less sites of contention than signs of accomplishment. The three learned men remain in the Cameroon Grassfields but, at the same time, Allégret represents them as having entered another world, one of Christian pastoral authority. In many ways, the work of this photograph is to register the distance travelled by the pastors.

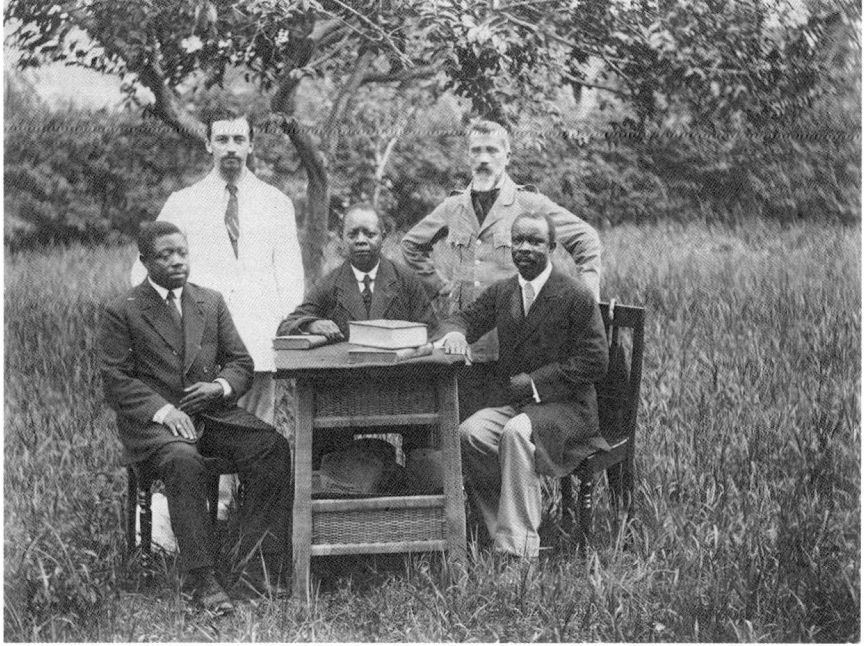

Figure 0.2. Élie Allégret, 'French missionaries and African pastors in Cameroon', photographic print, c. 1918-1919.

This photograph is now part of the archive of the Société des Missions Évangéliques de Paris; it has a pendant in the archive, showing the three pastors flanked by two missionaries [Fig. 0.2]. Allégret stands to the proper left of the seated men and his younger colleague, Charles Maître, is to the right. Maître wears the white jacket often favoured by members of the missionary schools and Allégret is uniformed because he held the rank of captain in the French army, revealing one imbrication of the mission with colonial structures of power.

There are different ways of reading the relationship between these five figures. In missionary photographs of this period, teachers tend to stand by their seated pupils and fathers by seated wives and children; Allégret was undoubtedly familiar with such pictorial conventions. So here he is figured as a father of his flock, and the photograph therefore claims a place alongside other images of patriarchal authority. Even so, the picture should not be understood reductively, as a diagram of uninflected colonial power, for this would be to see Allégret's photography far too much from the outside. The first of the two photographs may well have been intended for use by the missionary society while the second may have been made as a souvenir for the African pastors, a token of their friendship with Allégret and Maître. Or it might have been the other way around; the point is simply that the existence of two variant photographs suggests different uses and different configurations of social relations. In the early twentieth century, as now, photography was often called on to participate in rituals of solemnisation and so often marked out gradations of formality and familiarity. A pertinent analogy for Allégret's images might be found in a series of photographs taken at a wedding, beginning with the newly married couple and growing to include ever more friends and ever more family members, ever more distantly related.

In missionary photographs such as Allégret's the private and the public are not very readily separated. A good missionary should serve as an exemplary figure for his flock and his relationship with his family was thus also a model. Accordingly, the missionary's house and its immediate surroundings were stages for playing out these roles, with some liminal spaces, such as the verandah, used for performances that could move smoothly enough between the private and the public.[4] This fluidity is one of the reasons why it is difficult to assign any particular photograph by Allégret to a specific role. In the case of the pastors' two portraits, it seems that both poses and props have been transferred from interior to exterior. This is unlikely to have been done for reasons of convenience. If the missionary house was one stage for performance, the unmown meadow could be recognised as another. Allégret and his friends were certainly able to turn such a setting into a metaphor. When Allégret arrived in Fumban after the First World War to re-establish the French Protestant mission, he recorded the grateful words of one of the faithful: "We were lost in the wilderness, you have come and we are rescued. Do not abandon us now!"[5] If, in transcribing this, Allégret allowed himself to be cast as a saviour, in making the photographs he perhaps gave similar roles to the pastors; this could be one way of accounting for the incongruity between their poses and their surroundings. After all, had the pastors not endured a long struggle towards Christ? And was this not done in order to rescue others?

Of course, Kuo, Ekollo and Modi Din had their own agency and their own authority; the latter, to take just one example, played an important role in re-establishing Allégret's mission in Fumban.[6] This must be acknowledged and, accordingly, the two photographs should not be collapsed into a single perspective on the colonial encounter. Yet nor should they be held too far apart. Allégret certainly considered there to be a hierarchy of educators and those who were to be educated, and his photographs have a negotiated place in this hierarchy. He seems to have been content enough with this, as is made clear by his decision to present himself in uniform.

A version of Allégret's confidential report eventually found its way into print in 1923 in the form of an essay in the *International Review of Mission*. As one would expect, here he redrafted his earlier account in order to conjoin or articulate more firmly the work of the missionaries with that of the French state. He wanted to make explicit the contribution that the missionaries were making, and still had to make, to the creation of a Greater France:

> A request often made before has been repeated to me in one way or another with growing insistence: 'Give us your aid. This is the moment when all men of goodwill must come together to mould the France of tomorrow. We need a picked race, and you alone can really give them that moral education without which we run the risk of producing only failures.'[7]

The stake here is not simply the development of Cameroon but of France. And the logic is clear: the making of "a picked race" of men will be the making of a glorious future France and the former task has to precede the latter. Thus Allégret saw his missionary work as political as well as religious; his efforts were enabling the greater work of the French Third Republic and he quotes the French minister for the colonies, Albert Sarraut, precisely to this effect: "We do not oppress, we liberate."[8] In fact, Sarraut's views were not entirely congruent with Allégret's but, nevertheless, the colonial minister also saw his work as a creative one of shaping, moulding and sculpting. In a striking metaphor of 1921, Sarraut noted of his colonial policy: "It models the face of a new humanity from the shapeless clay of the primitive masses."[9] Here a higher power is imagined at work on an Adamic clay; such is the project of moulding the France of tomorrow. But what was entailed in this making of men? My central concern in this book is to answer this question, which I understand as an ethical one. A second question is implicit in the first. One cannot simply ask: what does it mean to conceive of and model a new humanity? The further question is: what did it mean to find oneself so conceived? One can perhaps already glimpse part of the answer in the portraits of the pastors.

Frantz Fanon and Aimé Césaire offered their own answers to this twofold question long ago (and here the former quotes the latter):

> I begin to suffer from not being a white man to the degree the white man imposes discrimination on me, makes me a colonized native, robs me of all my worth, all individuality, tells me that I am a parasite on the world, that I must bring myself as quickly as possible into step with the white world, 'that I am a brute beast, that my people and I are like a walking dung-heap that disgustingly fertilizes sweet sugar cane and silky cotton, that I have no use in the world (...).'[10]

This is how it feels to be treated as shapeless clay. And yet it cannot simply be assumed that the pastors in Fumban would have shared this view. They could be described as having been baptised into a "white man's religion", insofar as Christianity came to the Grassfields with the Germans, but this a very narrow description. Their experiences were not the same as Fanon's and I shall not attempt to make one the explanation of the other. There are many experiences and many ways of making men. There are also many uses of the available materials. It follows that it would be unwise to condemn European modes of representation as straightforward mechanisms of oppression, as mere means of adequating the colonised to the colonisers' ideal; this seems too hasty a judgement on the images of the pastors. Nevertheless, it would be wrong to dismiss as empty Sarraut's metaphor of modelling "the face of a new humanity", for he was in earnest. What I want to show is the importance of this metaphor of modelling. It was central to the French imagining of their colonial task.

The shape of the project

The present book addresses the period when the French empire reached its greatest extent, that is to say, the first four decades of the twentieth century. The French state celebrated what would transpire to be the apogee of empire with the *Exposition colonial internationale* of 1931, but the interwar period also saw the emergence of new forms of anti-colonial struggle. I want to examine both the structure of French colonialism and the challenges posed to it and to do so I will attend to the fissures and failures of a set of photographic projects, focusing on three moments in which photography played a crucial role in mediating relations between France and Africa. Across the three principal chapters of this book my perspective moves from that of the French in Africa, to that of Africans in France, and finally to that of Africans as they encountered the French in Africa. Juxtaposing these perspectives seems to me the most effective way of addressing the twofold question raised by colonisers' attempts to make a new humanity.

This task of modelling humanity is outlined in the first chapter. I argue that its matrix is the great formula of *liberté, égalité, fraternité*, and my contention is that under the Third Republic — and above all under the ministries of Jules Ferry in the 1880s — this formula became entwined with a French mission to assist "oppressed" races towards civilisation. Ferry sought to secure the liberation of France and this example was to be spread across the world; an ideology of liberation — a Republican imaginary — was to find its fulfilment in a colonial imaginary.

If France was to be exemplary in fulfilling this task, so also were Frenchmen. Thus my first sketch of the colonial imaginary is complemented by an account of portraiture as the art of the exemplary. An exemplar is precisely a model and, as Sarraut well understood, models have a central place in the colonial project. Allégret and Maître clearly felt it their duty to act as models of this kind, and so also, in their own way, did Kuo, Ekollo and Modi Din. Their portraits were to take their place in a longer tradition of imaging the self, a European tradition which involves a quite specific convergence of personhood and pictorial procedures.

The following three chapters tease out the implications of this European tradition, in three case studies. The first examines the journey of André Gide and Marc Allégret — Élie's son — through central Africa. This journey stretched from July 1925 to May 1926; Gide's meticulous and sometimes anguished record was published in two volumes, *Voyage au Congo* and *Retour du Tchad*. For his part, Marc Allégret made a 114-minute film during the course of the journey and also took some 2000 photographs (64 of which were reproduced in an illustrated edition of Gide's journal). In different ways, these records work and rework the tropes of European exploration and of the African journey as a voyage of discovery and self-discovery. A crucial part of this process was the uncovering of the various abuses perpetrated by the companies holding state concessions for rubber production. On his return to France, Gide was to lead a fight against their corrupt practices and, as such, he contributed to nascent anti-colonial campaigns. Yet Gide's attitude to colonialism was profoundly ambivalent and for this reason his texts are particularly revealing of the many tensions and contradictions within the French colonial imaginary. There is a cognate ambivalence in the images that Allégret made during the African journey. Some follow established conventions for the depiction of the colonised whilst others occupy much more unstable positions. Here the very category of the portrait is put under pressure.

My second case study is shorter but pivotal. It addresses the *Exposition coloniale* of 1931, an event intended to showcase the successes of the French colonial project at its centenary. In its realisation, this exhibition had a much more fraught history than its predecessors, in part because the French Communist party had by this date taken up much more actively the anti-colonial campaign to which Gide had already contributed. The exhibition may be understood as the converse of the African journey; if the latter could be presented as a movement through an exotic spectacle, in the former exotic peoples were transported to Paris to be displayed. While such displays had previously been accommodated in earlier exhibitions, even as recently as the *Exposition nationale coloniale* of 1922, in 1931 the use of human exhibits was contested. Now there was a new resistance to being made into a representation, to being treated as an image.

The final chapter explores further the experience of the colonised. Returning to the Grassfields and Élie Allégret's mission, this chapter traces the history of the Bamum of the Cameroon Grassfields; it examines how Ibrahim Njoya, King of the Bamum, appropriated European modes and practices after his first contact with German forces in 1902. He adopted European uniforms for his troops, built palaces in European styles, developed new forms of art patronage, posed for numerous photographs and sometimes practiced photography himself so as to make self-portraits. Through analysing this material, I demonstrate how the Bamum sought to negotiate the terms of their encounter with the Germans, the British and, finally, the French, who effectively dismantled the Bamum Kingdom and then exiled Njoya in 1931. The chapter concludes with an analysis of Njoya's own history of the Bamum and the portraits accompanying this text. Here photographic materials were appropriated and turned to new ends.

Taken together these chapters probe the ways in which colonised subjects participated in or resisted portrayal. A brief epilogue returns to metropolitan France in 1935, following the journey of Charles Atangana, who a few years previously had been Njoya's host during his exile. Atangana's visit coincided with a major exhibition of material from Cameroon at the Musée du Trocadéro in Paris; here he was photographed contemplating one of Njoya's thrones. He was in a number of respects an exemplary viewer. Contemplating his image allows me to return to the implications of portraiture, the business of looking, and the making of men.

In each of the three case studies the photographic record offers a particular point of entry to an exploration of the colonial encounter.[11] There are good reasons for taking such an approach. Okwui Enwezor and Octavio Zaya have argued that photography has played *the* key role in creating "visual fictions of the African continent", and from this it follows that there are particular benefits in studying photographs generated in this context.[12] Yet this also throws up quite specific problems. Photographs were part of a broader traffic between the metropole and the colonies, and in order to understand how they operated it is necessary to address the quite different ways in which they mediated the colonial encounter.

The status of photography as a mediating practice had been secured with the ascendancy of Fox Talbot's positive-negative process over the Daguerreotype. With this process photographic prints could be readily multiplied and the possibilities this created were quickly seized on, beginning with the range of uses Fox Talbot demonstrated in the first photographic book, *The Pencil of Nature*, published between 1844 and 1846. In the following decades various experimenters tried to find new ways to exploit Fox Talbot's process. The experiments were largely concerned with speed, from increasing the speed with which chemicals responded to increasing the speed with which the photographic image could be reproduced alongside newsprint. Such increases created new aesthetic and commercial possibilities; photography's mediations diversified, above all through developments in the technology of the printing press (from the duo-tone process to variants of rotogravure). As a result, by the beginning of the twentieth century most viewers encountered photographs not as individual prints but as reproductions, as postcards, or in books, newspapers and the periodical press.[13] With these developments photography became far more ductile than other media, more readily conscripted to other discursive practices and also, for this reason, subject to specific disciplinary measures.[14]

Portrait photography necessarily shares this ductility and so I have chosen to examine it not as an independent or coherent category but rather in its interactions with other visual and textual practices. If, in Gide's account, portraiture appears in many respects an import into Africa, it was closer to a prerogative in the colonial exhibition, where it was one aspect mediating relations between centre and periphery, between metropole and colony. And yet for Njoya in the Cameroon Grassfields the situation was different again, as photography could be appropriated according to a specific, indigenous, logic of practice. Portraits — like people — work differently in different contexts.

The shape of the field

In recent years there have been a number of attempts to move the discipline of art history beyond the horizon of the European. There has been a great increase of interest in global art history and world art studies, and there have been significant efforts to understand the entire compass of artistic traditions. Ambitious pan-cultural accounts (as opposed to merely comprehensive surveys) have sought to establish frameworks which might embrace all artistic traditions without distinction or hierarchy.[15] Such frameworks have considerable merit and have been taken up — albeit in different ways and sometimes rather loosely — to write new histories of exchange, appropriation and negotiation. My studies of the photographic mediation of France and Africa are intended as a contribution to this work.

Narratives of photography in Africa and of photography by Africans have also been carefully reassessed and these histories are now much more closely intertwined, a result of critical engagements with photography in the wake of the slow process of decolonisation. In this context, the first reassessments of the problematic relationships between photography and anthropology came in the late 1980s.[16] There followed a number of critical studies examining the relations between photography and colonialism.[17] Subsequently, there have been attempts to establish more nuanced accounts of interaction.[18] These latter studies were impelled at least in part by recognition of the work of African photographers, a recognition in turn stimulated by an archival impulse in contemporary African photographic practices.[19] So recent work in the history of photography has produced much more complex views of the different agencies implicated in the colonial encounter. This review of agency brings the history of photography closer to recent histories of empire and recent histories of anthropology.[20] If this postcolonial scholarship has not yet had its full impact in France, it has nevertheless stimulated a vitally important engagement with the French colonialism and its afterlife.[21]

Much of this critical work has attempted to move beyond the binarism of coloniser and colonised. In fact, this was a task already addressed in Albert Memmi's work of 1957, emphatically titled *The Colonizer and the Colonized*. Yet there remains the challenge to the historian to "treat metropole and colony in a single analytical field".[22] Whilst it is a challenge that has long been recognised, it has not always been adequately met. This, finally, has implications for how one should organise such work.

Ethics and structure

The twofold question — of what it means to make men and what it means to find oneself so created — addresses an act in which the other is remade in the image of the self. The issues involved here have been carefully examined in the work of Emmanuel Levinas, perhaps most pertinently in *Totality and Infinity*. In that book, Levinas distinguishes between absolute and formal alterity, a distinction which is fundamental to his view of ethics. He acknowledges that the very world we inhabit is other in relation to us, and may appear foreign and hostile, but he describes this otherness as merely formal because "this alterity falls under my powers", it falls under "the *sway* of the I".[23] Here the other is reduced to the same, to what Levinas identifies in Hegelian phenomenology as the "imperialism of the same".[24] Absolute alterity escapes this grasp. The absolutely other is free. "Over him I have no *power*."[25] The relation with the absolutely other is produced for Levinas "as a *face to face*".[26] Consequently, the face-to-face relationship calls into question the very notion of sameness, and this is what Levinas names ethics. "The strangeness of the Other, his irreducibility to the I, to my thoughts and my possessions, is precisely accomplished as a calling into question (...) as ethics."[27]

The production of such ethical relations is inhibited — to say the least — by the structures of colonialism. Under colonisation, with the recognition of otherness there is also an attempt to overcome difference. The relation between coloniser and colonised is one of formal alterity because in this relation the other falls under the sway of the colonising power. The colonised are to be remade, divested of absolute alterity, produced as a usable other.

Resisting this, Levinas argues that in the ethical relation the other is recognised as such. The historian must attempt to reach towards this recognition, and this is my reason for asking the twofold question concerning the making of men. It is also why addressing this question entails moving between France and Africa, and between different perspectives without, I hope, reifying them. Of course, it is necessarily also the case that my responses will not have a conventional rhetorical coherence; the different studies in this book will seem in some regards to be quite separate texts. Yet operating with such divisions is a means of at least indicating the responsibility to the other presented in the philosophy of Levinas.[28] What follows, then, is in a number of ways a fragmented and fraught account. It is fragmented because different positions need to be respected. And it is fraught because I seek to offer not simply a narrative of colonial operations but also an account of their contestation. Tracing this has demanded working at a level of detail which should itself be taken as a methodological principle, for the detail

is part of what serves to create friction. Whilst I believe I have consulted a sufficient range of sources to generate such a level of detail, the present work does
not pretend to be exhaustive. My focus is the French colonial project elaborated
during the Third Republic; a particularly focus, then, yet also a means of bringing into view a larger picture of the entwined histories of Africa and Europe.

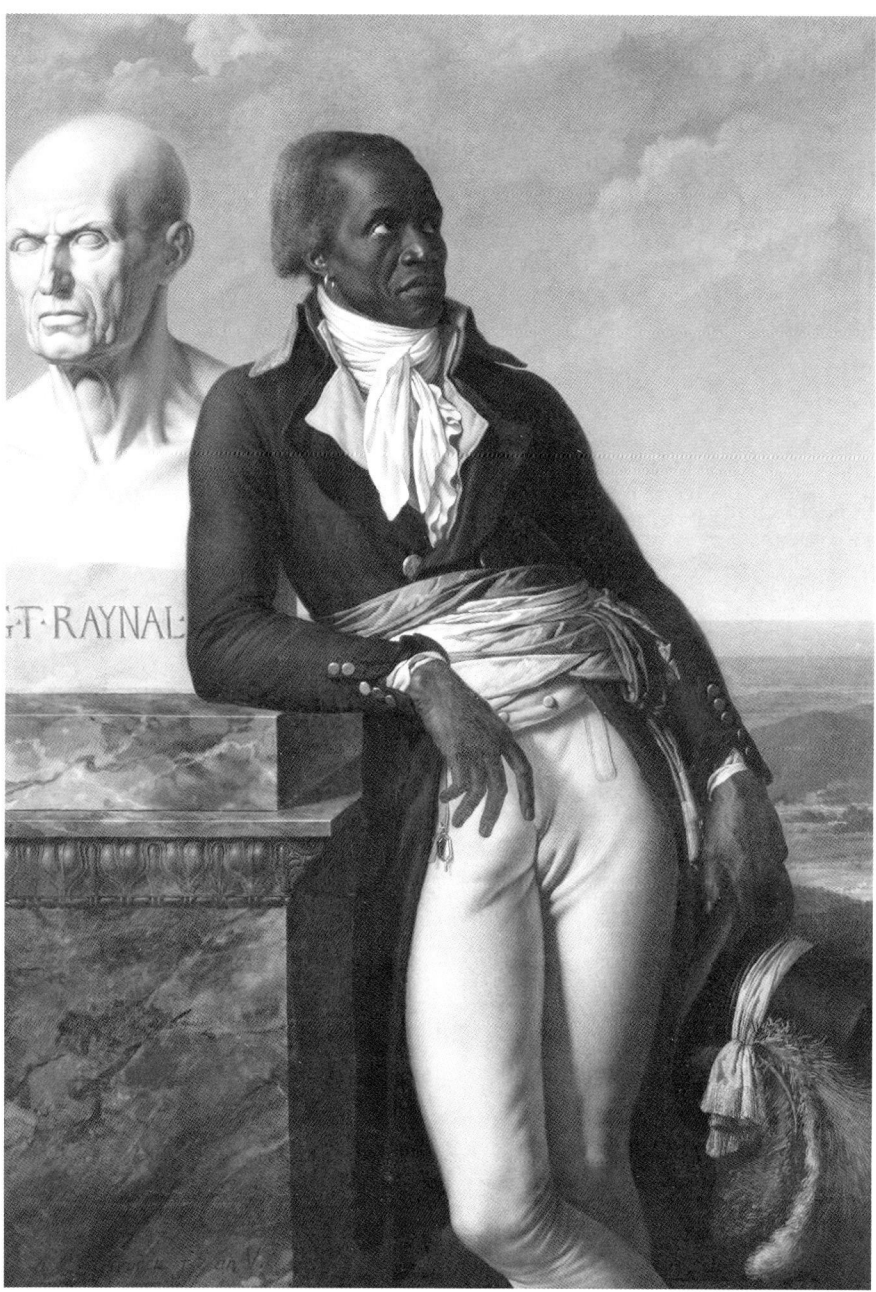

GT·RAYNAL·

Figure 1.1. Anne-Louis Girodet de Roucy-Trioson, 'Portrait of Jean-Baptiste Belley', signed, dated Year V, oil on canvas, 159×113 cm. 1797. Musée National du Château de Versailles, MV 4616.

1. Making men
Citizens and subjects

The great formula of *liberté, égalité, fraternité* was foundational for the Third Republic. The promise of the Republic was to complete of the work of the French Revolution, something which remained an urgent task for equality was not yet equally distributed. The history of the French abolition of slavery indicates this clearly enough and so reveals the vicissitudes of the colonial imaginary.

The first abolition was declared by the National Convention on 4 February 1794. This declaration was preceded by a signal event, when three delegates from the French colony of Saint-Domingue were formally introduced to the Convention. They were Louis-Pierre Dufay, Jean-Baptiste Mills and Jean-Baptiste Belley; the delegates were greeted with these words from Simon Camboulas:

> Since 1789 a great action has remained unresolved: the hereditary aristocracy and the sacerdotal aristocracy had been wiped out, but the aristocracy of skin still held sway. The latter has now expired. Equality has been ratified.[1]

By 1794 the language of revolution could generate a number of effects and in this speech the abolition of slavery is presented as rehearsing earlier moments of transformation. Following the *Declaration of the Rights of Man and of Citizens*, a further universality was now proclaimed. Skin was to have its rights.

The declaration of abolition was itself understood to make an epoch, to divide a past and its prejudices from the present and its equalities. To enact and secure such divisions were the great revolutionary tasks and Citizen Belley had played his part here. He was a revolutionary and was to be figured as such. Accordingly, the division of past and present is crucial to the portrait of Belley completed by Anne-Louis Girodet in 1797 [Fig. 1.1]. Nonchalant in pose and dressed in the costume of a representative of the people — with tricolour sash and cockade — Belley is shown leaning against a plinth supporting a bust of Guillaume Thomas Raynal. The latter was the author of *L'Histoire philosophique et politique du commerce et des établissements des Européens dans les deux Indes*, a text which amongst other things condemned the treatment of slaves in the colonies. Raynal had died the

year before Girodet's painting was finished and the inclusion of his bust serves
as his memorial, and as a commemoration of his resistance to the injustices
meted out to former slaves such as Belley. So there is in the painting an acknowledgement of past iniquities, but there is also an emphatic signalling of the revolutionary present; Girodet depicts Belley in the costume of a deputy and shows
that the black population of Saint-Domingue has won political representation.
Belley had been instrumental in this victory; he had been an infantry captain and
had taken part in the revolt led by Toussaint Louverture which would result in
the founding of Haiti. He had asserted his rights. Yet what were the conditions
for his portrait's division of past and present? And how might Belley have understood his image in 1797? Sketching a response to these questions will serve to
introduce the larger themes of this chapter.

Belley is relaxed and his gaze is slightly elevated but somewhat abstracted;
combined with his proximity to the bust of the *philosophe* this might suggest the
model of the individual scholar portrait. (Girodet was familiar with this format,
as is shown by his portrait of Giuseppe Favrega of 1795.) Yet Belley is standing,
not seated at a desk, and is without the accoutrements of pen and paper. And
nor is he ensconced in a study. Belley and the bust are positioned on an emi-
nence commanding a view to a distant shore. So if features of the painting might
evoke the scholar portrait, this model is not secure. Whilst it would be tempting
to ascribe this to an instability or equivocation in Belley's status, this is, I think,
a temptation to be resisted.[2]

Almost nothing is known of the portrait's genesis and so one cannot appeal
to the details of a commission to establish firm foundations for an interpretation.
However, it is clear that Belley was properly sensible of his own status; in Paris
the deputy from Saint-Domingue made eligibility for portrayal — the right to
representation — a significant part of his political campaigning. In denouncing
the anti-abolitionist deputy Benoît Gouli, Belley emphatically rejected what he
described as Gouli's "bizarre portrait" of blacks.[3] Gouli had compared the colonised to brutes and reproached them "for *having souls without physiognomy*"; in
making this charge he had recourse to the familiar racist claim that blacks were
lesser beings and that whatever souls they might possess were barely discernible
as such.[4] So in important respects, for Gouli blacks were unrepresentable. Belley
did not simply refute this charge; instead his tactic was to draw on the language
of revolution and make an inversion. He denounced Gouli's reproach as perverse,
asserting that to deny the humanity of the enslaved was "to profane nature" and
was moreover to contest the laws of the Republic and reject the "sublime decree"
of 4 February 1794.[5] Equally, it was to flout the *Declaration of the Rights of Man*.

Those who chose to do so renounced their own humanity. As such they could no longer be portrayed; they had disqualified themselves from representation and were, at best, mere masks. This is what Gouli revealed of himself to Belley, who concluded: "you show clearly enough that it is your physiognomy that is without a soul".[6]

Belley was intent on defending his accession to representation and Girodet's portrait may be understood as part of this defence; in effect, it figures this revolutionary accession. This is the task performed by the temporal division within the painting. Raynal's bust is commemorative but as such is oriented to the past; in contrast, the image of the deputy of Saint-Domingue belongs to the present and is oriented to the future. The painting pairs these portraits: the turn of Belley's right shoulder is matched by Raynal's left, and the verticals formed by Belley's right upper arm are aligned with the left edge of Raynal's bust. This makes an axis, a conjoining of the two portraits which constitutes them as a kind of Janus image, a *Janus bifrons*. Such images, of course, face both to the past and the future. This double orientation has various uses; it may signal a basic temporal division but may also be used to establish spatial limits. The Janus image may be used to mark a threshold, its placement creating a division at once in time and space. And indeed the bust of Raynal has the sculptural form of a herm, a boundary marker in antiquity. Girodet's pairing of portraits may be understood, then, as marking a significant threshold. Crossing this threshold is a rite of passage, insuring a change of condition or status, and this is what Belley has accomplished.[7] He has moved from slavery to freedom. And in his new condition he has won the position of deputy; he has acceded to representation in the fullest sense. The work of the painting is to mark this. It does not simply represent but *stages* the accession to representation. This is what the *Janus bifrons* achieves. Thus, if the abolition of slavery made an epoch, Girodet's painting is similarly inaugural. When greeting the deputies from Saint-Domingue, Camboulas had proclaimed equality ratified and universal rights properly extended; Girodet's painting makes a similar acknowledgement. The painter, like many others of his time, would claim his art as a "universal language", and so it was indeed only proper to extend this art to Belley's portrayal.[8] Here a universal language is used to proclaim a universal right.

Belley moved across the threshold from slavery to freedom. This movement returns me to the twofold question of what it means to conceive a new humanity, and what it means to be so conceived. Belley is liberated and portrayed as such; his image thus stands as a counter-example to the slave portrait. But there are profound difficulties with this formulation. Consider: the slave portrait is an oxymoron. As David Bindman has argued, many portraits have as their defining purpose "the affirmation of the sitter's subjectivity, autonomy, and integrity" and these are precisely qualities denied to slaves.[9] They are possessed rather than self-possessed and it follows that images of slaves will not, by strict definition, be portraits "proper". Hence the oxymoron of the slave portrait. Belley's portrait is a counter to this. Unlike so many earlier images of enslaved Africans, here Belley is unquestionably the principal subject. He is turned away from Raynal's bust and is emphatically not presented as a mere foil to the commanding figure of a white master. As noted, he is, if anything, nonchalant, and certainly not the kneeling supplicant of abolitionist imagery. However, to suggest that Belley's portrait is a sum of refusals is to define it against an other, and this is what remains problematic.

Belley's portrait belongs to a particular, and fleeting, moment. Slavery had been abolished in France in 1794 but it was reintroduced in the French colonies in 1802 and the final abolition had to await the revolutions of 1848. By that date France had acquired new colonies and also new apologists prepared to defend colonialism as an ongoing project of liberation. Whilst it might be the case that with the second abolition one term of the contradiction of the slave portrait was annulled, this did not mean that contradiction was finally resolved. Annulment is anything but resolution. And it is not surprising that the year 1848 did not herald a triumphant revival of portraiture in the mode of Girodet's image. If the second abolition of slavery marks an epoch in the history of the French colonies, it nevertheless remains a chapter *within* the history of the colonised. Those in the colonies might no longer be enslaved but they were not yet free. On the basis of all this, one may recast the question of portrayal: what did it mean to find oneself between Belley and Modi Din, between the figures of oxymoron and metaphor?

Fanon, in approaching this question, saw the colonised as between "two frames of reference", with a conflict between one set of customs and an imposed civilisation.[10] Nevertheless, in the conclusion of *Black Skin, White Masks*, Fanon refuses to be defined by these frames of reference. He refuses to be a slave of the past. He would not accept that his own actions should be confined to a "Negro mission", even if this mission was given its most heroic aspect. Alluding to the actions of Toussaint Louverture and Belley, Fanon states: "I am not responsible solely for the revolt of Saint-Domingue."[11] This is a refusal to remain caught between slavery and freedom. In one sense, this is even to refuse Belley's portrait. Of course, Fanon had excellent reasons for his refusal. Yet the questions posed by Belley's portrait persist, and not least because many people remained material for metaphor, to be shaped by those such as Allégret and Sarraut. The present chapter is concerned with this work, with what the portrait means in the coloni-al context, both as a European object and as a threshold.

A new humanity

Allégret and Sarraut thought it appropriate to describe the colonisers' task as one of sculpting and moulding a picked race. However, this is not an adequate description of the colonial encounter because this encounter was understood by some — if not by all — to be mutually transformative. Allégret certainly under-stood his own missionary work as having implications for himself. He believed that the modelling of a new humanity also required profound changes in the modeller; as he saw it, the task could only be undertaken by those prepared to dedicate themselves to God and so receive some measure of God's strength. In 1889, when Allégret had just finished his training as a missionary, he wrote as much to his ward, the young André Gide:

> God grant you, grant us both, to become more and more *men* during this year, with the strength to resist all temptation, the strength to do our duty, and at the same time the strength to have compassion for all those who suffer, in such a way that our life might be worth something.[12]

Allégret's letter is datable to early January and is clearly an attempt to encourage Gide to form appropriate resolutions for the coming year. However, Allégret was aware that in February he was due to depart for Gabon and his letter also indicates his own spiritual preparations for the work ahead of him. This involved nothing less than fulfilling Christ's missionary charge:

> And Jesus came and spoke to them, saying, 'All authority has been given to Me in heaven and on earth. Go therefore and make disciples of all the nations, baptising them in the name of the Father and of the Son and of the Holy Spirit, teaching them to observe all things that I have command-ed you; and lo, I am with you always, *even* to the end of the age.' (Matthew, 28: 18–20)

According to the theology of the Incarnation, God was made man in Christ and those who are to follow God's command should also follow this example. As I shall show, a great deal turns on this. For those such as Allégret, to make of oneself a man was to have Christ's strength and Christ's compassion; it was to recognise oneself as made in the image of God. The young Gide was evidently envious of this powerful vocation. In a letter of 30 April 1889, responding to Allégret's exhortations, Gide assured his guardian that there was no need to fear he had proffered an excess of moralising: "I am completely convinced of the need to gather one's strength before launching oneself on life."[13] This was the preparation which Allégret had undergone and Gide was full of admiration for the missionary who had "already embarked on a career, labouring for the great harvest".[14] In this context, the colonisers' task of shaping the colonised could be understood as a mission for those who had first worked to acquire the requisite moral authority. Thus whilst the colonial encounter was not imagined to be a meeting of equals, it could nevertheless be understood as transforming not just the French colonies but also metropolitan France itself. Surely, this was what Allégret had in mind when he wrote of the moulding of a Greater France.

I want to examine the implications of this by pursuing two lines of enquiry. The first concerns the consequences of rapid colonial expansion in the early years of the Third Republic. During these years the idea of producing agents to collaborate in "moral and economic development" was given a new force, as the very idea of a civilising mission was elaborated. The second line of enquiry concerns what it meant for missionaries like Allégret to imagine becoming "more and more *men*". What kind of subjectivity was imagined here? How was it to be represented? Whilst at first glance these two lines of enquiry might seem to address rather distinct sets of issues, in fact they offer two different kinds of purchase on the same phenomenon: the making of men. In turn, I want to argue that the discipline of art history can contribute a new and productive understanding of this phenomenon. This will, however, require some rethinking of the discipline, in order to position it *as* a history of subjectivity. This is what is needed if one is to understand images of the colonised together with their frames of reference.

The Republican imaginary and the colonial imaginary

Elié Allégret was a willing participant in what should be considered a distinctively French colonial enterprise, the principal architect of which was the Republican politician Jules Ferry. In France, Ferry was responsible for the laws securing freedom of association and freedom of the press, and for thus enshrining the liberties fundamental to the very notion of the French Republic.[15] The modelling of a Greater France is to be understood in this context, as a Republican project, one advanced with the greatest energy during the consolidation of the Third Republic in the 1870s and 1880s.

On 28 July 1885 Ferry rose in the Chamber of Deputies to defend his view of France's colonial duties and his own actions as an imperialist. It was during Ferry's administrations in the early 1880s that the most rapid expansion of the French empire had occurred, with the acquisition of Tunisia, the seizure of Madagascar and extension of control in Equatorial Africa and Indo-China.[16] All this activity had led to much criticism of Ferry, and he was attacked in particular for his naked opportunism. This was why his speech of 28 July had to be a powerful exposition of the principles underlying his colonial policies; he was obliged to be cogent and systematic for to be otherwise would be to play into the hands of his enemies. Accordingly, Ferry carefully laid out "the motives and the diverse interests which justify the policy of colonial expansion".[17] He wanted to present these interests within a "tripartite system of principles: economic principles, principles of the highest level of civilisation, and principles of a political and patriotic order".[18] First, Ferry made clear that the colonies had huge potential for economic development, and in particular offered scope for expanding markets, something of great importance in the new era of protectionism.[19] Yet having established as much he turned from economic considerations to humanitarian duties. In respect of the latter, "one must plainly state the fact that the superior races have rights over inferior race".[20] Of course, such notions of superior races and privileged rights were fundamental to the ideology of empire, yet Ferry's claim provoked much opposition. Jules Maigne, a Radical at the extreme left, made the obvious retort: "Oh! You dare say that in the country where the Rights of Man were proclaimed!"[21] Other deputies also protested, leading Ferry to counter: "Can you deny, can anyone deny, that there is more justice, more material and moral order, more fairness and more social virtue in North Africa since the French conquest?"[22] Ferry's reply carried echoes of earlier debates over the rights of the colonised, even though in 1885 he was turning the arguments of others to his own ends.

Already in 1791 the Abbé Grégoire had anticipated Belley in appealing to the National Assembly to grant civic and political equality to French colonial subjects, asking: "Would you really dare to say that only white men are born free and equal in rights?"[23] His question retains its force. Could the extension of order, fairness and virtue ever justify one people exercising rights over another? Ferry, at least, was in no doubt about the answer. It was precisely because France was the country of the Rights of Man that it was the ultimate duty of the French to extend to all peoples the formula of *liberté, égalité, fraternité*. Brushing aside any alternative views of the great formula, in his peroration Ferry claimed a great role for his Republicans. For in its relatively brief time in government his party had shown that:

> it quite understands that one cannot propose for France a political ideal of the sort that might be appropriate for a nation such as free Belgium or republican Switzerland; France requires something else. It is not enough for France to be a free country: France must also be a great country, it must exercise an influence over the destiny of Europe, and must spread its influence across the world[.][24]

Ferry believed that France had revealed a destiny for itself with the Revolution, and it was the duty of the Republicans, as heirs to the revolutionary Jacobins, to fulfil this destiny. To fail in this would be nothing less than a betrayal of "the greatness of France".[25]

This pursuit of empire and its elaboration as a coherent project belonged to Ferry; if it had begun with the conquest of Algeria in 1830, it was in the early years of the Third Republic that it was consolidated. During these years, what the French termed their civilising mission became closely entwined with Republican myths and ideals. Nevertheless, the mission had its own lineage. Condorcet, the last of the Encyclopedists, had used the rights of man to make cogent arguments for the abolition of slavery whilst also imagining how European nations might assist oppressed races towards civilisation.[26] So in some respects Ferry's speech was far from empty rhetoric. He was no doubt an opportunist, but he wanted to establish that the projects of French Republicanism and French colonialism were linked and that this relationship was not simply a result of temporal conjunction, or indeed, mere opportunism. Rather, for Ferry, the Republican and colonial projects rested on particular and aligned ideas of freedom. If the task for Ferry was to promote the great formula of *liberté, égalité, fraternité* across the world, it is clearly necessary to understand how this formula was used, and to understand what "freedom" meant under the Republic.

French Republicanism contains a contradiction between the juridical freedom exercised by the enfranchised and the freedom to exploit as exercised by the capitalist. This contradiction has a complex history traceable through struggles both political and economic. What follows here is merely a sketch of this history, and one which necessarily suppresses much of the complexity.[27]

As is well known, the storming of the Bastille in 1789 led, eventually, to the creation of the First Republic in 1792. Subsequently the Jacobin Constitution offered universal suffrage as the means of realising the will of the people but this was short-lived. Then the language of Republicanism was given voice again in February 1848, with the proclamation of the Second Republic. Now, as Marx observed, all classes of French society were forced "to act for themselves on the revolutionary stage".[28] However, the proletariat was soon defeated, in June 1848. The consequences of this were made clear in the constitution drafted between 4 September and 23 October of that year; it was this document which gave "political power to the classes whose social slavery it is intended to perpetuate: proletariat, peasants and petty bourgeoisie".[29] Thus Marx clearly identified the contradiction between a form of political freedom and a form of slavery.

For Marx, this social slavery was itself the product of a perceived realm of freedom and equality, that of the marketplace for labour-power. His cutting analysis of this particular marketplace revisits the language of rights and parodies the foundational *Declaration of the Rights of Man*. With reference to the second article of that *Declaration*, Marx notes:

> The sphere of circulation or commodity exchange, within whose boundaries the sale and purchase of labour-power goes on, is in fact a very Eden of the innate rights of man. It is the exclusive realm of Freedom, Equality, Property and Bentham. Freedom, because both buyer and seller of a commodity, let us say labour-power, are determined only by their free will (...). Equality, because each enters into relation with the other, as with a simple owner of commodities, and they exchange equivalent for equivalent. Property, because each disposes only of what is his own. And Bentham, because each looks only to his own advantage.[30]

The partners in the sale and purchase of labour-power are free to exchange, yet there are strict limits to this freedom. Workers have in fact only their labour-power to sell and they are therefore obliged to submit to the conditions imposed by capital. Their labour is consumed by the capitalist in production and the fruits of their labour belong to the capitalist. This, then, is a form of social slavery and it is this condition of exploitation which stands in such marked contrast to the political freedoms conferred by the constitution of 1848. In this context, *le peuple* defined as *les hommes français* (in itself a problematic category in its exclusion of women and children) are free to exercise their will as political subjects at the ballot box but *le peuple* defined as *le populaire* remain an exploited class; this was the contradiction Marx correctly identified in the Second Republic.[31] Under the Republic, "freedom" was never absolute or even straightforward. It was always

divided. Grasping this is crucial to a proper understanding of the related structures of French republicanism and French colonialism.[32]

Again, as is well known, the Second Republic was short-lived, and so the
contradiction identified by Marx did not reappear nor develop fully until after
the débâcle of the Franco-Prussian War and the capitulation of Napoleon III in
1870. The Third Republic then emerged with the suppression of the Commune
in 1871. As such this version of Republicanism is best described as a perverse
development of revolutionary Jacobinism; this is so because after the defeat of
the Communards the French bourgeoisie was victorious over both the revolutionary fractions of the working class and the vestiges of the *ancien régime*. Thus,
as Antonio Gramsci observed, "the internal contradictions in the French social
structure that took shape after 1789 were resolved, relatively speaking, only with
the Third Republic".[33] After the destruction of the Commune, democratic republican institutions could proceed more easily with the task of "softening the
antagonism between the two extremes of capital and wage-labour".[34] The revolutionary fraction had been defeated but now Republicans could hold out the
promise that the working class was to be freed by "the people" acting as political
subjects, expressing the will of the nation. Crucially, the contradiction identified
by Marx was recast as a project. "The people" as defined by class relations were
to be progressively liberated by "the people" as defined by universal suffrage,
that is, by the adult and male section of the population.

This paternalistic project of latterday Jacobinism was, in turn, meant to secure a relationship between Republican ideology and those subjected to it. I have
termed this relationship the Republican imaginary.[35] The relationship between
ideology and subject has been characterised by Louis Althusser with reference to
the relationship between the individual Christian and the Godhead, designated
as "subject" and "Subject", respectively.

> Were not men made *in the image* of God? (...) God needs men, the great
> Subject needs subjects, even in the terrible inversion of his image in them
> (when the subjects wallow in debauchery, i.e. sin).
>
> Better: God duplicates himself and sends his Son to the Earth, as
> a mere subject 'forsaken' by him (the long complaint of the Garden of
> Olives which ends in the Crucifixion), subject but Subject, man but God,
> to do what prepares the way for the final Redemption, the Resurrection of
> Christ. God thus needs to 'make himself' a man [.][36]

I am returned to the divine model for the making of men espoused by Allégret. For Althusser, this is the model for the very structure of ideology. Here is the crucial part of his account, in all its density: he argues that ideology "*subjects* the subjects to the Subject, while giving them in the Subject in which each subject can contemplate its own image (present and future) the *guarantee* that this really concerns them and Him".[37] The relationship of subject and Subject is one of apparent reciprocity, governed by rituals which ensure "the mutual recognition of subjects and Subject, the subjects' recognition of each other, and finally the subject's recognition of himself".[38]

Within the Republican imaginary, the casting of the vote at the ballot box is one such ritual of subjection, both a recognition of and acquiescence before the state. During the Third Republic, the voting individual, the enfranchised male, would perform his own citizenship and, in the process, claim his place amongst peers as one member of a polity. Moreover, in this ritual of the ballot box, the sovereignty of the popular will is enacted, democratic institutions are reproduced and the tasks of these institutions confirmed. Of course, votes may be cast for different candidates, who might have different conceptions of how the tasks of state are to be approached, yet it is this diversity which permits the act of voting to appear as if it is autonomous, an exercise of will which "really concerns" the voter.

Such is the autonomy of the citizen. In effect, in the French Republican imaginary the citizen chooses his representatives and thus helps to determine how *le peuple*, shaping the will of the nation, should approach the liberation of *le populaire* as a class. Here, as I have already noted, Ferry would play a decisive role. As well as securing freedom of the press and freedom of association, Ferry made primary education secular, free and mandatory for boys and girls; and to these achievements he added his colonial policy. All were to be understood as works of liberation. For Ferry's larger ambition was the eventual participation of all in the Republican project and one may consider his democratic institutions as designed to fulfil this ambition. Through his legislation Ferry wanted to enable exchanges between leaders and led and to permit all male citizens "to act for themselves".[39] To use Althusser's description, Ferry was "one of the high priests of the ruling ideology".[40]

From all this it should be clear that in the Republican imaginary freedom is at once present, ensured by the masculine autonomy embodied in the act of voting, and cast to the future, a prize to be pursued through ongoing sufferings and struggles. What I want to argue is that the colonial imaginary had a similar structure. France's civilising mission was to liberate "inferior races" oppressed by what was held to be their backward conditions; such conditions would be transformed by contact with the agents of progress. So there is a fundamental, constitutive relationship between Republican and colonial imaginaries because both are based on putative principles of Enlightenment and progress: the promise is that the "people" will rescue the "people" and "humanity" will elevate "humanity".[41] Ferry was certainly not the first to see this work as the exalted duty of France; it is easy to identify earlier defenders of the programme amongst the Republicans of the 1830s and 1840s.[42] Yet it was Ferry who played a crucial role in consolidating the colonial imaginary, just as he consolidated the Third Republic. However, consolidation is not necessarily completion. Ferry's project, like progress itself, was ongoing. He was happy to claim that French colonialism brought more justice and more material and moral order but, implicitly, it had not yet brought enough. A Greater France was still in the making.

The colonial imaginary renewed

Debates in the Chamber of Deputies were at some remove from the improvisations, misunderstandings and violence involved in the quotidian experiences of colonisation. Nevertheless, the claims made on the floor of the Chamber by those such as Ferry produced their own effects. The colonial imaginary may be understood as the attempt to organise the claims for justice and moral order; this was what was involved in the task of progressive liberation. Yet once articulated, the rhetoric of freedom was sometimes difficult to control; those to be liberated could use it to make their own claims. The colonial imaginary was, like other ideological structures, a site of struggle, and its rhetoric could be contested.[43] Such contests were provoked in the wake of crises, and this was the case in the aftermath of the First World War. And so Allégret expressed some exasperation in 1919 when he came to complete his report on colonial policy. At this date he was acutely aware that the very idea of a Greater France had barely survived. During the course of the War parts of the metropole had been devastated and France had become newly reliant on the colonies for both human and material resources. This came with its own problems for the colonial administration, as Allégret registered, noting of conscripted colonial troops:

> In the last few months we have told them so many times that they have saved France that they have become entirely unreasonable and many of those who have returned to their native lands are encouraging insubordination if not outright revolt.[44]

It was in response to this situation that, in 1921, Sarraut would reaffirm the project of liberation and renew the colonial imaginary, and, with it, the fantasy of sculpting "a new humanity from the shapeless clay of the primitive masses".[45]

Sarraut had been appointed minister for the colonies in January 1920 and was immediately confronted with an extremely complicated situation; he attempted to address this in a *Projet de loi portant fixation d'un programme général de mise en valeur des colonies françaises*. Sarraut saw his colonial policy as a contribution to the economic regeneration of the metropole.[46] However, like Ferry before him, Sarraut proudly asserted that his policy was not merely economic, it "assigns a place to works of instruction, education, [and] health".[47] Thus Sarraut drew on Ferry's legacy as both a colonialist and a reformer. Whilst his project was directed towards the material development of the colonies, and in particular towards the development of industry, he proudly asserted to acknowledge that "there are other riches that the French 'protector' will take and seek to increase: the races we protect have a human wealth, a moral and social value, the *value of humanity*".[48] So Sarraut was an heir to Ferry but was also concerned to transform the work of his predecessors. He declared:

> The work is no longer unilateral: it is conceived for the advantage and benefit of both parties. There is no longer the exploitation of one race by another, but *association*, to use the happy formula that has become the watchword of our colonial policy.[49]

Such a policy of association necessarily went beyond earlier conceptions of the colonised subjects.[50] Sarraut asserts: "French colonial policy sees our protégés as *men* and not as an anonymous and servile mass, whatever the colour of their skin, however arrested their development."[51] The colonised are here endowed with a new status, even whilst they remain under the tutelage of their French colonisers. And Sarraut was clearly not in doubt that those he considered under his protection were in a backward condition; in his vision much remains to be done by both parties in working towards the common goal of modelling "the face of a new humanity". The task of making men was literally affirmed. Moreover, Sarraut is explicit about the origins of his doctrine, as he was pleased to term it: "if it is the virtue of the Third Republic to have formulated it explicitly, one must allow that the Republic has found the elements of the doctrine in the oldest traditions of France".[52]

Yet access to these traditions remained restricted. Sarraut was circumspect regarding indigenous rights to French citizenship.[53] This circumspection is one aspect of what was a fundamental distinction between the colonial and the republican imaginaries. For the exchanges between leaders and led that characterised the popular sovereignty of the Republic were only ever to be glimpsed in the colonial imaginary. The colonised were not citizens and the possibility of their self-government was cast to a distant future. For Sarraut, this creates something of a paradox, the servitude of liberation; in the struggle toward the future, colonialism had "to legitimate itself each and every day through its actions, to 're-establish' itself unceasingly in its strength and authority".[54] In this conception of France's imperial destiny, agency is unequally distributed because the colonial subjects are not citizens and not players on the stage. They are not yet "to act for themselves".[55] So the colonised in the colonial imaginary remain fully subaltern, without the access to power that fully franchised Frenchmen enjoyed under the constitution of the Third Republic. Of course, in registering this one should also register that agency was unevenly distributed in the Third Republic as women were not enfranchised. In this respect there was a homology between the status of women in France and the status of colonised populations. This could be said to be present in repressed form in the very idea of "making men". As much was recognised by some at the inception of the Republican project; it was not a coincidence that Olympe de Gouges, author of the *Déclaration des droits de la femme et de la citoyenne* of 1791, was also an abolitionist and produced works such as *Réflexions sur les hommes nègres* of 1788.[56]

If the freedom of the colonised remained cast to a future in the colonial imaginary, what of that other freedom, that of the worker? What of the marketplace where labour and wage are — at least notionally — freely exchanged? Here, again, the situation is complex. For the conditions for the sale of labour-power were only imperfectly implanted in the colonies. The campaign against slavery, which culminated in France in the final act of abolition of 1848, was a campaign against a barbaric form of property. It had as one end the creation of new conditions in which individuals were able to dispose freely of their labour-power, that is, were free to enter into the relations of wage-labour. Yet if the abolition of slavery created new property relations it did not thereby create a new sense of the individual as one able and free to dispose. Instead, French colonisers would lament that their colonial charges simply lacked a conception of possessive individualism; Thomas Paine may well have celebrated the universal and innate rights of man but the colonisers often complained that it fell to them to inculcate a sense of these rights.[57] Missionaries such as Allégret also wished to see Paine's rights promulgated, yet at the same time they also sought to mitigate the worst effects of "a new spirit of acquisitiveness".[58] In Allégret's view the "noblest and most idealistic" course would be "to make known the *Declaration of the Rights of Man* as interpreted by St Vincent de Paul"; Allégret would have the *Declaration* interpreted as a work of charity.[59]

By now it should be clear that the progressive task of liberation central to the colonial imaginary was to be pursued along two paths. Making men involved programmes of education to create a masculine elite which might, one day, accede to citizenship and it also involved the creation of individuals able to participate fully and freely in economic exchanges. As much was implicit in Allégret's sense of his role as one dedicated to making "men capable of collaborating in the moral *and* economic development of the country".[60] When this task was eventually completed, the colonised would finally be men in a sense that Paine might have understood.

Having established at least something of what was involved in the French colonial project of making men, it is time now to take up my second line of argument and consider their representation. I turn to consider the status of those who — rather than being merely depicted — might be portrayed.

Portraits, points of view, and representation

What is a portrait? To say that the *sine qua non* of the portrait is the production of "a likeness of a particular individual" is in fact to offer only the barest sketch of an answer.[61] Yet this sketch has at least the virtue of indicating that the preconditions for a portrait are a category of individuated personhood or subjectivity together with some agreed procedures for the representation of that category. The category itself and the attendant procedures may be related in different ways in different traditions, and the agents effecting this may also be understood in different ways. Portraiture is not a static entity. What I shall argue now is that, in the European tradition, portraits come with a quite specific convergence of personhood and pictorial procedures and this, in turn, has consequences for the representation of Europe's others. Here it is helpful to return to the portrait of Citizen Belley [Fig. 1.1]. In it, Girodet has mobilised a set of conventions — and indeed thematised them through the inclusion of Raynal's bust — and then directed them to an unprecedented end: the representation of an individual who was a former slave and also a citizen and a deputy. Given this, it is not surprising that Belley is turned from the bust of Raynal and placed at the centre of the painting. He is not a mere foil and his subjectivity is essentially his own. But what is the nature of this subjectivity? And what is specific to the European procedures for its representation? Finally, what is the relationship here between subject, artist, and viewer? The answers to these questions are hardly straight-forward; as will become clear both subjectivity and its mode of representation have their own entailments. I shall begin with the latter then turn to the former. (This order of exposition inverts the standard account of the emergence of the European portrait, which begins with the emergence of the individual; it will become clear why that is an unhelpful point of departure.)

A first, basic, contention: the precondition for the creation of a "likeness" is some agreement about the status of "sightlike" configurations.[62] These configu-rations came to a new prominence in Europe in the fifteenth century, as images were increasingly made to correspond to optical experiences (or at least select-ed parts of these experiences). Visual configurations came to resemble views or scenes more and more; this form of naturalism depended on "the analysis of vision into elements of light, dark and colour in a field of vision".[63] Such a transcription of optical experience then enabled new forms of artistic vision, including the creation of images at once fantastic and optically credible.[64] On a conceptual level, this involved a shift in the role attributed to the imagina-tion, a faculty which gradually ceased to be understood as recollecting "forms" from memory in the service of reason, a point of view ultimately derived from Aristotle.[65] Instead, now the imagination painted pictures.

David Summers argues that with this work of "pictorialization",

> it became more difficult to distinguish the rational from the fantastic by appeal to nature, and the borders between mental faculties dependent on image metaphors — sensation, memory and imagination — became hard-er to draw, simply because all had the same optical basis.[66]

Here an old argument is turned on its head, for one might think that optical naturalism served to entrench the authority of the sense of sight. However, in Europe, the new science of optics, and the modes of picturing it fostered, gradu-ally led to a reordering of sensation and intellection:

> Vision, with the deepest and most basic possible consequences, was sep-arated from the basis of the traditional work of reason, and it became necessary to describe the activities of vision (and the other senses it had long represented) in relation to the activities of mind and soul in very different terms[.][67]

In this manner, the "forms" originally identified by Aristotle were replaced by descriptions of "traces in vision".[68] In these, the emphasis was placed more on internal activities of mind and less on external forms and, as a result, Réne Descartes could come to insist that it is the mind that sees and not the eye.[69]

This was to have manifold consequences. The fact that configurations might correspond to features of actual optical experience did not necessarily mean that artworks should or did conform to what was actually seen. On the contrary, the rise of "sightlike" configurations did not narrow the spectrum of possibilities for art practice but broadened it. At one end of this spectrum, as artistic forms came to be understood to arise from the imagination, they also came to be understood as *expressive* and, as a result, different configurations could be understood to express idiosyncrasies. Put differently, an artist's style could convey an individual point of view. And at the other end of the spectrum, forms could be made to conform to the seen through carefully constructed metric naturalism, the making of resemblance according to measure and ratio. In due course this practice was elaborated into one-point perspective, and thus there emerged a rather different sense of the artwork as organised according to a single "point of view".

The implications of all this remain in the many everyday uses of the words "perspective" and "representation", and in the language of much art history. Here one often finds the assumption that artefacts are representations, either in a primary sense of being representational or in a secondary sense of being representative of a worldview. Indeed, with the elaboration of the sightlike model of configuration this secondary sense of representation as worldview became fused with the primary sense of the term. Accordingly, the word "perspective" now has uses which extend far beyond referencing pictorial constructions of spatial recession to include descriptions of an individual point of view on any given matter, visual or otherwise. The fusion of these two different senses of representation means that the aforementioned working assumption in art history is eminently reasonable, at least in the many European contexts where sightlike configurations still hold sway, including, of course, photography. However, it should be recognised that the assumption remains that: it is an assumption, not a given. From this it follows that even if questions of representation are central to the history of European art, they need not be central to the history of all art. Representation — in both the senses referred to here — is a condition artefacts may arrive at; it may be fashioned or attributed and need not be considered as being an essential or indispensable property.

Recognising this has profound implications for how one might understand the ranking and comparison of artefacts. This is most readily demonstrated by

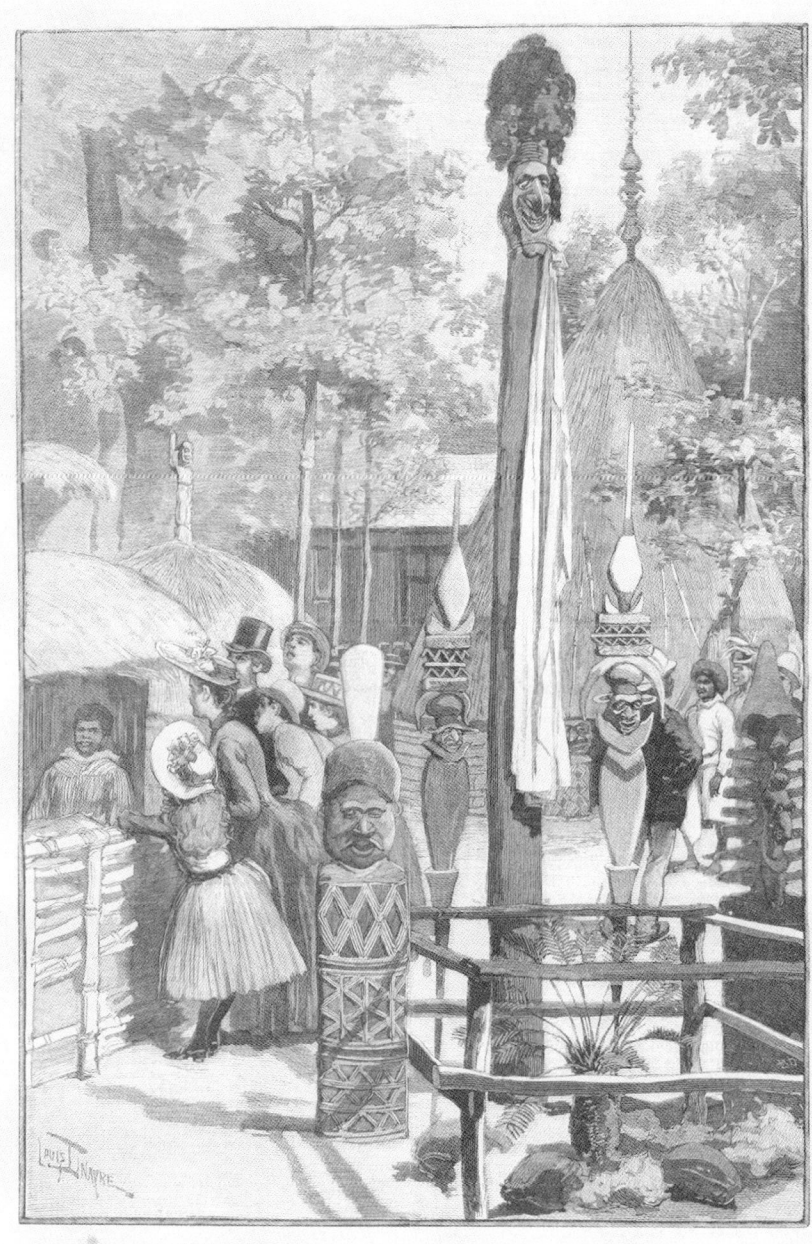

EXPOSITION UNIVERSELLE. — LE VILLAGE CANAQUE A L'ESPLANADE DES INVALIDES.

(Dessin de M. LOUIS TINAYRE.)

Figure 1.2. Louis Tinayre, 'Exposition universelle: The Kanak Village on the Esplanade des Invalides', wood engraving after drawing, *Le Monde illustré*, 1687, 27 July 1889, 56.

turning to an example, one deliberately chosen to introduce two closely related issues: hierarchies of representation and hierarchies of subjectivity.

As part of its coverage of the Parisian *Exposition universelle* of 1889, the weekly magazine *Le Monde illustré* reproduced a drawing by one Louis Tinayre [Fig. 1.2]. This shows one of the villages recreated on the Esplanade des Invalides, inhabited by people transported from various French colonial possessions, including New Caledonia and Tahiti. For Tinayre, the drawing was part of a developing pictorial vocabulary, since he would later become a professional of the picturesque in the employ of Albert I, Prince of Monaco.[70] The colonial villages were among the attractions which also drew André Gide, although in anticipating such pleasures he followed the general tenor of his youthful correspondence with Allégret and was careful to register his anxiety at potentially being distracted from his studies.[71] As is clear from Tinayre's drawing, the villages of the Esplanade featured not only indigenous populations but also indigenous artefacts. This means that they were amongst the first displays in Europe to present Oceanic arts "in context".[72] In turn, it seems to have been this context which stimulated Paul Gauguin to travel to Tahiti (even if, of the Parisian displays, he was most enthusiastic about the "Javanese" village).[73] So the colonial villages certainly have their place in histories of modernism and primitivism. And in these histories much has been made of the role of imagery such as Tinayre's, and its construction of an opposition between the "civilised" and the "primitive".[74]

A critical examination of this construction is surely important but this should not be undertaken at the expense of neglecting the larger part of the cultural work done by this type of imagery. For Tinayre's drawing clearly functions within those European traditions of representation that I have just outlined. Once represented within this tradition, objects such as the Oceanic sculpture could be positioned and perceived in fundamentally European terms, that is, as visual configurations which ought to be sightlike. Thus the opposition unfolded in Tinayre's drawing is not just between the "civilised" and the "primitive" but also between a putatively correct representation — one conforming to the "proper" conventions of optical naturalism — and another order of imagery, which would be judged backward, having not yet attained this sophistication. This is a crucial point. Note that this is not a case of presenting and comparing two separate orders of representation. Instead, one is presented *within* the other; the European tradition is simply the given framework for Tinayre and is as unquestioned and unquestioning as Ferry's account of the virtues and blessings of civilisation. Such is the operation of hegemony. As much should be acknowledged when one analyses this type of imagery. European modes of representation — however transparent and self-evident they may seem — are hardly neutral. Girodet's "universal language" of art was in fact contingent, and fragile.

There is, then, a considerable amount at stake in the optical naturalism employed by Tinayre. In images such as these, the framework of the European tradition serves to establish a hierarchy amongst distinct orders of representation. At the same time it also works to establish a hierarchy amongst subjectivities. This is so because of the status given to "form" in the European tradition. As noted above, when artists came to be understood to have styles, form itself came to be considered as expressive. These conceptions were elaborated (and variously contested) over the course of the early modern period and, as a result of a whole complex of forces, the pictorial and sculptural arts came to be understood as "fine arts".[75] If an artefact could both be representational and representative, a work of fine art was to be both formally expressive and express a point of view. And so it came to be that the fine arts, in both their production and their appreciation, became a sphere for the refined exercise of judgements of taste.

The elaboration of this subjective sphere of individual discrimination was matched by the development of one dedicated to the objective, namely the sphere of modern science, especially but not exclusively as it developed across the nineteenth century. Once that had happened, the spectrum of possibilities opened up by sightlike configurations was submitted to a new system of categorisation, in which the subjective and expressive were more readily opposed to the objective, geometric and mathematical and, accordingly, visual forms were much more clearly divided between those addressed to sensibility and those addressed to technical competence. Thus, whilst responses to the fine arts remained individual and subjective, an alternative was developed in the production and reception of artefacts such as axonometric drawings, which dispensed with the fiction of the individual point of view altogether.[76]

Eventually, the fine arts became a privileged arena for the exercise of subjectivity as both radical "point of view" and "free personal expression" and they could now be held to operate under a wholly modern form of the ancient tradition of representationalism, in which art corresponds to a mental image.[77] What is significant here is that the ancient tradition is "suitably modified", for whereas in its ancient form representationalism operated with a distinction between mental image and truth, that distinction does not obtain for the modern fine arts.[78] Artists are to work imaginatively and their viewers are to respond accordingly. Thus Summers concludes that the definition of art as fine art presupposes not just the expression of a subjectivity but also "presupposes an essentially *like* subjectivity as a 'viewer'".[79] And "such response on our parts makes us, not just viewers, but observers of the definition of subjectivity".[80] As much is clear in the implanting of art criticism as a genre, which institutionalised individual judgement as the appropriate response to works of art.[81] Taken together, these arguments show that the history of European art ought to be understood as the history of a quite particular, European subjectivity.[82]

Now that these implications of the European model of optical naturalism have been entangled a little, it is possible to characterise more forcefully the opposition constructed in Tinayre's image. In my first description, I suggested that there is not simply an opposition in what is shown — a contrast between "civilised" colonisers and "primitive" colonised — but also an opposition between orders of representation, and it is the significance of this which must now be drawn out. It is not necessary to be detained by a judgement as to whether Tinayre's image would be embraced as "fine art". The point is not whether this particular image should be raised to that status but rather that, by virtue of format and technique, it is at least eligible for such an elevation. In this the image is quite distinct from the Oceanic sculptures it depicts (at the time, the latter could hardly qualify for entry to a museum of fine arts and at best would be assigned to a museum of ethnography, such as the one founded at the Trocadéro for the *Exposition universelle* of 1878). The distinction here is not trivial; it is a not simply a matter of institutional classifications (as if these were ever simple). For to contemplate an image such as Tinayre's, which may be admitted to the category of "fine art", is to be an observer of a definition of subjectivity. Thus what is opposed in Tinayre's image is not simply the "civilised" and "primitive" in terms of behaviour and habitat. The larger opposition constructed in and by this image is between definitions of subjectivity, between Tinayre's modern, expressive subjectivity and that of the anonymous and putatively backward Oceanic maker. The former is deeply familiar and the latter quite alien, and was frequently considered to be somehow "arrested" in development.[83] It was perhaps so alien to exhibition visitors in 1889 as to pose a threat to their very understanding of subjectivity, especially as some excitable visitors imagined themselves to be encountering cannibals.[84]

Perhaps it is now clearer why I chose to discuss a printed image based on a drawing, rather than to develop my initial account of portraiture through an analysis of photographs like those discussed in my introduction. Before embarking on an account of photography it is necessary to establish the principles of optical naturalism and what they entail and imply. This is because photography would not have been thinkable without these prior and much older principles; it was elaborated to conform to them, although this involved both effort and considerable difficulty.[85] Thus, whilst the advent of photography complicates the account I have offered so far, it certainly does not confound it. Nevertheless, photography introduced new processes of image-making and these made the new technology difficult to classify; the result was that the status of photography as an art had to be clearly asserted — again, a process which took some effort — and the role of subjectivity within this particular process had to be articulated and defined.[86]

Now, as a reproductive technology, photography came to take its place alongside other processes of mass production. One version of the history of photography is that of a technology first emerging as a specialised process — requiring various kinds of competence — but eventually becoming an industrialised and de-skilled activity (particularly after the launch of the Kodak camera in 1888). This transformation is one small and quite specific iteration of the development from manufacture to large-scale industry.[87] Of course this meant that, for much of the late nineteenth and early twentieth century, photography was often placed in opposition to the arts and for this reason photographic work gained entry to museums of fine art only with some difficulty.[88] Yet one should not therefore assume that photographs and the Oceanic sculptures discussed above had equal status; whilst both were initially excluded from the museum, the exclusions were for quite different reasons. Photography was understood as a scientific achievement, indeed as one of the "great scientific conquests" of European civilisation, and thus was held to belong in an entirely separate register from that occupied by "primitive" productions.[89] In this understanding, scientific achievements were invariably and essentially European. Meanwhile, scientific methods, defined as those which derive conclusions from repeatable experiments, belonged in the objective sphere, established against the subjective sphere of the fine arts. Therefore, as a product of both optics and chemistry, photography was originally assigned a place in the sphere of modern science. Those who would struggle for photography to transcend this status were faced with a long campaign.[90] By 1889 photography had at least gained an ancillary rank in relation to the fine arts, and at the *Exposition universelle* it was classified amongst the materials and processes of the liberal arts.[91] As such, photography even merited an allegorical representation on the principal façade of the Palais des Beaux Arts alongside those other mediators of knowledge, *Education* and *Printing*.

All of this has a bearing on how one should understand photographs of the *Exposition universelle*. Like Tinayre's image, the photographs taken in 1889 could participate in structuring oppositions. However, their places in these structures were often rather unstable. Consider, for example, a further scene from the

Kanak village [Fig. 1.3]. In Tinayre's image, one order of representation was presented within another, with the enfolding European tradition as the given and unquestioned framework, and at first glance this might also seem the case for this photograph. At this date, whatever it was that was being photographed, the photograph itself was considered a European product. This was not simply because of the pictorial conventions used, but also because of the very technology that both reproduced and reinforced those conventions. However, when photography is understood in this manner, as profoundly embedded in European traditions of thought and production, it emerges as an unstable combination of the subjective and objective, as a product of individual points of view but also of mechanical and chemical processes. In different circumstances, one term or

Figure 1.3. Anon. 'Exposition universelle, 1889: Esplanade des Invalides: Kanak Village', albumen print, 1889.

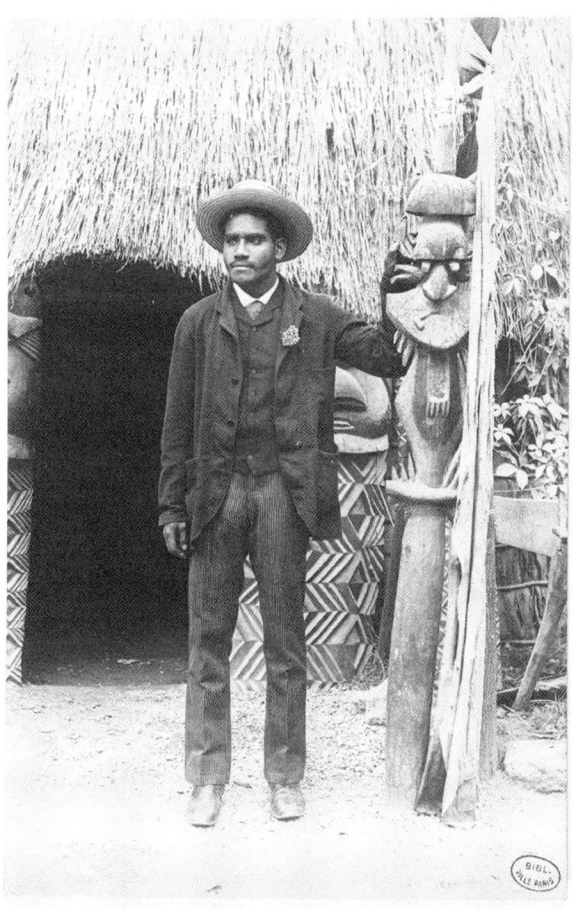

the other in this equation might be asserted to have some privilege, in an attempt to introduce some stability into individual photographs as either artworks or as impartial and reliable documents. These assertions were often somewhat capricious authorisations and indeed photographs have a tendency to move between classifications, sometimes in strange ways. What needs to be registered at this point is simply that photography was not simple; mediators — even mediators of knowledge — often have an ambiguous status. So the photograph of the Kanak village is, ultimately, difficult to classify. And the Kanak man photographed in a European suit is also difficult to place. The photograph and the man as photographed could both be submitted to regimes of classification but they might also evade these regimes because they are both difficult "subjects", that is, with difficult relations to subjectivity. Here attempts at classification produce what might seem a surprising convergence between the status of photography on the one hand and that of the indigenous peoples displayed at the *Exposition universelle* on the other. At this date there were a number of authorities devoutly hoping to classify such images and such people, yet their attempts to locate and define subjectivity were often fraught. Where was it? And how could its effects be identified? These questions haunt much of the present book precisely because they exercised those enjoying authority in the colonial period.

Here it is instructive to attend to the different attitudes displayed towards the inhabitants of the Kanak village. If some visitors considered those exhibited to be cannibals, others were far more circumspect. For instance, in the commentary in *Le Monde illustré*, the author, one G. Lenôtre, describes how far the "villagers" are from savages. Not only do they speak excellent French, but one of them, Badimoin, is a teacher of the language and "is profiting from his visit to France to study our manners, our theatre and our literature".[92] A contrast is established between the refined individuals from France's empire and the vulgar "gawping mob" crowded around their huts.[93] Something of this may also be detected in Tinayre's drawing. However, whilst Lenôtre presents the villagers as civilised, he also recognises that the village is not without its "picturesque" aspects, including the "*tabous*", the "roughly hewn" blocks of wood standing guard outside the huts.[94] This is how Lenôtre understands the Oceanic sculptures shown in Tinayre's image and in the anonymous photograph of the village, where the Kanak man stands next to one, resting his hand on it with something of a proprietorial air. The man is neatly dressed, with a flower in his buttonhole, and thus the contrast implicit in Lenôtre's account is drawn out, a contrast between the cultivation of the villagers and what the commentator takes to be their rather coarse sculptural tradition. It is particularly striking how the man's self-presentation is quite distinct from established pictorial conventions used for the presentation of native villagers at this point in time.[95] In this photograph, there is a seeming paradox: the man has something of the comportment later assumed by figures such as Pastors Kuo, Ekollo and Modi Din, and yet he does not appear to have entirely abandoned the beliefs of his forebears.

As Lenôtre's account suggests, the presence of the *tabous* indicates a set of devotional practices alien to the gawping metropolitan mob. In turn, this suggests that my account of the (varying) degrees of difference between the "civilised" and "primitive" remains incomplete or, more precisely, without content. For the opposition between image-makers like Tinayre and the Oceanic maker is not simply between the familiar and the alien, it is also, implicitly, an opposition between a Christian worshipper and a pagan other, an "idol-maker". That is to say, the opposition between different traditions of making is also organised by divergent religious traditions, each with its own modalities of personhood. This is why I now turn to an analysis of personhood in the Christian tradition, to complete my account of the entailments of portraiture in the European tradition.

Portraits and subjectivities

The formation of Christian models of subjectivity is an enormous topic and the reader will doubtless be relieved that in what follows I restrict myself to a rather narrow of treatment of the most relevant themes. These may be broached by considering in a little more detail the status of the anonymous Oceanic maker of *tabous* introduced above. I have suggested that, at least in later nineteenth-century France, the idol-maker might not have been considered as wholly human, as having full subjectivity; such recognition was usually withheld because idol-makers were taken to live in a state of unfreedom, bound as they were to superstitious cults. Certainly, writers such as Allégret and Sarraut readily contrasted this state of unfreedom with that of Christian congregations. After all, these authors concurred that they were not seeking to oppress but to liberate. Yet what liberation was this? In what sense may Christians be said to be free? And what are the implications of this for the portrayal of Christians?

These are distinct questions yet they are — once again — related, precisely because they are approaches to the same phenomenon: the making of men. The relationship is established in the philosophical system of Georg Wilhelm Friedrich Hegel. Even the crudest sketch of this system serves to give some purchase on the phenomenon and its entailments.

For Hegel, the coming of Christ inaugurates a new historical era. Christ, as the true image of God, the incarnate deity, yet also as man, brings a new actuality and dignity to the individual and thus gives a new character to portraiture; such is the argument developed in the *Aesthetics*:

> The Divine, God himself, has become flesh (...) Christianity alone introduces this actuality in flesh and spirit as the determinate existence, life and effectiveness of God himself. Now therefore this body, this flesh, is brought into honour (...) Just as man was originally the image of God [Gen. 1: 26], God is the image of man, and who sees the Son sees the Father, who loves the Son loves the Father also [John 14: 9, 21]; God is to be known in an actual human being.[96]

The actuality introduced here has profound consequences for art; as a result of it, Hegel argues, Christian art received a divine impetus to move beyond the anthropomorphism of Classical Antiquity.

> Christianity has pushed anthropomorphism much further; for, according to Christian doctrine, God is not an individual merely humanly shaped, but an actual single individual, wholly God and wholly an actual man, drawn into all the conditions of existence, and no merely humanly shaped ideal of beauty and art.[97]

For Hegel, beauty is no longer, as in the Classical era, a question of a unity in which inner life is expressed and entirely embodied in corporeal shape. With Christianity this unity is lost. And with "this indifference to the idealizing unification of soul and body there enters essentially, for the more special individuality of the external side, *portraiture* which does not blot out (...) particular traits and forms as they actually exist".[98] Yet, crucially, Hegel argues that portraiture is not the result of a simple indifference to the ideal, something which merely permits the depiction of the peculiarities (and imperfections) invariably attendant on specific physiognomies. Instead, he is at pains to emphasise that human external appearance, "the shape of common life", is brought into a new honour as one of the consequences of the Incarnation.[99] Christ, the living and fully human image of God, enables the individual human to become visible in a new way; and this gives the artist a new task. Now "the human being, as actual subjectivity, must be made the principle".[100] Thus for Hegel it is only in the Christian era that proper or true portraiture can even exist as an artistic possibility. To draw this point into concert with the arguments made earlier: within the European practice of portraiture, optical naturalism is deployed in the service of a particular sense of subjectivity as inwardness. Thus, with the portrait, an ontology is morphologised.[101]

For Hegel, the consequences of the Incarnation are profound because not only does it introduce a new era for art it also has a literally epoch-making role as the origin of what he considered the fourth and final phase in world history. This is so because the Incarnation has enabled "subjective freedom" to determine itself, a type of freedom which Hegel distinguishes from "substantial freedom", the latter simply being the rationality of the will developed within the confines of the state, with its commandments and laws.[102] As is well known, Hegel describes the advance towards freedom as an adventure, as the "history of Spirit", of Spirit departing from a state of nature to become finally "conscious of itself and aware of its own nature".[103] This is what is achieved with the Incarnation; Hegel describes this in *Phenomenology of Spirit* in a manner which adumbrates his account in the *Aesthetics*. The Incarnation creates a great shift of consciousness: "Spirit is *immediately present* (...) as an *actual man*".[104] So "the believer is immediately certain of Spirit, *sees*, *feels*, and *hears* this divinity. Thus this self-consciousness is not imagination but is *actual* in the believer".[105] It is with the birth of Christ that self-consciousness can become actual and immediate, rather than as it was previously, when, in Hegel's account, it was merely thought or imagined.[106] Subjective freedom, as inwardness, as self-consciousness, can only arise with this stage of Christian development.

I have already cited Althusser's description of this process. "God thus needs to 'make himself' a man".[107] (Althusser described Hegel as an admirable but unwitting "theoretician" of ideology.[108]) Althusser concludes his account of ideological structures with a consideration of free subjectivity but does not do so to proclaim a freedom but rather to emphasise "the ambiguity of the term *subject*".[109] The subject is "author of and responsible for its actions" yet also "a subjected being".[110] Thus, there "*are no subjects except by and for their subjection*".[111] This is what it means to understand oneself as made in the image of God. If the Incarnation inaugurates portraiture, it does so as subjection.

Hegel's account of subjective freedom has many implications: one consequence needs to be confronted immediately, that concerning the unfolding of world history. Here Hegel is explicit: "World history travels from east to west; for Europe is the absolute end of history."[112] He continues:

although the earth is a sphere, history does not move in a circle around it, but has a definite eastern extremity, i.e. Asia. It is here that the external and physical sun rises, and it sets in the west: but it is in the west that the inner sun of self-consciousness, which emits a higher radiance, makes its further ascent.[113]

In this account, self-consciousness can only arise in the Christian era, it cannot exist without the concept of the Incarnation. In this way the West is held to constitute the true horizon of historical development. Thus not all peoples will evolve to Hegel's fourth and final stage; when figures such as Sarraut claimed that those outside Europe were arrested at earlier stages, they were both following and reiterating this line of argument. Moreover, some peoples were thought not to have even begun the process of development at all and were therefore without history. Famously, Hegel consigns Africans to this condition: "What we understand as Africa proper is that unhistorical and undeveloped land which is still enmeshed in the natural spirit."[114] Here, then, is the ultimate articulation of a difference between "primitive" and "civilised".

Of course, in their own ways, missionaries and colonisers wanted to initiate the process of historical development.[115] Allégret and Sarraut imagined such a project. They wished to foster the freedom — as they saw it — born of moral education and conversion to Christianity as well as the freedom which enabled participation in economic exchanges. But their imaginings were derived from European conceptions of freedom and thus only confirm the need to escape from this view of history. In sum, this was the history that Fanon would refuse. He would not be a slave of a past defined by pervasive, fundamentally European models of devotion, development and representation.

The present task may now be defined more clearly: it is to scrutinise this history — rather than merely reproduce it — and the study of portraiture is a means to this end. For the portrait defined as a likeness of an individual is not at all neutral in the context of colonialism. "Likeness" depends on a tradition of naturalism which is bound up with a history of European subjectivity. In this history, a portrait is an individual performance, one which entails the representation of a subjectivity and, at the same time, it is a performance directed to "an essentially *like* subjectivity".[116] Portraiture, as a distinctive interplay of subjectivities belongs wholly within the paradigm of the European fine arts.[117] In both form and content, the portrait is a theatre for performances of subjectivity. All those gilded frames are so many proscenia. Many of those outside Europe remain excluded from the performance; many, but not all, as Belley's example shows. The proscenium frames a space which is difficult to access but may, nevertheless, be traversed. One may cross a threshold and accede to portrayal.

In the Republican and the colonial imaginaries freedom was cast to a more or less distant horizon, a prize to be won through struggle. Whilst the French themselves were understood to have made greater strides forward than those under their charge in the colonies, nevertheless, the advance for both was ultimately to be towards the same horizon, one of fully liberated — that is, Christian — personhood. If the colonial imaginary took colonised peoples as objects, the duty of colonial authorities was to lead them towards the status of subjects, to lead across the threshold. In the chapters to follow, I examine various attempts at such leadership and also show how such attempts were resisted.

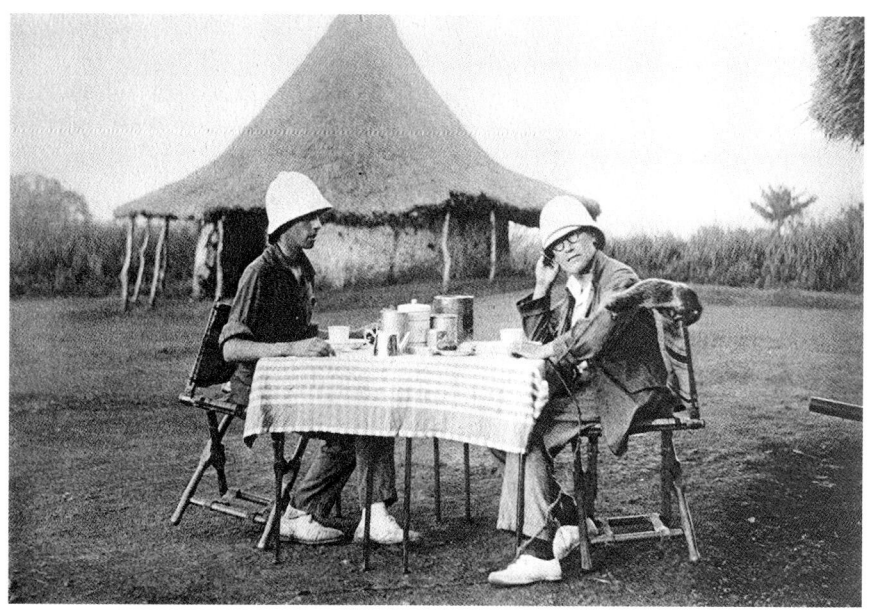

Figure 2.1. Marc Allégret, 'André Gide and Marc Allégret at a halting point', frontispiece in André Gide, *Voyage au Congo*, Paris: Gallimard, 1929.

2. Perception, apperception and disavowal

André Gide and Marc Allégret in the Congo

The illustrated edition of André Gide's *Voyage au Congo* has as its frontispiece a photograph of the author and his companion taking tea. The image is simply captioned: "André Gide and Marc Allégret at a halting point" [Fig. 2.1]. Gide and Allégret, lovers as well as travelling companions, are both every inch European explorers, complete with pith helmets and the paraphernalia and comforts of civilisation, including a folding table and a checked tablecloth. As explorers they have come in search of the new and unfamiliar and whatever is in the hut in the background of the photograph will, in all likelihood, be quite different to the objects set out on their table. So there is something slightly comic in this situation, not just in the awkwardness of postures but in the incongruity between the ritual of the teatable and the setting in which it is enacted; one is not at ease in one's drawing room. To grasp this scene as the occasion for a photograph is to recognise its comedy and be prepared to signal it to the viewer. Something is staged here. The European may or may not be something Gide and Allégret will attempt to overcome on their journey but it is certainly something they take with them (in many senses) and they do not pretend otherwise.

The titlepage of Gide's illustrated edition declares that it includes 64 previously unpublished photographs by Marc Allégret but this is not quite the case. For one can make out that the frontispiece is actually by Gide; the shutter-release is hidden in his left hand but its lead is visible snaking from the table edge and out of the frame towards the tripod. And it is Gide, the eminent writer, and senior member of the teaparty, who looks toward the camera, controlling both himself and his composition. Thus, if the photographs accompanying Gide's text are by Allégret, this frontispiece suggests that the terms for the collaboration were established by the writer. Of course, the image shows both author and photographer, and this suggests that there may be some congruence between the points of view presented in the text and those offered by the photographs. Yet the first image remains Gide's performance.

The comedy of this frontispiece suggests tensions rather than harmony — comedy, after all, being the management of tensions. These tensions are also signalled in the elaborate textual framing given to the frontispiece. First there is the titlepage announcing *Voyage au Congo suivi du Retour du Tchad* and so suggesting a journey upriver and down; on the next page is a dedication to the memory of Joseph Conrad, and in this way the present volume of African travels is brought into association with the river journey traced in Conrad's *Heart of Darkness*. In that novella the meeting of the European and the African is utterly destructive and, even if little of this is evident in the frontispiece, the dedication adumbrates a similarly fraught encounter. For on the page after the dedication is a quotation from one of John Keats' letters: "Better be imprudent moveables than prudent fixtures."[1] This particular invitation to voyage nicely points up the awkwardness of the travellers in the frontispiece on the following page. Perched as they are on chairs so badly matched to their teatable as to oblige them both to tip forward to squeeze their knees under it, the men are certainly not prudently fixed. Finally, opposite the frontispiece is a quotation from King Louis XVI's instructions to the explorer the Comte de la Pérouse: "It is required that all crew members maintain good relations with the natives, to win their friendship by good conduct and proper consideration (...)"[2] This royal injunction is presumably one which the two pictured explorers will obey. Taken together, the dedication and quotations suggest that Gide and Allégret, even whilst venturing into what is for them the unknown, are also following in the footsteps of others. Further, the framing of the frontispiece intimates that Gide's text will be shaped by a literary inheritance, one embracing the fictional as well as the biographical and autobiographical. In sum, the prefatory matter is reflexive, in accord with the staging of Gide's photographic self-portrait. Surely, a third party could have been found to release the shutter but this would not have served to reveal the carefully mediated character of the representation itself. A straightforward, seemingly transparent photographic document would not be to the author's purpose. For here it is not simply a matter of showing or revealing; the image instead offers the scene of its own making.

This careful staging is of a piece with the comedy. That is to say, the production of the photograph — the point of view, the theatricality — is of a piece with the awkwardness, the paraphernalia of tea things and tablecloth and their incongruity before the hut, the marker of the exotic. The choice of frontispiece and the manner of its framing put the project of Gide and Allégret at once inside and outside the standard narratives of the European encounter with the African. The difficulties in sustaining this liminal position, and what it reveals of the colonial imaginary, are the subjects of this chapter.

At one level Gide's narrative is the familiar one of an awakening to purpose: the author-as-hero encounters iniquity and strives to defeat it. In this case the awakening will involve Gide's discovery of the corruption and cruelty of those working for the companies extracting rubber. This discovery would profoundly change the direction of Gide's work and his attitude to French colonialism and, on his return to France, would lead to a political campaign. Below I shall trace this narrative in some detail but the first object of my attention will be the manner in which Gide chose to narrate it. If something of the narrative structure of Gide's text is familiar, what is unusual is the role played by the author; he is not simply the hero and his account is not organised merely around actions but around his own reflections on his perceptions. As much is indicated by the reflexive frontispiece, which is Gide's own performance. The occupiers of the hut in the background of his self-portrait may well have been in the vicinity during the taking of the photograph yet they are not pictured; in the prefatory matter they are not fully objects of attention, present only as objects of royal solicitude in the instructions to La Pérouse. Instead, it is Gide's performance and his perceptions that are made central.

This prompts the question of how "the natives" will be depicted in Gide's text and Allégret's photographs. What will be their role and status? The question becomes only more pressing if the photographic frontispiece is compared to the very first image included in the illustrated edition, that of a young woman reproduced on the title page [Fig. 2.2]. The figure has been excised from its pictorial context and sits isolated on the page, in a melancholic pose with downcast eyes. The lighting gives the figure a clear, strong modelling and thus a sculptural presence which lifts it further from the titlepage. Such procedures for isolation emphasise the introspection of the figure whilst also depriving this mood of a discernible source. A connoisseur — after all a quite likely purchaser of the luxury edition — could find in the figure's pose references to Dürer's *Melencholia*, and perhaps also to the Spinario and Cnidian Venus, yet these would not seem to have a great explanatory value. At best they might serve to distance the female figure from a stock imagery of dancing, smiling Africans, and so might suggest that Allégret's photographic project will depart from at least some conventions. At any rate, the frontispiece of the teaparty seems replete with detail when compared with this first illustration. The comic awkwardness of the teaparty also stands in contrast to the introspective mood of the isolated woman. This might, in turn, indicate some circumspection on the part of Gide and Allégret regarding their understanding of the Congo, that is to say, it might serve to introduce their liminal position.

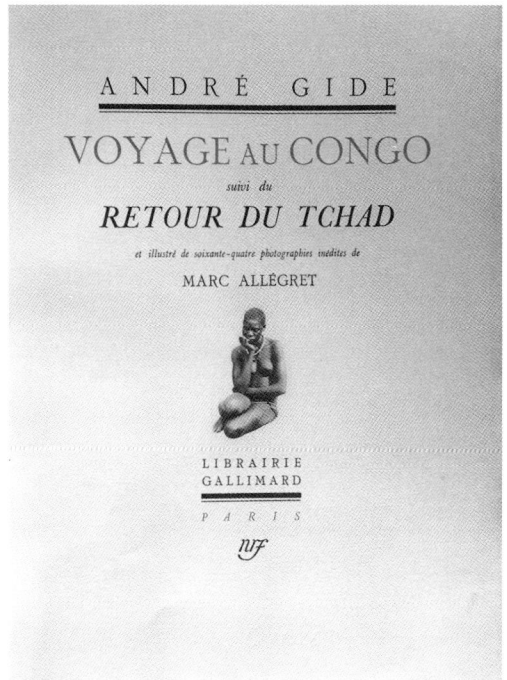

Figure 2.2. Marc Allégret, titlepage, in André Gide, *Voyage au Congo*, Paris: Gallimard, 1929.

The position of Gide and Allégret's needs to be explored with some care; the long tradition of simplifying *Voyage au Congo* was inaugurated by Léon Blum very soon after the work was published. In a discussion in the socialist paper *Le Populaire*, Blum presented Gide simply as a courageous witness: "Gide is a man who knows how to see, and nothing will stop him from stating plainly what he has seen."[3] But, as I have already suggested, Gide's project was much more complicated than this; his witnessing would turn out to be fraught and compromised. And so understanding what was involved in bearing witness demands more than tracing the journey taken by Gide and Allégret: it requires an analysis of the conditions which shaped their different accounts of that journey. The works which Gide and Allégret made public — texts, a film, and photographic illustrations — were not only carefully edited, they were constituted by processes of elision, suppression and disavowal. These processes are already generating their effects in the first chapter of *Voyage au Congo*. Yet before turning to this text, I need to introduce more carefully both the author and the photographer, and the means at their disposal for negotiating the colonial imaginary.

Gide's queer disposition

A preliminary to exploring Gide's *Voyage au Congo* is some consideration of the very shape of the writer's œuvre. Ranging across many forms and genres, Gide's writing presents particular challenges to interpretation. Roland Barthes, who remains one of the best guides to the œuvre, is prepared to confront this diversity, and begins by granting that, in approaching Gide's work, incoherence is preferable to an "order which deforms".[4] Yet if the work should not be constrained or reduced to a formula this places some difficulties in the way of those attempting exposition. So it is perhaps useful for me to anticipate: in what follows, rather than constructing a system I will trace a movement through the network of Gide's texts. My purpose in doing so is to establish Gide's disposition and the manner in which it turns on relations to the other. Specifically, I shall argue that Gide's wish is to sustain reciprocity and to produce relations "face to face". This had a profound impact on his ability to perceive Africa.

A network does not have a given point of entry and nor is there is a given pathway through it. That said, one can attempt to describe a network's elaboration and extension, although in Gide's case the network is daunting in its scale and complexity. Alongside his journals and voluminous correspondance, there is an enormous span of published works, which stretches from 1889 to beyond his death in 1951.[5] To find a way through this I shall begin with the briefiest chronological survey. Gide began his *Journal* in 1887.[6] A work entitled *Journal: 1889-1939* first appeared in 1939 but it would be entirely misleading to suggest that this was the first publication of the text. Many expressions in Gide's first book, *Les Cahiers d'André Walter*, of 1891, were transcribed directly from the *Journal*.[7] Yet even to describe this as Gide's first book is problematic as the first edition was signed "P. C.", the initials of a pseudonym of Gide's friend Pierre Louys.[8] Already one has entered "a hall of mirrors".[9] In 1897 Gide published the work by which he was most often judged, to his own annoyance: this was *Les Nourritures terrestres*, another book which is difficult to classify but is at least in part autobiographical.[10] In the course of 1920-21, Gide published two volumes of memoirs, *Si le Grain ne meurt*. Then, in 1925, he completed his one "true" novel, *Les Faux-Monnayeurs*, which, when finally published in 1926, was joined by an account of its production, *Le Journal des Faux-Monnayeurs*.[11] These are the key works which precede *Voyage au Congo*. This latter text was published in the form of a journal, with dated entries, and so is presented as reportage; it was first serialised in the *Nouvelle Revue Française*, from November 1926, before being published as a book in 1927.

Le Retour du Tchad, Suite du Voyage au Congo: Carnets de route appeared in 1928. The illustrated edition, my principal focus, was published in 1929.

Even a cursory reading of this restricted list will reveal a complex relationship between unpublished and published texts, and thus a relationship between the private and the public, between the "life" and the "work". It is this complex relationship which led Barthes to view the Gidean œuvre as a "network of enunciations" rather than as a product of a stable authorial identity.[12] Thus, for Barthes, the *Journal* is not some uncompromising record of an individual's opinions; it is a much more subtle work than a confessional:

> Gide's *Journal* always has its own inflections; it is more often a dialogue than a monologue. It is less a confession than the story of a soul in search of itself, responding to itself, reflecting on itself (in the manner of St Augustine's *Confessions*).[13]

The *Journal*, then, is not simply a chronicle, or record of external events, yet nor is it a narrowly conceived interior monologue. It is dialogical in character and Barthes notes that whilst the dialogue might be internal it may also be sustained with a whole range of Gide's contemporaries, such as Valéry and Claudel, and also with earlier writers such as Goethe and, above all, Montaigne.[14] These dialogues are fluid; that between Gide and Montaigne is one of "undulation [ondoiement]".[15] It is in such movements that Gide "escapes the sclerosis of systems".[16] One should remember that Gide liked to read Montaigne whilst walking.[17] Gide's debt to Montaigne lies in the essayist's concern not with propositions but with his own disposition, which itself is fluid and "changeable [ondoyant]".[18] This is a point Barthes takes care to emphasise, "movement remaining for Gide the best of man".[19] Of course as much is signalled in Gide's quotation of Keats as the introit to *Voyage au Congo*. But why is it prudent to be moveable? What is the value of fluidity? What does it enable? Gide himself makes an approach to these questions in the first pages of *Voyage au Congo*.

The book opens, as many travel accounts do, on board ship. The first entry is dated to the third day of sailing, 21 July 1925, and among Gide's very first reflections is the observation that because he was not rocked in a cradle as an infant he is "particularly prone to seasickness".[20] There is, then, at least the suggestion that to embark on this journey is to experience a second birth. And, like a birth, the journey seems not willed but of its own momentum. This is so much so for the author that he is "on the point of forgetting that it is nothing but a 'project of youth realised in maturity'", a project conceived when Gide "was not yet twenty".[21] Élie Allégret, Gide's guardian, first mentioned the Congo to him in a letter of 9 July 1888 when Gide was, indeed, just nineteen.[22] It is this project of youth which sets Gide apart from his travelling companions, the "administrators and traders".[23] Of those on board ship, he and Marc are "the only ones travelling 'for pleasure'".[24] This prompts a question:

> — What are you going out for?
> — I'll see when I get there.[25]

An earlier response to this question of what it means to travel without purpose is offered in one of the last essays of Gide's dedicatee, Conrad. In "Geography and Some Explorers", completed in 1924, the novelist defends travel for pleasure. He argues that

> geography finds its origin in action, and, what is more, in adventurous action, of the kind that appeals to sedentary people, who like to dream of arduous adventure in the manner of prisoners dreaming behind their bars of all the hardships and hazards of liberty, dear to the heart of man.[26]

Gide clearly had some sense of this connection of the sedentary and the arduous when staging his photograph of awkwardly seated adventurers. Indeed Conrad's essay moves across a similar terrain to that presented in Gide's photograph; he also pauses "in the shade of an enormous African tree (species unknown)" close by a "village of grass huts".[27] Conrad goes on to establish that his most cherished adventurers had the virtue of innocence and were in the service of a geography which was "the most blameless of sciences".[28] This branch being for Conrad quite distinct from a "geography militant" which directs itself to the service of conquest and greed, thriving on "the fears and cupidities of men".[29] Some of those bound for Brazzaville with Gide were involved in this service. By identifying his fellow passengers as "administrators and traders", Gide recognises their roles and the objectives they move towards, whilst preserving for his own mobility a different character. He travels without purpose and this freedom clearly has its own value. Yet this is only the first part of an answer to the larger question of the value of movement in Gide's œuvre. As Barthes recognises, it is a crucial aspect of Gide's writing and it needs to be illuminated if one is to understand his project in *Voyage au Congo*.

Earlier, in October 1924, when Gide had decided to postpone his departure for Africa, he had some cause to reflect on voyaging; at this moment he made the following entry in his *Journal*:

Some people direct themselves towards specific goals. Others simply fol-
low their noses.
For myself, I don't know where I'm going, but I'm going forwards.
Perhaps I'm just an adventurer.[30]

Gide distinguishes himself from others and does not direct himself as others do. His movement forward could be held to be the thrust of the *Journal*, this move-ment, then, is that of the text. For Gide understood the project of writing to be coextensive with life and to guide it, even whilst remaining in some tension with it. As much was established very early on in his writing career; already in January 1892 Gide had observed to himself that the artist "must not simply narrate the life he has lived, but live it just as he will narrate it".[31] Gide made this observation in his journal just over a year after he had set down similar thoughts in *Les Cahiers d'André Walter*.[32] Significantly, this book takes the form of two journals written by a young man, that is, a form which is resistant to a simple opposition between fact and fiction. *Les Cahiers* was one kind of experiment and the *Journal* was another and as much seems to be what the youthful Gide recognised in January 1892. He was no longer to consider the *Journal* as a record of lived experience but rather of what it meant to live his life as text. This is a crucial moment in the elaboration of his network. Gide was to be on the side of writing. A life lived in this way cannot be taken to be egotistical — a refrain of Gide's critics — for it is opened as a dialogue. The artist does not write as a form of self-presentation, he is written.[33] Gide becomes, in Barthes's happy phrase, "an actor of writing".[34]

Gide's subsequent writings in their proliferating forms — tract, memoir, novel — are further elaborations of the network, as the texts extend the dialog-ical potential of the *Journal*. Gide's successive works continue the project "to exhibit, successively, different aspects of the self".[35] Yet Barthes emphasises that Gide's network is one "of mobile points" and subjectivity here should not be considered "as a river, even an everchanging one, but as a discontinuous (and yet unabrupt) mutation of sites".[36] This was explored by Gide with some care during the period when he was writing the novel *Les Faux-Monnayeurs*, the book which immediately preceded *Voyage au Congo*.

Thus, in December 1924, Gide reflects in the *Journal* that there is "a certain *sense of reality* that I lack."[37] He continues:

I can't rid myself of a certain astonishment that things might be as they are; that they might all of a sudden be different would not astonish me any more. To me, the real world always remains a little fantastical.[38]

Thus "German philosophy finds in me a fertile soil. When I read Schopenauer's *The World as Will and Representation*, I said to myself straightaway: Yes, that's it!"[39] Nevertheless, he goes on to insist that this is not really a philosophical position and is rather, quite precisely, a matter of his disposition: "it's the *feeling for reality* that I do not have".[40] However, this is not to say that the author is living a fantasy when he goes on to register that the world is no more real than a novel, such as *Les Faux-Monnayeurs*. Whilst this is a judgement one might expect from an actor of writing, Gide makes it in order to underline that others are not for him mere ciphers, to be arraigned and arranged according to whim.[41] Quite to the contrary, in a related journal entry, he asserts:

> The triumph of objectivity permits the novelist to borrow the 'I' of others. I have been a little too successful in this and some have been taken in; they have read my books as a series of confessions. This renunciation, this poetic depersonalisation, which makes me feel the joys and sorrows of others so much more deeply than my own, no-one has spoken of this better than Keats (*Letters*.)[42]

A character in *Les Faux-Monnayeurs*, Édouard — another author — shares these sentiments. His "heart beats only out of sympathy" and he has "a singular faculty of *depersonalisation*" which enables him to feel other people's emotions as if they were his own.[43] In the *Journal des Faux-Monnayeurs*, Gide returns to (or anticipates) Édouard's sentiments: he notes that his own heart "beats only through sympathy".[44] However, it is far from being the case that Édouard is Gide, or in any straightforward way his *porte-parole*. In an entry made at the end of the *Journal des Faux-Monnayeurs*, that is, in June 1925, just before departure for the Congo, Gide cites with approbation a remark by Albert Thibaudet: "The authentic novelist creates his characters according to the infinite directions of his possible life (...) The genius of the novel makes the possible come to life; it does not revive the real."[45] Again, it is not surprising that the actor of writing would be happy with these lines. And in an appendix to the *Journal des Faux-Monnayeurs* Gide has another character, Lafcadio, summarise these thoughts in an internal dialogue with Édouard: "This need I have to be on the move, to offer myself (...) is after all possibly only a need to escape myself".[46] So this is the value of movement. Gide's movement is continually away from himself, yet as Barthes notes, the movement is also a return, an aspect of the writer's disposition.[47]

Now, this piling up of perspectives and *personae* — which I have to a degree mimicked in the paragraphs above — is the defining Gidean effect. It is a desta-bilising effect, but also an enabling one. This is what Lafcadio understands when he reflects on what it means to "prefer someone else to myself".[48] The move-ment is of desire. The implications of this were already set down in 1897, in *Les Nourritures terrestres*. Towards the beginning of this text the unnamed narrator declares: "A mind only interests me in what makes it different from others".[49] Difference is asserted, quite baldly, as a principle; yet it becomes clear that it is not simply a means of differentiating the self. It emerges at the end of the text that this difference is also constitutive of love: "It is because you differ from me that I love you; the only thing I love in you is what differs from me."[50] And if the narrator loves what is different he is repelled by those who lack differen-tiation, those who repress what is different about themselves. Such people are, in a sense, unrecognisable. They have nothing in them which the narrator may love. They have nothing with which to reciprocate. Against those who repress difference, the narrator asserts to his companion: "the sincerity of my pleasure, Nathaniel, is my chief guide".[51] Pleasure is not to be constrained. And this, in the end, is what Barthes understands when he notes that Gide's writing must not be enclosed in a system. "Nathaniel, I will teach you that all things are divinely natural."[52] Yet arriving at this view was hardly a straightforward process for Gide.

The writer's epochal moment is recounted in the memoir, *Si le grain ne meurt*. This text is once again concerned with movements, it is a narrative of "the move-ment of my heart and mind".[53] These movements will not be down preordained paths; Gide is clear that he is charting his own course. "In the name of what God or ideal do you forbid me from living according to my nature?"[54] Again, this is not a simple egoism, and much less, Gide asserts, a question of mere license. On the contrary, it is a struggle with Christian morality, yet one in which Gide comes to doubt whether God "really exacted such constraints".[55] These reflec-tions are offered as part of the introduction to an account of Gide's experiences in Algiers in January 1895, which would prove decisive for the course of his life.

In Algiers, the young Gide encounters Oscar Wilde, whom he had first met in 1891. In a café, Wilde and Gide see two youths playing music and the Irishman senses in Gide a desire, which at first the young man cannot articulate. Leaving Gide in the café, Wilde organises a liaison with the help of a guide. He then re-turns to fetch Gide to a hotel.

> Wilde took a key out of his pocket and showed me into a tiny apartment
> of two rooms, where we were soon joined by the vile guide. The two
> youths followed him, each of them wrapped in a burnous that hid his face.
> Then the guide left us and Wilde sent me into the further room with little
> Mohammed and shut himself up with in the first with the *darbouka* player.
> Every time since then that I have sought after pleasure, it is the memory
> of that night I have pursued (...) I had found my normal at last. There was
> nothing constrained here, nothing precipitate, nothing doubtful[.][56]

This is Gide's momentous discovery: the realisation of a queer disposition. The
liaison is not, strictly speaking, Gide's sexual initiation, but it is his first sexual
experience that is not shadowed by remorse and as such it is marked as the true
beginning of his pleasure.[57] The liaison with Mohammed is what frees Gide from
the hell of his attempt at "normalisation".[58] For the whole day after his night
with Mohammed, Gide experiences "a joyfulness, a kind of lightness of body and
soul".[59] Yet his moment of pleasure is haunted. His experience is shadowed by
some sense of its source in the unequal relations between Gide and Mohammed.
A familiar form of the colonial encounter is played out here, although barely
acknowledged as such. Instead, the moment of pleasure is recapitulated in what
Gide finds an horrific form. Immediately after his description of "joyfulness",
he wrenches the structure of his memoir to leap forward two years to a second
meeting with Mohammed. Gide, now accompanied by one Daniel B., retires
with Mohammed to a hotel room, ostensibly for a drink. There, Daniel siezes
Mohammed and carries him to the bed:

> and soon I saw nothing but two slim legs dangling either side of Daniel.
> He had not even taken his coat off. Standing there in the dim light besides
> the bed, with his back turned and his face hidden (...) Daniel appeared
> huge, hunched over the little body he covered, like a great vampire feast-
> ing on a corpse. I could have screamed with horror.[60]

Gide is paralysed, he presents himself as not able even to scream, much less able
to act in response to Daniel. Accordingly, the description is abruptly broken off
at this point for more abstract reflections on the loves of others. After some pe-
riphrasis Gide returns to the play of his own desire:

> For myself, I only take pleasure face to face, and as mutually enjoyed and without compulsion. I am, like Whitman, often satisfied with the most furtive contact and so I was horrified both by Daniel's behaviour and by Mohammed's complacent submission to it.[61]

For Gide it is not simply Daniel's swift and brutal reduction of Mohammed to a passive, sexual object that is horrific, it is also what he assumes to be Mohammed's complicilty. This he sees as an effacing of reciprocity by both parties.[62] Gide's horror means that he does not seem able to consider that he may be witness to the resignation of the less powerful, which is something quite distinct from complicilty. It is the case that Gide would tend to repress his own role as a sexual tourist and seek absolution from roles of dominance; to do this he establishes a clear distinction between his own behavior and that of men such as Daniel. Gide may be rejuvenated by his encounter with Mohammed but convinces himself that this will not be at the cost of becoming a vampire.[63]

Gide's queer disposition resists submitting to imposed norms but also resists demanding the submission of others. This disposition enables reciprocity; it precisely enables Gide to feel so deeply "the joys and sorrows of others", rather than effacing them.[64] And in rejecting any "normal" other than his own Gide discovered what is productive in lacking a sense of reality. He will resist the "natural" as a source of truth. Reflecting on this as what might be termed a queer resistance, Barthes comments: "Who knows if this insistence on the plural is not a way of denying sexual duality? The opposition of the sexes must not be a law of Nature; therefore, the confrontations and paradigms must be dissolved, both the meanings and the sexes be pluralized."[65] And thus there will be "only *homosexualities*, whose plural will baffle any constituted, centered discourse".[66] Against the *doxa* will be set the heterodox and this will be Gide's movement. It will run in different directions; it will be heterodomous.[67]

Gide's own position was of course unstable, and problematic; as much will already be clear from the narrative of his two encounters with Mohammed. I need, then, to refine my initial observation concerning the place of Gide as at once inside and outside the narratives of the European encounter with the African. It is better to describe Gide's position as involving both resistance and complicitiy. As Robert Aldrich concludes: "Gide might be castigated for perpetuating a kind of sexual colonialism, but he was also one of the singular Europeans who tried to reach across the great cultural and political divide."[68] If Gide does not share the motivations of his fellow passangers on board ship, it does not follow from this that he is simply disengaged; the absence of purpose in his journey enables engagement. This will lead, ultimately, to his political campaigning and to his challenges to at least some of the orthodoxies used in defence of colonialism. Yet Gide would meet with difficulties in prosecuting his campaign and some of these were of his own making. During his African journey he did not achieve a complete triumph of objectivity, and would reach the limits of reciprocity.

Allégret's apprenticeships

Whilst Gide's journey was to be a project of youth realised in age, Marc Allégret's journey was more straightforwardly a project of youth; he was 24 when they took ship. However, this does not mean that Allégret's project was without complexity. Precisely because he had not elaborated an authorial disposition his activities, and their traces, were diverse and sometimes ill-sorted. Here is a brief inventory. There are photographs including 490 on glass plates and around 1500 exposures on Kodak film.[69] There is a documentary film which exists in various states, of which seemingly the most complete runs to 114 minutes.[70] Then there is a written record, focused mainly on the period between 5 September 1925 and 26 April 1926. This record is divided into three separate types of manuscript: a personal journal, a documentary record of distances covered, payments made and so forth, and, finally, a series of fieldnotes which could contribute to an ethnographic account; some of the latter were used to draft a *Note sur les Massa-Mousgoum*.[71]

These different productions could be turned to different ends. The *Note sur les Massa-Mousgoum* has a level of detail and a slightly laboured scholarly tone which make it comparable to the *Mémoires* produced at this date by students at the École coloniale.[72] Yet the fieldnotes could also be worked up into more or less ambitious pieces of journalism for publications such as *Le Monde Colonial Illustré*.[73] And it is evident from Allégret's correspondence that his photographs were always to lead their own lives; he expended much effort in circulating them.[74] Nevertheless, it is also clear that a collaboration with Gide and ideas for an illustrated volume were sketched out quite early on. Gide's third entry in *Voyage au Congo* has the two travellers on shore in Dakar but obliged to return to their ship to collect a camera; one may draw the inference that from the outset the journey was to have both a textual and a visual record.[75] However, this sense of a possible destination for his images did not saturate Allégret's practice nor constrain its commercial potential. From his contact with photographers such as Man Ray he would have known how to maximise the profit to be drawn from a negative and also how to exploit a position at the edge of different but only occasionally overlapping social circles, in Allégret's case including the ambit of Marcel Duchamp and the members of the Société des Missions Évangéliques.[76]

All this is to say that, while Allégret was in many respects the junior partner in the journey, his activities were not wholly subservient to Gide's writing. Of course, at one level Gide and Allégret were engaged in cognate tasks, both converting impressions and experiences into traces and both beginning with immediate records, jottings and snapshots. However, the very idea that these records are "immediate" presents its own problems. First, the reception of photographs tends to collapse the instant of exposure with the subsequent print (if the latter is ever developed). Second, the 64 photographs in the illustrated edition were selected for reproduction long after exposure and this selection was made according to principles which were only nascent at the moment the photographs were taken. Of course, as much is also true for Gide's text, which preserves a sense of immediacy whilst being the result of careful editing. In effect, the illustrated edition is as much a product of Paris as of Bangui and Fort-Archambault and thus the photographs may be described as both preceding and following the textual account. There were conditions for the final assembling of illustrations but there were also preconditions for Allégret's photography. If Gide had precursors in Conrad and La Pérouse, Allégret had a precursor in his own father, who had taken numerous photographs whilst in Africa, including, unsurprisingly, images of his own family.[77] Marc Allégret's photography may be said to be shadowed by Élie's. Yet as I shall show, the precedent of missionary photography was something Marc frequently resisted. And in turn Marc's project should be understood to complicate Gide's. For the first time this author was to travel with someone photographing and filming and, accordingly, his text came to stand in tension with these other records. In fact, different modes of viewing — and difficulties of viewing — came to play an important role in structuring Gide's account. They are central to the opening chapter of *Voyage au Congo* and Gide's first African encounters.

Perceiving the African

Here is the opening line of *Voyage au Congo*: "Inexpressible langour. Hours with neither content nor contours."[78] The languor nicely anticipates the calm reflections on cradling that Gide entertains whilst at sea, with attendant thoughts on infancy. If there is an implied rebirth at the beginning of the journal, it is related to a need for rejuvenation. Here are the last lines of the previous journal:

my apathy. I have given up on anything but the Congo to get me out of it (...) Recently, my sight has weakened considerably. Spectacles help with this. If only the brain could wear them too! Today the difficulty my mind has in 'focusing' on an idea is analogous to the weakness of my eyes. The outlines remain blurred.

8 June

Finished *Les Faux-Monnayeurs*.

14 July

Departure for the Congo.[79]

The continuity between the two journal entries is striking. On board ship Gide is in a state of limbo and this is not merely the condition of the traveller between departure and destination; it is also the state of the habitual writer suspended between a completed novel and an as yet unarticulated sense of a new project. In this state neither eye nor mind can focus. Exploring this condition is the business of Gide's first chapter and it is of a piece with the writer's stated lack of purpose. As such, it recalls something of the condition of Conrad's Marlow in *Heart of Darkness*, another narrator on a steamer travelling down the west coast of Africa. Marlow feels the "idleness of a passenger, my isolation amongst all these men with whom I had no point of contact".[80] And indeed this isolation keeps him, like Gide, "within the toil of a mournful and senseless delusion".[81] Escaping delusion is not easy.

Gide's first experience of Dakar is not encouraging, and in this rehearses a movement of anticipation and disappointment that is a staple of travel literature. "Dakar by night. Narrow, deserted streets. A dreary, sleepy town. One can't imagine anything less exotic, or more ugly."[82] To have travelled so far for this! Even when Gide and Allégret leave "the French town" they do not leave French influence behind; on a sidestreet they chance on an open-air cinema but once seated Gide finds behind him "a big Negro" who "reads aloud the text on the screen".[83] Thus the very first "African" voice Gide hears is not just reading French but also narrating an imported entertainment.

Naturally, these are first impressions, they will come to serve as counterweights to other experiences. If sea journeys have a particular role in travelwriting, so do ports as liminal spaces. Gide will have his rejuvenation. The reading of French intertitles will soon enough be replaced by the overlapping couplets and refrains of those ferrying the travellers ashore at Mayoumba, rhythms Gide will learn to compare with those of the Chad region.[84] And when he does first enter the forest, at Mayoumba, he is elated. "If I had been twenty my pleasure would not have been keener."[85]

So the journey proper seems to begin. And it is at this point that the first illustration is introduced, a view from a riverbank [Fig. 2.3]. Such views were common in missionary photography, precisely because they were an effective way of picturing the journeys undertaken in the service of God. Images like this could be particularly striking if they showed at once an exotic means of transport and a broad expanse of river, suggestive of the scale of the African continent. Élie Allégret took such photographs and it would be surprising if Marc was un-familiar with them [Fig. 2.4]. These photographs might prompt reflection on the wonders of God's creation. They could also accompany a trope of Christian mis-sionary narratives dating back to the New Testament: the deliverance from dan-ger whilst travelling.[86] Such images and narratives were shaped on the mission stations but were for consumption in the metropole; what was significant was the missionaries' distance from home and from those underwriting their work. The first illustration in *Voyage au Congo* operates differently, as proximity rather than distance is what is made salient.

The image is simply captioned: "The banks of the Djoué". In the text a more precise location is given, that of a fishing village at "the confluence of the Congo and the Djoué, about six kilometres from Brazzaville".[87] This specification is important and is matched to a close description of the location photographed.

> Strange dry river-bed, traced by an incomprehensible accumulation of almost black 'boulders'; it looks like a glacial moraine. We jumped from one of these rounded stones to another until we reached the banks of the Congo. A little path, almost at the river bank; a shady creek, where a big canoe was lying moored.[88]

The text describes what one sees in the photograph, the rocks, the shady creek, the canoe. At this point there is then a conjunction of word and image (and this conjunction was important enough to lead to the inclusion of what might oth-erwise seem a rather unsuccessful photograph with a tilted horizon). The text is enumerative; the reader is given a location and then a progress, along a river bed, with boulders, followed to the Congo. Writer and photographed are positioned, more or less as in the frontispiece. And the point of view adopted by the camera is wholly explained. The reader arrives at it. In the text, the reader is arrested at this point, before the rocks, at the path to the river. The creek and the canoe are held at a distance in the final sentence I have quoted; a set of features are

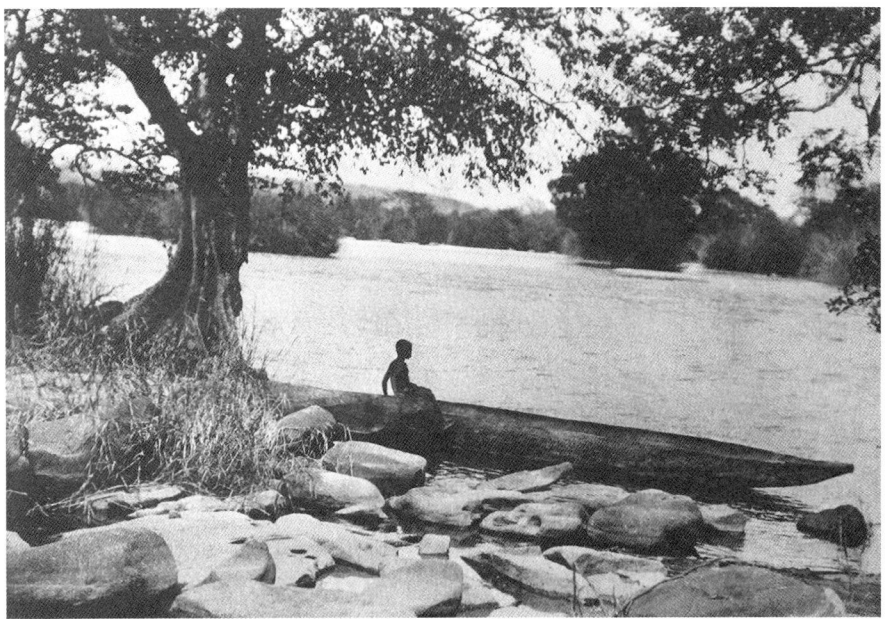

Figure 2.3. Marc Allégret, 'The banks of the Djoué', illustration at p. 16 in André Gide, *Voyage au Congo*, Paris: Gallimard, 1929.

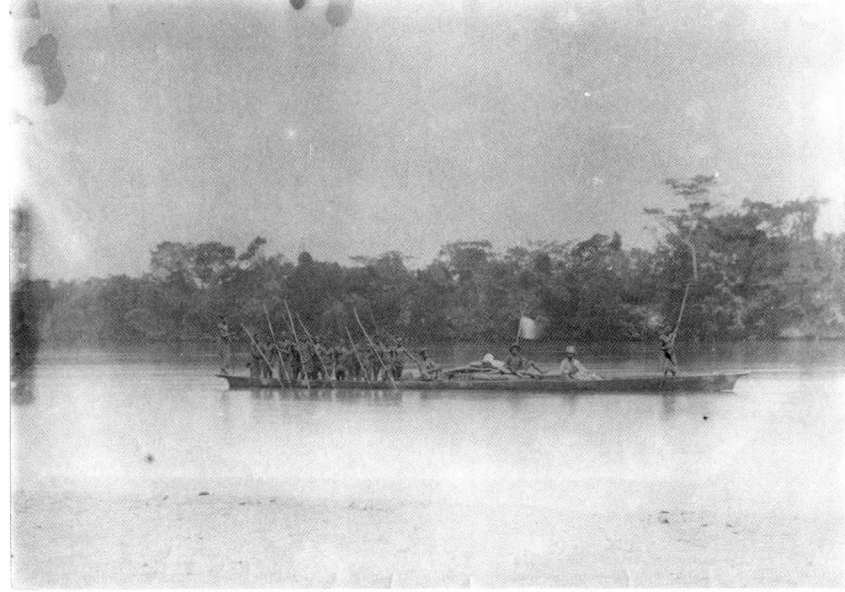

Figure 2.4. Élie Allégret, 'Canoe on the Ogooue river, Gabon', photographic print, 1889.

gathered into a view, that which is given by the camera. This seems, then, to fulfil something of the promise given by the frontispiece, of both a hierarchy of agency and a degree of collaboration. The procedures here are simple and congruent even though the congruence of views is not complete; the text does not mention the figure in the canoe. Nevertheless, the congruence seems important. Saying and seeing are held together without too many problems. In contrast to Gide's condition on board ship, here things are in focus.

Yet the focus established here is to prove fleeting; difficulties in maintaining it are encountered quickly. In the very next journal entry Gide records his return to the Congo rapids, this time in the company of Alfred Chaumel, amongst others. Chaumel had been charged with a mission to make films celebrating the colonial project. He was to be (like Louis Tinayre) a technician of the picturesque.[89] Yet this is a role which Gide resists, even whilst standing on the banks of the Congo before a spectacle "more majestic than romantic".[90]

> 'And would you believe it' — said one of the guests, looking at me — 'such a spectacle still awaits its painter!' This was an invitation to which I shall not respond. Art requires temperance and enormity is repugnant to it.[91]

This exchange — or, rather, the refusal to enter into an exchange — serves to signal Gide's preferences. As his account unfolds, the reader will discover that this signalling is important. The merely spectacular is repugnant and its celebration is a weakness, an unreflective response where a more measured one is appropriate.

The next entry begins with a terse paragraph: "The Sambry trial."[92] Here there is an abrupt shift of register, something which the journal form readily permits. In the dock in Brazzaville is "an unfortunate administrator", whom Gide judges to have been given too difficult a posting at too young an age.[93] Finding himself in such a position, and, according to Gide, lacking any natural authority, Sambry resorted to a reign of terror. The administrator's weakness of character is introduced with a formulation which will become a refrain: "The less intelligent the white man, the more the black appears stupid to him."[94] In the context of the trial this is easily read as a condemnation of Sambry, who evidently failed to be judicious in exercising the authority conferred on him. In framing the failure of Sambry in this way, it is quite possible that Gide was recalling Élie Allégret's view that the task of making men could only be undertaken by those prepared to dedicate themselves to God and so receive His strength. For after all Gide's first contact with the Congo had repeatedly brought him back to the moment when Allégret had made this observation. So in one sense Gide is inverting the terms of the civilising mission; he sees that instead of the "white" elevating the "black", the stupidity of the former only advances the degradation of the latter. Yet what is really being judged here? In Gide's formulation the agency of the black is not in question. What is at stake is the perception of the white and the appearance of the black. This is to say that if the terms of the civilising mission are inverted, they are by no means dismantled; the actions of the whites may ennoble or debase, but the province of action remains theirs. Here the black is a passive object, formed in the perception of the white. It will become clear that Gide's experience of the trial will prompt him to reflect on his own perceptions and whilst he will not completely reject the terms of the civilising mission nor will he simply reproduce them.

The day after the trail, Gide is visited by one of the judges, referred to as Monsieur X: "'Do you want to know the meaning of all this?', he asked me. 'Sambry slept with the wives of all the militiamen under his command. There is nothing more imprudent.'"[95] Thus Sambry lost his authority and his control over the militia. Monsieur X continues: "Almost all the cruelties which Sambry was accused of were committed by them. But they testified against him, as you saw."[96] Now Gide's judgement is unseated. Immediately after noting the revelations of Monsieur X, Gide observes: "I am taking these notes too much 'for myself'; I now see that I have said nothing about Brazzaville."[97] If on the voyage out he was led to confess that he did not know why he was travelling, he now at least is able to discern that he is not in Brazzaville for himself. A straightforward egotism is acknowledged as a limitation. Gide realises that he felt at first an "excess of astonishment and could find nothing to say. I did not even know what to call things. I admired without discriminating."[98] He now understands that his elation on first entering the forest was, precisely, intemperate. "One doesn't write well when drunk."[99] He recognises he has not met the standard he had set for himself on the banks of the Congo. He has not comported himself as art requires.

This failure of comportment is not quite the failure to bring things into focus that beset Gide before embarking, nor is it the failure to discern distinct contours which he experienced on board ship. There remains an inability to discriminate but this is not a matter of blurring; it is rather a result of the visual field becoming overcharged. Whilst the earlier failures were a result of Gide's lassitude, which impeded acuity, the later realisation of failure is prompted by what is apprehended. Once this is realised, it becomes a challenge and is made over into something like a task. Thus, with the acknowledgement that Gide is not in Brazzaville "for himself" but, implicitly, for others, a sense of a new role begins to emerge. Perception becomes a project. Now difficulties of apprehension and comprehension must be addressed. So what Gide finally manages to write of Brazzaville is:

> Above all, I realise that it is impossible to make contact with anything real; not that things here are factitious but that the screen of civilisation interposes itself and everything is filtered.
> I don't doubt that much could be learned of the machinery of the administration, in particular, but in order to understand it properly it is necessary to know the country already. Yet what I am beginning to grasp is the extraordinary complexity, the great entanglement of all the colonial problems.[100]

Of course, an epiphany of this nature will necessarily be incomplete. Nevertheless, it is inaugural. This is registered with an extended footnote, which departs from the habitual tenses used by the journal-keeper to acknowledge — in retrospect — the importance of this moment. In the note, Gide emphasises that the Sambry trial revealed to him "these distressing social questions" which would become "the chief interest of my journey".[101] Yet, even as this is acknowledged, there remains the difficulty of bringing things into view. So, still within the note, Gide returns to his excess of astonishment:

> A traveller arrived in a country where everything is new to him is arrested by indecision. Everything is equally fascinating and to begin with he registers nothing, being unable to register everything. How fortunate the sociologist is, being interested only in manners and customs, or the painter who contents himself with the country's aspect, or the naturalist who occupies himself only with insects and plants! How happy the specialists are! (...) I will be forgiven, then, for only being able to look at these new things with a hesistant, uncertain gaze.[102]

One now realises that, in his first chapter, Gide has been assuming and discarding the various roles he describes here, attending to the rhythms of local song at Mayoumba, reflecting on the invitation to paint as spectacle the rapids of the Congo, noting the varieties of butterfly and so forth.[103] For each individual role must be rejected. The narrow focus of the specialist will not permit Gide to grasp the dense knot of problems created by colonialism. "Focus", which Gide had previously struggled to attain, is now presented as problematic, if by the term one understands the action of isolating elements or holding them at a distance.[104] So his project remains nascent. It is not simply discovered as an external object; that would hardly do for a writer who is proud of the fact that he does not know where he goes. An external object would compromise Gide's disposition. Instead, he finds it preferable to maintain some hesitancy and a less than steady gaze. In this context, the focus of the photograph of the creek becomes suspect, as does the congruence of seeing and saying. And this, I think, is the reason why this manner of pairing word and image does not recur in the illustrated edition. The mutual reinforcement of text and illustration becomes undesirable. From this point onwards, the sequence of reproduced photographs begins to be uncoupled from the narrative of the journal. Better not to be prudently fixed. There will, on occasion, be a measure of correspondence between word and image, and this will be striking; yet the photographic will not serve as Gide's model. This is part of what is unseated.

The heart of things

Once difficulties of viewing have been properly acknowledged, Gide's perceptions oscillate between apprehensions of the familiar and the unfamiliar. Yet recognition of the familiar sometimes seems a form of redundancy. On 8 September Gide notes: "The spectacle is beginning to become more as I expected it to be; it is becoming *like*."[105] Nevertheless, at least to begin with, some form of the spectacle is able to sustain itself. On 28 September Gide finds himself in a village "so strange, so beautiful, that we felt we had found here the very reason for our journey, and had entered the heart of things".[106] But this is only seemingly the case and it will soon become abundantly clear that Gide and Allégret have only taken the first steps on their journey. Indeed, as much is implicit in the very combination of the beautiful and the strange, which provides only a schema, the formula of the exotic.[107]

A similar formula is to be found in the illustration inserted at this point [Fig. 2.5]. This is captioned: "A chief's daughter having her hair arranged by a servant (Oubangui)". There is no commentary, space, or scene in the relevant chapter to which this image can be linked, and in this it is quite unlike the first illustration, of the banks of the river. Nevertheless, the image of the chief's daughter is one which fulfils expectations, as in the manner of the spectacle registered on 8 September. It could be understood readily enough as combining the beautiful and strange. To be sure, the basic act of fashioning a coiffure is familiar but the manner in which it is shown here is sufficiently peculiar. The photograph's depth of field is narrow and in the version of the image cropped for publication the figures are tightly framed and as a result little is revealed of their setting, beyond the fact of it being a relatively clear and open space. These straightforward compositional choices serve to focus attention on the figures, their quite different degrees of bodily adornment and their perhaps contrasting moods of relaxation and attention.

What I offer here is more a description than anything else but that seems

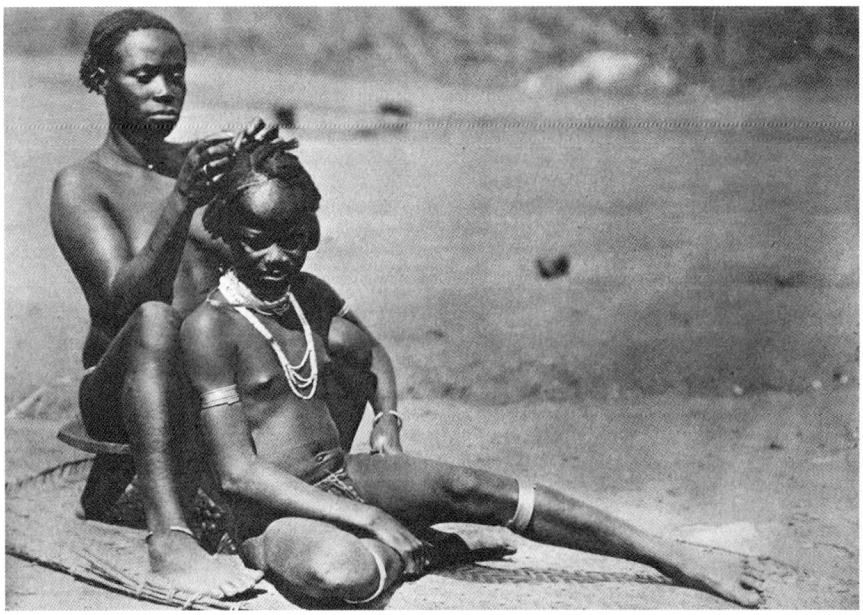

Figure 2.5. Marc Allégret, 'A chief's daughter having her hair arranged by a servant (Oubangui)', illustration at p. 40 in André Gide, *Voyage au Congo*, Paris: Gallimard, 1929.

appropriate, at least at one level. For this is a descriptive image, that seems designed to be brought under a classification such as "native habits and customs". This is a world seen from the outside. And as such it is brought close to a certain order of knowledge in which terms such as "lineage' and 'hierarchy", "privilege" and "service" may do their work. Details of coiffure and adornment may be registered as exotic or, more precisely, as regionally distinctive. So the details could be shuffled into a context to be ranged with, for example, the markings and decoration of the sculpture produced in Oubangui. All this is to say that the image may be understood in relation to the procedures of the "ethnographic".[108]

However, Allégret has attended to the ways in which hierarchy and service could be physically related. It would be a lazy or unfair description which did not extend to the relation of the daughter's pose and the servant's. For the daughter is not really relaxed; to maintain her pose she has right hand on her right shin and her left arm held over her servant's knee and her left hand braced on her own thigh with her leg thus pushed forward under tension. A number of other photographs in the volume show a similar attention; in these figures are set within environments and given activities, rendering walls or holding up the results of the hunt, as the case may be [Figs 2.6 and 2.7]. Bodies and actions are attended to as distinctive.

But is this what the travellers are searching for, images of such ready conformity? After all, Gide has already rejected the perspective of the sociologist. The very way in which the image of the chief's daughter fulfils expectations thus presents its own difficulties. To the extent that it may be assimilated to existing

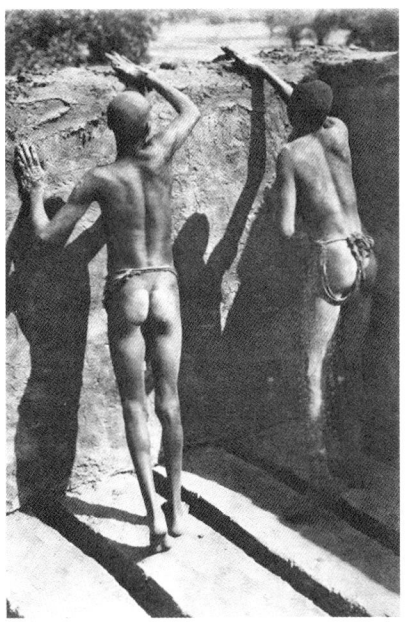

Figure 2.6. Marc Allégret, 'Masons at Fort-Lamy', illustration at p. 150 in André Gide, *Voyage au Congo*, Paris: Gallimard, 1929.

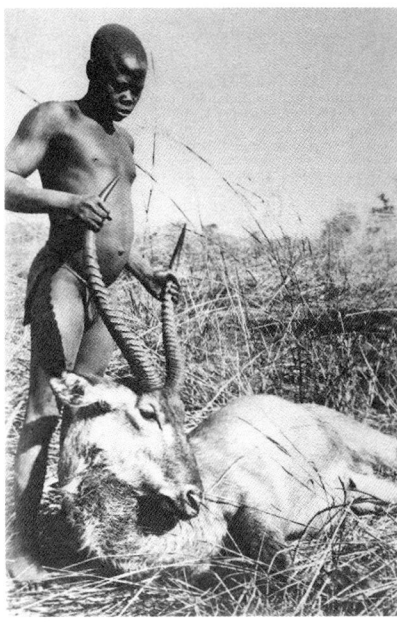

Figure 2.7. Marc Allégret, 'A katembourrou', illustration at p. 164 in André Gide, *Voyage au Congo*, Paris: Gallimard, 1929.

registers, it may be as disappointing as the first impressions made by Dakar. Gide acknowledges as much a little further on in the journal, when he notes that his

> image of this country was so lively (I mean that I imagined it so vividly) that I wonder whether later, this false image will not compete with my memories and whether I will see Bangui, for example, as it is or as I first of all imagined it to be.[109]

In offering such reflections, Gide acknowledges that he remains caught up in the play between anticipation and experience he had registered in Dakar, that is, he remains concerned with the business of travelwriting. Yet within the trajectory of the journal such reflections are the necessary preparation for the next steps, when conventional travelwriting will be abandoned as the travellers "will truly begin the journey".[110]

Gide declares: "What we really want to do is get off the beaten track, to see what one does not ordinarily see, to enter more deeply into the country."[111] It is difficult to imagine a more banal desire for the extraordinary. Nevertheless, if the desire is familiar, this moment is marked by shifts in Gide's habituated perceptions of the European. Through the course of his journey thus far Gide has registered both approbation and disquiet at the actions of the Europeans he encounters. One the one hand there are those engaged in finding new methods to treat leprosy and sleeping sickness, on the other hand there are those attempting to extract rubber at the lowest possible prices, through scandalous methods, thus serving themselves by meeting the demands of European industry. These divergent practices may be juxtaposed in the space of a short journal entry, as, for example, in that dedicated to Bambari, where a visit to a dispensary is followed by a survey of the monthly rubber market.[112] Thus the activities of Europeans in Africa have different aspects, technical and ethical, which are presented in unstable combination. And Gide's own observations are implicated in this, made possible as they are by the products of European industry, by the steamers on the Congo, by the cars on the roads specially laid for motor traffic. However, Gide and Allégret decide — rather unsurprisingly — that they will not proceed by the "usual" route from Bangui to Archambault and on 27 October they abandon most of their entourage and their cars, which in any case have run out of both petrol and oil. They now leave the more accessible roads and also leave Oubangui-Chari and the relatively benign rule of Governor Auguste Lamblin. This movement beyond the immediate compass of the colonial infrastructure will indeed make possible a more profound acquaintance with the character of

French colonialism, something foreshadowed on the morning of the 27th, when the travellers breakfast with the administrator of Boda, Georges Pacha, who is introduced as "the sinister Pacha".[113]

Gide and Allégret depart Boda for Bambio; they spend the night in a wayside hut maintained for travellers and there, in the early hours of 28 October, they are awakened by the sound of footsteps and a voice. "We called out in Sango: 'Zo niè?' (Who's there?)"[114] The visitor is an important chief, Samba N'Goto, who is desperate to gain an interview with the travellers. He wants to report the conduct of one Sergeant Yemba. The latter, acting under the orders of Pacha, had been sent to exercise sanctions against the villagers of Bodembéré, who had refused to obey an order to relocate their settlement. On 21 October, Yemba and a small detachment under his command entered the village and tied 12 villagers to trees. These 12 men were then shot. Women were killed with machetes. Five young children were herded into a hut which was then set on fire. In all there were 32 victims.[115]

The next day, Gide seeks out a chief of Bambio, who confirms the narrative of Samba N'Goto and adds another, concerning the punishment meted out to workers of the company holding the concession for rubber production, the Compagnie forestière Sangha-Oubangui (C.F.S.-O.). Gide then takes up the narrative from a further source, the journal of a riverboat captain turned hunter, M. Garron. His journal records that workers who had failed to deliver the allocated amount of rubber

> were condemned to circle the factory under a burning sun, carrying very heavy loads of wood. If they fell down, whipping by the guards forced them back onto their feet.
> The 'ball' began at eight o'clock and lasted the whole day with Pacha and Maudurier, the company's agent, looking on.[116]

In turn, it is made clear that this is only the most recent of a series of violent repressions in which the colonial administration has worked in tandem with the representatives of the concession.[117]

Gide's account of these events is terse to the point of being elliptical, for he is circumscribed by his sources. He is at pains to note that he only reports what has been related to him directly or what he is able to confirm independently. The access he requires to gather this information is delivered as a result of his earlier, banal desires. He notes that as "a simple tourist I may well often see and hear things" which the governor, preceded by his entourage, will not.[118] Yet this singular, naïve perspective has its own limitations and Gide now reminds himself of the "terrible entanglement of problems which is not for me to resolve".[119] He returns to the reflections which followed the Sambry trial. Elaborating on his earlier, partial epiphany, with these new revelations of violence and abuse Gide confirms himself in his role. He will bear witness. He will concern himself with "certain definite facts, completely independent from the difficulties of a general order".[120] Here the role of witness is not so much assumed as imposed, and, in being imposed, the role is like the African journey itself. Gide draws the two together; embracing his role as witness, he is able to answer the question put to him when bound for Brazzaville.

> Now I am overcome by a great sadness; I know things to which I cannot reconcile myself. What demon drove me to Africa? What was I looking for here? I was at peace. Yet now I know: I must speak.[121]

Previously, Gide had prided himself on not knowing where he is going. Now he no longer has that luxury. It is this which makes an epoch, in changing his relationship to his writing. "Up until today, I have always spoken without any care as to whether I was heard or not"; but henceforth he must speak and he must be heard.[122] So, to recall his youthful letter to Élie Allégret, Gide now has to conduct himself in such a way that his "life might be worth something".[123]

Having accepted his mission, Gide pursues his investigation of Pacha's administration and the prison maintained at Boda. "I want to go behind the scenes, to the other side, to know what is hidden there, however horrible it might be. I suspect as much and now I must see."[124] In effect, Gide and Allégret embark on a new relationship with those for whom they bear witness. Here is the beginning of Gide's entry for 29 October: "This morning I went to see one of the native chiefs who had come yesterday to meet us. Long conversation."[125] At first glance there would seem to be nothing remarkable here. Then one realises that, following the narrative of Samba N'Goto, this is the first iteration of a dialogue with an African that Gide has actually recorded. Previous encounters have been mediated by merchants, doctors or administrators, or limited to visual contact.[126] For example, at the edge of the beautiful, strange village which had once seemed at the heart of things, Gide and Allégret had dined surrounded by about 40 children, who "stayed there, watching us eat, as a crowd at the Jardin d'acclimatation gathers to watch the sealions being fed".[127] The point is that the children would no more think of addressing the travellers than would the visitors to the zoo attempt to exchange greetings with the sealions. So the Sango question,

"Zo niè?", now assumes its full significance; it is the first occasion on which the reader is presented with the opening of a conversation. As such it inverts the situation at the cinema in Dakar, when the voice of a Senegalese man is heard, but only reading French intertitles.

Gide now meets a number of chiefs and holds a series of long conversations; the frequency of interaction with the local populations is greatly increased.[128] And this project of witnessing has a corresponding photographic mode. It is introduced with an image captioned: "Natives of Baya come to the entrance of our hut" [Fig. 2.8]. The caption indicates a space of encounter and helps to explain the composition of the photograph; it becomes clear that the mass at the right of the image is a pillar forming part of the entrance to the hut. This pillar is a marker, one serving to create a sense of an interior space. It also helps to suggest the presence of the travellers within the hut, by at once framing and partially blocking their outward view. In turn, this prevents the image appearing as one mastered by the camera, controlled and ordered by the apparatus, as is the case with some of the earlier images. This photograph is not made wholly on the terms of the photographer; whilst the viewpoint of the camera is that out from "our hut", the image is not governed by this. Rather, this view is met by others.

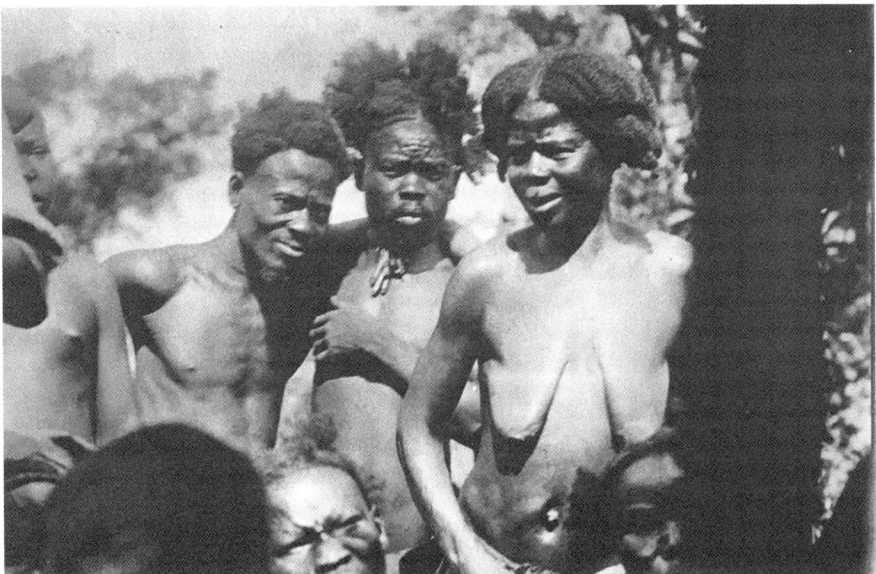

Figure 2.8. Marc Allégret, 'Natives of Baya come to the entrance of our hut', illustration at p. 64 in André Gide, *Voyage au Congo*, Paris: Gallimard, 1929.

Of the six faces visible, there are at least four different directions of gaze. These divergences are important; they create disorder within the image, an informality also present in the way one man drapes his arm across the shoulders of another. Such informality is also evident in the narrow depth of field which divides the image into different, compressed registers rather than presenting a clearly ordered space. Registers, looks and gestures all confirm that the figures before us have not been summoned, they have not been brought before the camera but present themselves. The various informalities in the image should be understood as defining the interaction between villagers and travellers; together they constitute a sociability.

Describing the image in these terms and matching it to a rhythm of social interaction implies some relationship between the journal entries and photographic representation. On the page before the photograph, an entry for 1 November reads: "At each stop in a village, we speak with the chief."[129] And on the page opposite the photograph, Gide describes an encounter in which "men flock round us in order to make appeals".[130] So there is here some congruence of seeing and saying. Earlier this had been suspect, when Gide had first begun to recognise "the great entanglement" of the colonial situation. However, at that point his project was yet to be defined; now, however, he must speak. A new relationship to speech is perhaps registered in the photograph of the entrance to the hut for, at this moment, speech is no longer Gide's alone; here it is not a matter of conjoining word and image, as was the case with the photograph of the creek. Now, Gide's speech and his mission are the result of his conversations with villagers and chiefs and Allégret's photograph works with this. There are, then, different types of speech implicit here; the man at the centre of the image has a quizzical expression and it is at least possible to imagine him formulating his own variant of the question: "Who's there?"

If this question is formulated here, then the photograph is in its own way inaugural. The image is of an entrance, a liminal space, and Gide and Allégret look across this threshold at a world that is not theirs. But what I have tried to show is that this world is not straightforwardly an object for their gaze. The people before the hut are not presented as reducible to a set of categories or knowledges, as is perhaps the case for the image of the chief's daughter and her servant. Instead the photograph represents an encounter which may be described as "*face to face*".[131] The people outside the hut have their exteriority but this is perhaps recognised as such, as irreducible, and in this the image may be said to have an ethical dimension. Here one is faced with an Other "refractory to categories".[132] The photograph acknowledges the "strangeness of the Other, his irreducibility to the I".[133] For Levinas it is precisely the case that this face to face relation is effected in speech, in conversation. For Levinas it is vital that "the face speaks".[134] "Conversation, from the very fact that it maintains the distance between me and the Other (...) cannot renounce the egoism of its existence; but the very fact of being in a conversation consists in recognizing in the Other a *right* over this egoism."[135] In exercising this right, the Other calls into question the same, "this is precisely accomplished as a calling into question of my spontaneity, as ethics".[136] One may say that this is what happens to Gide at this moment; he is imposed on.[137]

Allégret's photograph presents an encounter which is quite distinct from those presented in the missionary photography to which he was heir. In many of the photographs taken by his father figures are marshalled and brought before the camera; the conventions are stable and recurrent. For example, in an image of young catechists, taken by Élie Allégret in Gabon, the neatly dressed Christians have been arranged in rows, seated and standing, and submit to the protocols of the European group portrait [Fig. 2.9]. For the young men are present in a capacity, and they now share a world with the missionary. The distance between the photographed and the photographer has been diminished. There is not the imposition which is entailed in accepting the ethical role.

Within the account unfolded in *Voyage au Congo*, Gide accepts his role; he wants to see and there is a sense in which the photograph at the hut entrance is the first image in which he is figured *as* seeing. And this is not simply a matter of the creation of an implied view from the hut, it is also, and more importantly, a matter of his being called into question. This is what distinguishes this image from the previous ones in the illustrated volume, each of which had a controlling viewpoint. Gide and Allégret were present to take in the view offered in the photograph of the river bank, but they were present in a landscape that was in effect depopulated. The figure in the canoe was not registered, or was registered only as staffage; this person did not face them. As viewers they were placed and commanded the scene. But as viewing subjects one could say that they were shut up in their interiority, and not questioned. Now, however, they do not command but, rather, they are seen. This is what will enable them to see in the fuller sense of bearing witness. Gide now sees because he is seen.

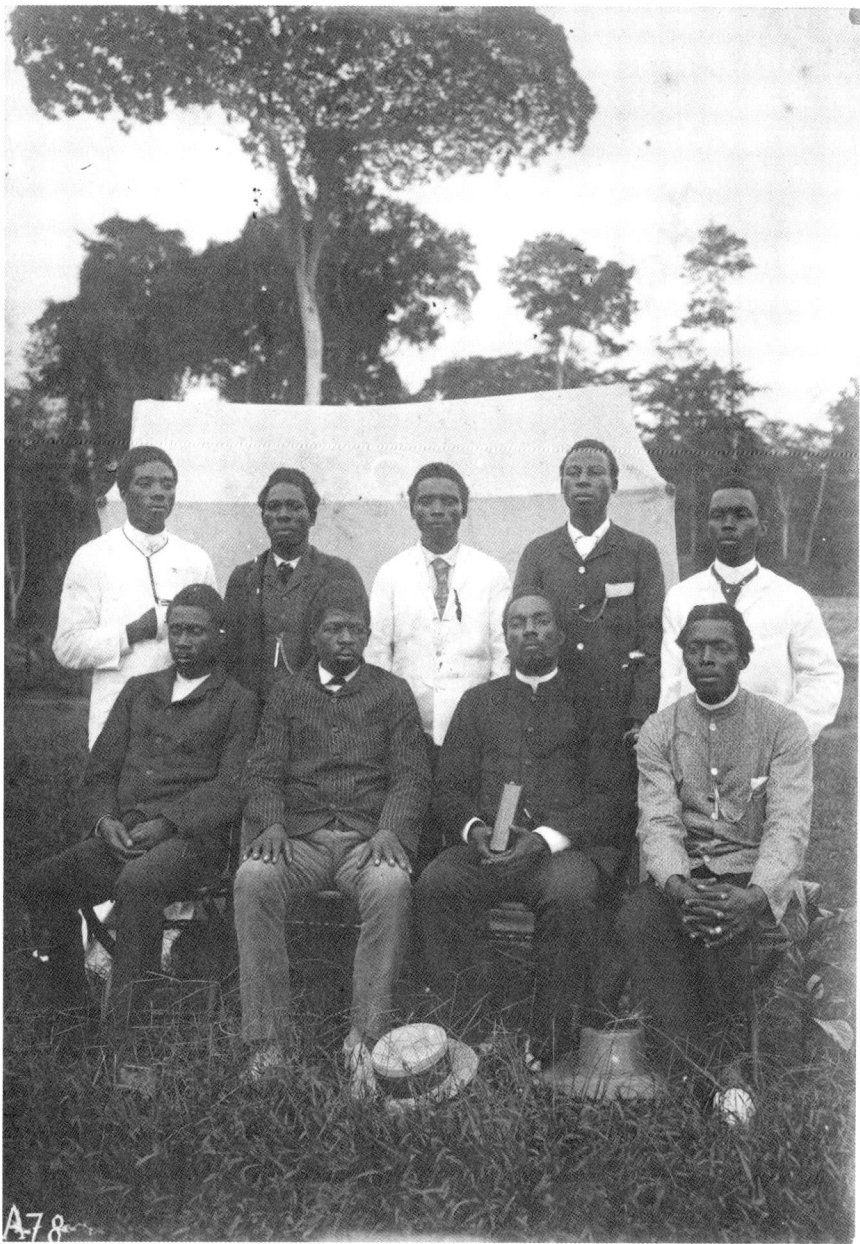

Figure 2.9. Élie Allégret, 'Galwa catechists in Gabon', photographic print, c. 1895-1904.

Difference and differentiation

After the encounter with Samba N'Goto there is an increased rhythm of exchanges with villagers and chiefs. However, it soon becomes clear that the rhythm is unsteady and is one that Gide finds difficult to sustain. Through the course of these difficulties, he will gradually come to his own accommodation with the colonial imaginary.

If previously the novelty of Gide's experience had induced a kind of drunken wonder, now his knowledge modulates his perceptions. His response to the landscape is qualified as he begins to understand what he sees, and its causes. At the edge of Pacha's subdivision of Boda, Gide surveys enormous "fields of *unharvested* manioc (...) and further on fields of castor-oil plants, also unharvested, all the men being at work gathering rubber, or in prison, or dead, or run away".[138] As he attempts to deepen his understanding of the entanglement of problems, he is sometimes thwarted. At Katakuou, the chief "hurried up to present his book, in which we read: 'Incompetent chief, totally without energy, cannot be replaced; none of the other villagers any better.'"[139] And shortly thereafter, on 3 November, he notes: "I tried to question the chief of a village where we stopped, a stupid man (like the chief of last village and of the next one) who held out his book where I read once again: 'Incompetent chief, without authority over his people.'"[140] The only communication sustained in these encounters is the chiefs' unwitting presentation of an administrator's judgement of their inadequacy. The communication is transferred from one Frenchman to another whilst the chiefs are reduced to being intermediaries in the weakest sense; they are in effect deprived of speech.

The oppositions established in earlier chapters of the *Journal* are now revised. Gide encounters agents of the C.F.S.-O. who appear honest. However, he immediately adds that their honesty will redound against them as the company prefers those who make the most money to those who make it honestly.[141] Then Gide meets a Doctor B. who at first criticises the concessionary company and its evasion of its responsibility to provide healthcare. Yet the next evening — after Gide has made him privy to his charges against Pacha — the doctor, now perhaps drunk, takes pains to defend the colonial administrators. He protests against the bad practices of a few being used as the means of tarring the reputation of the many. Gide concedes that this is a problem but, as the evening wears on, the doctor labours his point and makes increasingly bizarre and extravagant claims in defence of the use of force.[142] The long conversation with the doctor and the interviews with agents are of a piece because they offer two sides of the same coin. The latter serves to demonstrate the fundamentally corrupt nature of the concessionary companies whilst exonerating at least some of the individuals in their pay and the former demonstrates the fallibility of other individuals, including Doctor B. himself, whilst allowing Gide to refrain from condemning French colonialism as a whole. So, if there is refinement of some of Gide's judgements, these entries in the journal are in conformity with his earlier observations; agency, whether exercised humanely or brutally, remains with the whites.

Given the brutality, cupidity and cynicism Gide has encountered, and given his role as witness, it may seem at the very least strange that the writer does not adopt a more robustly critical attitude towards the colonial regime. Why should he have travelled towards the heart of things in order to respond in this way? The answer is given at the climax of the first volume of the journal but a preliminary response may be found in a set of remarks Gide makes about his relations with his own entourage. These remarks are made on 10 November, in the entry which follows that describing the views of Doctor B. Again, the comments offer two sides of the same coin. First, Gide affirms that those in his temporary charge cannot be praised highly enough; treated well, they respond admirably. "A mutual accord and confidence have spung up between our servants and ourselves, and all, without exception, are as attentive to us as we are affectionate to them."[143] Yet limits are then placed on this potential for reciprocity. Gide concludes this journal entry by describing the progress he has made in the reading lessons he is giving his "boy", Adoum; this is his own project of making and one he takes to be exemplary. Praising Adoum's progress is the occasion for Gide to denounce the foolishness of whites. "What stupidity the white man displays when he is angered by the stupidity of the black!"[144] Gide here elaborates on his earlier observation: "The less intelligent the white man, the more the black appears stupid to him."[145] In the earlier instance, this was a matter of the perception of the white and the appearance of the black; now dullness of white perception is replaced with the display of white idiocy. Yet even whilst making this denunciation, Gide circumscribes its effects. He writes of the Africans he has encountered: "Yet I believe they are hardly capable of mental development, their brains are dull and sluggish, kept in darkness — but how often the white man makes it his business to hold them back!"[146] So here the colonial imaginary is reinscribed; given the diminished capacity ascribed to Africans, the need to make men remains. Although many whites may show themselves to be unequal to it, the struggle to liberate must continue.

Tacit acknowledgement of the limits of reciprocity is made by limiting the photographic modes used in the illustrated edition. The mode proffered with the image of the entrance of the hut does not recur. Instead, the dominant mode is the ethnographic one established by the image of the chief's daughter. What is not pictured is part of the response to what is encountered at "the heart of things".

Gide's reaction to his own entourage is only preliminary, for it contains further questions. What does it mean to be plunged in darkness? What threat is contained therein? These are not questions Gide raises directly; they are however ones his text now works to answer, or perhaps to forestall. In the same entry in which Gide offers his reflections on the stagnant brain he also relates his own experience of the environment, which seems to produce this mental lethargy.

> Every day we sink a little deeper into strangeness. I spent all of today in a
> state of torpor, barely conscious,
> *as though of hemlock I had drunk*
> losing track of time and place, and even myself.[147]

He now experiences his own progress as one of being plunged ever further into darkness. Thus the forest becomes oppressive to Gide. It is disorientating, depriving the senses of their operation; this he experiences as derangement, a threat to the self.

Gide is therefore relieved when, on 12 November, the travellers move into a new terrain; to underline the sense of liberation, as the landscape changes there is a corresponding change in the people the travellers encounter. "Before reaching Pakori, we passed through four or five villages, each one stranger than the last, with the villagers growing ever more excited. I fear I will only have confused memories of all this; it was too strange. At last we are out of the nightmare of the forest."[148] The villages now visited are the most beautiful the travellers have seen and the villagers are appropriately more robust and vigourous.[149] Alas, even these beautiful figures, in their very welcome, are threatening. "And all these people pressing down on one, jostling for the joy of shaking one's hand, all shouting and laughing, in a delirium of affection. It's almost cannibalism."[150] So the escape from the forest becomes entrapment, a further threat to the self.

This is now established as a pattern. In the next entry, Gide again records relief after suffocation. "At last we can breathe. A fine crossing of open country, savannah with grass about ten feet high, studded with clumps of trees. The landscape is undulating, the views extensive."[151] The stifling atmosphere changes and breathing is no longer laboured; arboreal darkness and density of foliage are replaced with open views. Body and senses are liberated. But once again the respite is fleeting. Now out in the open, "as always in this immeasurably vast country, there is no focus; the lines run in all directions. All lacks definition."[152] The description here is the opposite of that which accompanies the photograph of the river bank; there the viewer commanded the view but now this is impossible. And of course there is no photograph to accompany this passage of description; it is precisely the point that no photograph could capture Gide's experience at this moment. As in the forest, here once again the landscape is overwhelming and cannot be reduced to a photographic composition. One disorientation is replaced by another and it is the repetitions of this pattern which Gide will not be able to sustain.

The next repetition comes on 30 November and is the initial part of the sequence which forms the climax of the volume. The journal entry contains an uncharacteristic locution for Gide, a qualification of his own word choice:

> A magnificent landscape; the word is too strong no doubt, for there is nothing enchanting about the site — which reminds one of a number of French landscapes — but such was my delight at finally getting away from the formless, at seeing defined hills, decided slopes, and clumps of trees harmoniously disposed...[153]

Banal, calculated, the description is acknowledgement of respite and less an embrace of the magnificent than a welcome of the familiar. This is placed in contrast to the preceding landscape of oppression. After an almost insupportable experience, Gide feels "a state of physical joyfulness such as to make me find pleasure, nobility and beauty in the least striking scenery".[154] Before arriving at the village of Dahi he is carried away by "an intoxication of health" to which he attributes "that word 'magnificent' that I used just now".[155] It is important, I think, that Gide's transport is described with a vocabulary similar to that he used to describe his feelings after his night with Mohammed, when he experienced "a joyfulness, a kind of lightness of body and soul".[156] Both transports are liberations.

Yet, once more, respite is brief; the journal entry on Dahi concludes with a description of the villagers, which repeats that of the villagers before Pakori: "There must have been a hundred of them, gathering at our arrival after nightfall, crowding around us with cannibal-like expressions, so close as to suffocate us."[157] The pattern, then, is one of different forms and forces which ensnare Gide. Both habitat and inhabitants threaten; escape from the former only seems to lead to entrapment by the latter. But what is this movement from fear of suffocation to fear of ingestion? What is the nature of this threat to the self?

Even someone like Gide can see no more than brute stupidity or a suffocating mass in the Congo and so reciprocity is frustrated. Gide cannot live in another, his heart cannot beat in sympathy because he cannot discern the heart of the other. Herein lies the threat. Gide would be one to feel such a threat profoundly. Selfhood was a complex, much mediated project for the writer. Fear of its destruction, fear of being devoured, returned Gide to an earlier foundational, moment.

When Daniel seized Mohammed he assumed the aspect of a vampire. It was for Gide a moment of horror as his own pleasure "face to face" is transformed into one body preying on another. Gide's crisis in the Congo has a similar character. His desire to get "off the beaten track" has vanished; now he flies in the opposite direction.

> After having moved for such a long time amidst the savage, larval and formless, the joy at finding a clean and tidy village, with a prosperous air and a decent chief in European clothes, which are not at all ridiculous, and with a newly whitened helmet, and speaking correct French, and with a flag raised in our honour — all this is I find absurdly moving, bringing me to the verge of tears.[158]

This moment — when the travellers re-enter the territory of Governor Lamblin — is not at all a moment of relief. Gide's absurd, extreme reaction shows this. Instead of a hundred cannibals, Gide is met by a smartly dressed chief; after the nightmare of the forest, there is not respite but disavowal as the hundred-fold threat is dissimulated and the author is brought almost to tears.[159] So Gide embraces a type of mimicry here, in the chief's neat clothes and his speaking good French. He embraces "a reformed, recognizable Other", viewed from Gide's angle, not with pity or contempt, or perhaps only with pity for himself.[160] The mimicry here provides more than a solace; it enables Gide to defend himself successfully against the threatening encounter with the other. As the account lurches violently from the larval to the European, from unformed to formed, mimicry comes to modulate difference for Gide.

Radical difference here is that which cannot be differentiated, the formless, to repeat Gide's earlier description. The writer is now able to acknowledge this. At the beginning of the next chapter, in a more tranquil mood, he offers these reflections:

> The absence of individuality, of individualisation, the impossibility of dif-
> ferentiating, which oppressed me so much at the beginning of my journey
> — from as early as Matadi — on seeing a crowd of children all alike, all
> equally agreable, etc., and in the first villages, all the huts alike, containing
> a human herd, with the same looks, tastes, customs, possibilities, etc., and
> then it is just the same with the landscape.[161]

Gide passes in review both people and landscapes and as with the former, so
with the latter; the monotonous, the uniform cannot be differentiated and therefore cannot be seen. This failure is a product of Gide disposition; it is not a
triumph but a failure of objectivity. Gide has assumed the role of witness and
has attempted to form relations "face to face"; this was an attempt to recognise
the other as irreducible but it could not be sustained. Gide came to feel increasingly threatened by that which he could not differentiate. His inability to sustain
reciprocity was experienced as a direct threat to himself and in the Congo this
could not be resolved but only disavowed. So the only escape was to reduce the
other to the same. Hence the embrace of the neatly dressed chief. To the extent
that the chief comports himself in a European fashion, his difference is made
merely formal. As Levinas describes it, this alterity is that which "falls under my
powers"; this reduction of the other to the same Levinas identifies as the "imperialism of the same".[162] In embracing a form of this imperialism, Gide makes his
accommodation with the colonial imaginary.

Crucially, it is after the disavowal that the place of racial difference is established in Gide's account. This may be discerned in the differential treatment
given to habitat and inhabitants; both had once threatened, but now Gide is at
least able to apprehend the landscape. Two days after his encounter with the
decent chief, he may contemplate the scenery around Kuigoré with equanimity,
reminding him as it does of the forest at Fontainebleau. Previously, when there
was "no focus" the result was disorientation. Now there is no longer the need to
"suffer" the landscape.[163] Thus Gide can continue his reflections on the absence
of individuality with a more tranquil response to the landscape: "Everything is
uniform — there is no preference for a particular site. I remained the whole of
yesterday without any desire to move."[164] The uniformity suspends desire. Whilst
this quality might be restful in a landscape it remains repellent in those who inhabit it. Gide concludes his reflections: "This notion of differentiation, which I
have acquired here, and from which proceeds at once a sense of the exquisite and
the rare, is so important that it seems to me the principal thing I have learned in
this country."[165]

Such knowledge is acquired at a cost and as much is evident in Gide's descriptions of the people he encounters. Here it is instructive to compare Gide's *Journal* with his fiction. In *Les Faux-Monnayeurs*, there is an almost complete absence of physical description. Indeed, in the first chapter of the novel Gide signals this absence by having two characters discuss the role of local colour and scene painting in fiction.[166] There is no need to describe the characters because Gide places the reader in their presence, as auditor to their dialogues, and thus their individuality is dramatised. Offering details of, say, the cut of their clothes would not add to this in any significant way. In contrast, those registered in *Voyage au Congo* are not described nor their speech transcribed. In Gide's account there is no description of an African face; at best, the face is figured as part of a larger ensemble. So of a group of Modjembo women Gide writes: "The face is ugly, but the torso admirable."[167] The individual is subsumed in the homogenous collective.[168] There is nothing in the text analogous to the photograph of villagers at the entrance to the hut. There is no attempt at a portrait of an individual. Gide of course valued individuality and considered it an achievement; it was to be set against the description of the uniform "human herd". So, in the end, the indigenous people Gide encounters in the Congo are placed lower on a scale. They cannot accede to that state of being which is the European, the portrayable.[169]

By now, Gide has travelled a long way from the beginning of his journey, when he felt it advisable to maintain an uncertain gaze. At the outset, it seemed to Gide that the unintelligent white could see in the black only a beast or brute. Yet at this later point in the journey, Gide can see only human cattle. Instead of seeing individuals, he sees something closer to fauna, creatures of environment (although without the close description he affords fauna). Within the larger arc of the narrative, what is confronted is the limit created by the colonial imaginary. Within that imaginary it is the "making of men" that creates visibility. Just as the African landscape becomes visible as it approaches the French, so do Africans themselves become properly visible when they approach European models. Yet the shaping of such an account has required its own repressions, as is clear from the text's complicated publication history.

The first publication of *Voyage au Congo* was in *La Nouvelle Revue Française*, with the section under discussion appearing in the January-June number of 1927.[170] This first version has an appendix following the entry for 8 December, thus directly preceding the passage cited above on the absence of individuality. This appendix was a long citation from a letter from one chief's son to another; it details the reprimands meted after an attempt to tell the truth about the manner in which goods are supplied to the colonial administrators. The author of the letter reflects on the rebukes: "It is certainly true that the remarks made were that much more hurtful for being addressed to me almost in public. But, on the other hand, I have a clear conscience. I did not lie to the Governor."[171] Here one individual reflects on his own probity, and the way it has been traduced. The correspondent is fully aware of his actions and their consequences for himself, however unjust. He concludes ruefully: "The truth costs you dear in the bush!"[172] Reading the passage, one registers how different this perspective is from those encountered thus far. This is the very first occasion on which an individual African speaks. Rather than quoting, Gide has reported the content of conversations with Africans, and then only fragments are given and there is certainly no attempt to reconstruct a dialogue.[173] The moment listening to the reading of intertitles in Dakar here takes on a new force, as it becomes clear that the Africans in Gide's account will not speak.

This excerpt of correspondence is, then, quite distinct from the tone of the rest of the journal. It seems to me that it was for this reason that it was later suppressed. A set of proofs for the first publication of *Voyage au Congo* in book form contains the appendix but it has been neatly crossed through.[174] This deleted appendix offers a glimpse of another kind of book, in which the individuals Gide encounters would have had their own voices. Yet in the end the indigenous people may not present themselves, they must be represented. Gide has assumed the role of witness and this role, it seems, is not to be shared. Whilst testing the limits of the colonial imaginary, Gide has also chosen to remain within them; he chose to preserve the overarching structure in which the black was defined by white perceptions. As I shall now show, this was also the case — in different ways and with different limits — for the work Gide and Allégret would undertake on their return to France.

Resistance and accommodation

On their return, Gide and Allégret did not resume their former roles or, at least, not in a straightforward fashion. Yet Gide felt himself called as a witness against injustice, and in his campaign against the concessionary companies he would deploy his carefully honed skills as a writer.[175] Meanwhile, Allégret was to see out his apprenticeship, complete his film, and become a journeyman. This is to say that the resources that the two men acquired during the African journey were to have their potential realised within existing structures for organising knowledge and experience.[176] The colonial imaginary would in this respect prove accommodating.

Gide's campaign had begun with a letter of 6 November 1925 to the interim governor of Afrique-Équatoriale Française, Mateo Alfassa. Here he makes one more iteration of his relative ignorance and contrasts this with the experience of the governor; Gide's modesty is thus turned to use. "Since arriving in the colony, I have been able to form a clear idea of the terrible entanglement of problems that only your intelligence and tenacity are able to resolve."[177] In his role as witness, Gide devoted the largest part of his letter to Pacha's cruelty but concluded with a short list of further concerns about the subdivision of Boda: the carceral regime; the working conditions on the Bambio road; the use of women and children as porters; the dishonest pricing practices of the C.F.S.-O.

Gide followed this letter with two to Mssrs. Poissenot and Weber of the C.F.S.-O. The campaign became properly public, however, with the first serial publication of his African journal, beginning in November 1926. At this moment Gide's concerns were articulated with a wider agenda. The man who would emerge as Gide's principal ally was no less a figure than Léon Blum, erstwhile lawyer and author, and now leader of the Section française de l'internationale ouvrière (S.F.I.O.), the French socialist party, and director of its newspaper, *Le Populaire*. It was in *Le Populaire* that Blum inaugurated what was to be a long tradition of simplifying *Voyage au Congo*.

Blum was an exquisitely sensitive reader but was also capable of being literal if he thought his journalism required it. He was certainly aware of how he was writing. When he began a series of articles on Gide, in July 1927, he prefaced his remarks in this fashion: "I am no longer a literary critic, and some of my friends regret this."[178] Blum might have counted Gide amongst these friends as they had attended the Lycée Henri IV together and Gide had succeeded Blum as literary columnist of *La Revue blanche*. Yet in his commentary on Gide's work Blum emphatically refused to respond to the regrets of others: "I will not speak of Gide's style; I will not attempt an analysis of this precious, limpid work."[179] Instead, he embraces Gide's portrait of himself as a witness, as "a man who knows how to see".[180] However, in this Blum neglects to register that sight is not secure in Gide's account.

Blum begins by considering what he terms the moral and psychological angles of the colonial question.

> We still live with a host of assumptions which, in reality, have barely changed since the time of slavery. The Black appears to us to have been put on this earth in order to work for the White, he is ordained to procure profits for the White.[181]

And where is the justification for this? "In a difference of colour, culture and religion; in our innate belief in a human caste system."[182] This of course is merely a justification. Blum continues:

> Nothing useful will be achieved until one addresses the notions which form the bases of colonisation, and, above all, the idea of a natural inferiority of certain races which justifies dependency and subordination. As Gide says: 'The less intelligent the Whiteman, the more the Black appears stupid to him.'[183]

In this context, the compass of Gide's observation is enlarged, to make of it something more than a verdict on the probity of one administrator. Again, it is a question of European agency, but this is no longer restricted to the local or particular. Blum wants to conceive of this agency as fundamental, but also as fundamentally misguided. In Gide's account the failure of probity was permitted by a failure of surveillance, it was a question of a poor deployment of ill-prepared individuals, but Blum wishes to move beyond this to reveal the injustice of the entire colonial system.

Such a conclusion, precisely because it went beyond individual perceptions and therefore individual cases, could form the basis for arguing that the colonies should be liberated. Blum was certainly prepared to denounce the sophistries of colonialists such as Joseph Gallieni.[184] He was also prepared to juxtapose Gide's views with those of a critic such as Victor Augagneur in order to argue explicitly that abuses were not merely a matter of isolated instances.[185] Blum would also declare himself "an enemy of the principle of colonial conquest".[186] In spite of all this, he did not make an argument for the surrender of the colonies or for the pursuit of a directly anticolonial policy. Understanding why this was so entails viewing Blum's stance on colonialism from the perspective of his socialism.

Blum's socialism was shaped by the distinctive history of the French party, and its relationship to both republican and revolutionary traditions. For Blum the Socialists were, like the Radicals, engaged in the march along "the true path of progress".[187] However, unlike the Radicals — the traditional guardians of Republican virtue — the members of the S.F.I.O. belonged to a revolutionary party. Blum's party was ultimately engaged in the struggle to break "wage slavery" and was not merely seeking to soften the antagonism between capital and labour.[188] Those in the party did not believe that the contradiction between social and political freedom could be resolved and so they were fully prepared to exceed the hegemonic framework of the Republican imaginary. Yet it did not follow that Blum would draw the conclusions of a Bolshevik; he saw his task as building the conditions for social revolution rather than inciting it prematurely.[189] Accordingly, Blum consistently repudiated the Communists' belief in violence:

> It is discipline and military hierarchy, the permanent mobilisation of shock troops, the preparation of the surprise attack, the provoking of civil strife and religious and racial intolerance, it is civil war and colonial war and foreign war. Everywhere the call to arms, everywhere faith in the use of violence.[190]

Blum would not embrace such faith. He could deplore the abuses of the current colonial system but, in his scrupulous logic, this system was to be engaged with precisely because of its tendency to violence and all that stems from it. It had to be engaged, for otherwise it would be exploited by the Communists. "Our work of colonisation and civilisation is undertaken in conditions such that we are the mercy of the first cry of revolt."[191] Yet rather than encourage such revolts, which Blum saw as the promotion of the basest of instincts, he wished to promote the noblest sentiments of justice; these sentiments would make the firmest foundations for the building of Socialism.

Whilst preparing these foundations, the S.F.I.O. did, however, attempt to address the concerns Gide had raised. In Blum's first article on Gide he mentions that Georges Nouelle and Étienne Antonelli, deputies for Saône-et-Loire and Haute-Savoie respectively, had just submitted a question concerning the situation in the Congo to Léon Perrier, the minister for colonies. As soon as Gide saw this article he hastened to encourage the Socialists by arranging for his publisher to send them copies of his book.[192] On 7 July 1927 Nouelle challenged the minister over the recruitment of indigenous workers.[193] Perrier attempted to respond but was shouted down and the debate was adjourned until the vote on the colonial budgets in the autumn.

Gide nevertheless continued his campaign and in October published a long article: "La Détresse de notre Afrique-Équatoriale".[194] The arguments made here were taken up in the debate in the Chamber of Deputies preceding the vote on the colonial budgets. On 23 November Henry Fontanier spoke on behalf of the Socialists, advocating renewed examination of the "tragic situation of colonial labour".[195] Following the principles set down by the great Socialist leader Jean Jaurès, he argued that the responsibility of a Socialist was to work towards the moment when the colonial project would be undertaken "not for the benefit of the Metropole but for the indigenous populations".[196] To make plain the magnitude of this task Fontanier read to the Chamber extracts from Gide's book. Yet, despite this, Perrier felt able to respond that Fontanier's programme was that of Albert Sarraut. This could certainly be taken as facetiousness but it underlined the fact that the Socialists operated within the colonial imaginary and its temporality. In his speech Fontanier observed that it would be "premature" to establish such things as trade unions in central Africa.[197] The civilising mission was far from complete, it could be undertaken only gradually, and for this reason the Socialists rejected what they saw as the overly simplistic proposition of an immediate evacuation.

The colonial imaginary thus absorbed individual criticisms. Indeed, these could be placed in its service. Even Gide's work could find a favourable reception in an organ such as *Les Annales coloniales*. There, one Marie-Louise Sicard also singled out Gide's observation: "The less intelligent the white man, the more the black appears stupid to him."[198] She felt able to present this as "a colonial gospel", serving to underline the high calling of the colonialist.[199] The choice of language here is hardly fortuitous for Sicard deploys the logic of the missionising. "One needs the soul of an apostle to create a colonial mentality equal to its task, for we have to acknowledge that this demands the highest qualities: experience and education, of course, but also moral conviction (...) and great strength of character."[200] Truly, those to make men must first make men of themselves. Even in the secular Republic, the Christian model retained its force. In this context the abuses and injustice detailed in Gide's account become revelations to guide colonial action.[201] Thus *Voyage au Congo* and *Retour du Tchad* are used — perversely — to confirm the *raison d'être* of colonialism. Like capitalism, colonialism seems able to absorb anything but its own destruction.

Allégret's editions

As Gide was revising his journal for publication, Allégret was editing both his film and his *Note sur les Massa-Mousgoum*. And just as Gide's campaign finally took its place within the colonial imaginary, so Allégret's projects were also shaped by it.

Allégret's *Note* certainly conforms to models previously advanced by missionaries. Of course, learning to model one's practice on others' is the business of the apprentice and here Allégret took as his master one Louis Perrier, president of the Société des amis des Missions et des indigènes. Perrier counselled that the task of civilising primitive peoples, if undertaken rationally, required the study of "their histories, their customs, their religion and psychology".[202] In light of this, members of Perrier's organisation had drafted an *Enquête* to facilitate their research. They hoped that individual studies could be assembled into a larger whole and therefore researchers were enjoined to maintain exactly the format of the questionnaire, the better to facilitate comparisons. Ideally, each study would proceed from physical contexts to social ones. Perrier's *Enquête* begins with the "Geographical Situation" and then proceeds under the rubric of "Sociology" to examine "Family", "Social Life", "Political Organisation" and "Material Conditions".[203] Allégret's text is largely derived from this template. His *Note* is divided into nine sections: Geographical Situation; Physical Location; Family Organisation; Birth and Birthrate; Children; Relations of Girls and Boys before Marriage; Chieftancy; Laws and Customs; Material Conditions.[204] Here, Allégret demonstrates that he can use a template creatively, making his own emphases and exclusions.

Allégret was, then, an imaginative but dutiful apprentice and this is also revealed clearly enough in his filmmaking. Amongst the models he followed was that offered by Alfred Chaumel. In his *Journal*, Gide had been careful to distance himself from this formally appointed propagandist by refusing to celebrate the majesty of the Congo rapids. However, this would not be the case for Allégret. At the beginning of July 1926 Allégret had begun to edit at the Cinéma du Vieux Colombier and, just as he began this process, he encountered Chaumel once again, as the Vieux Colombier was about to première one of the latter's films.[205] Chaumel, like Perrier, was supplied with clear views as to the ordering of knowledge, and the ordering of humanity. In an essay of 1924 he had set out the arc for a

> film 'for the general public', taking the viewer on a journey through French Equatorial Africa, its different regions and races, and its different landscapes: the hills and mountains, rivers, forest, savannah and bush. Thus would be passed in review the primitive peoples, from the almost naked animists to the Islamicised, with their ample boubous[.][206]

Allégret followed this arc. This meant that his film was to have a greater scope that that of the *Note sur les Massa-Mousgoum*; yet his film, like his text, made its accommodation with comparative methods, and so the two projects conformed to the hierarchies of the colonial imaginary.

In the film the hierarchies are established with a scale used to measure development and, above all, the development of technologies. Chaumel's essay had anticipated a film opening with embarkation, then "various scenes on board ship, the different ports, the mouth of the Congo, Matadi, the Belgian railway" and this is precisely what Allégret offers.[207] The film indeed opens "at sea" and then proceeds to the railway. A shot follows the progress of a train along a viaduct; with the camera mounted on the train, the viewer's perspective is quite literally created and maintained by the colonial infrastructure.[208] Of course, it is not surprising that a travelogue similar to that imagined by Chaumel would adopt the point of view of the European as conducted by a European infrastructure. This infrastructure *is* the scale. It measures development. As in Gide's text, once the scale is established there is a movement beyond the immediate compass of the colonial infrastructure. An intertitle in Allégret's film informs the viewer: "West of Bangui the roads cease to be passable. Travelling on foot will allow us to have closer contact with five of the more unusual tribes of this country."[209] The "tribes" in question are then introduced, and with them the main sequences of the film: "The Baya, Sara, Massa, Moundang and Fula".[210] This suite of encounters permits Allégret to move from fetishists to the Islamised, from the naked to the clothed.

Such is the arc of civilisation. It is transcribed with care in the film.[211] The first sequence, on the Baya, is concerned with matters of subsistence. Scrub is burnt to clear areas for the cultivation of manioc, and then the camera follows women through the stages of washing, drying and pounding required to transform the tubers into flour. The sequence is restricted to these processes; there is no suggestion of a social life beyond that implicit in a gendered division of labour. Shots alternate between relatively broad panoramas, which set figures in their environment, and closer views focused on the actions of the figures. There are no close-ups; nothing approximates a portrait. The camera is dedicated to the *chaîne opératoire* and not the operatives.

The next sequence, on the Sara, conveys a different perspective: "The Sara are particularly welcoming; they freely admit us into their private lives."[212] Individuals are now introduced, and a social life, in the form of a courtship. The woman who will become the bride is presented as "Kaddé". This name was actually a fiction; the actress was named Mariom, yet the Hebrew origin of that name perhaps complicated the smooth arc the film was trying to establish.[213] "Kaddé" is introduced with her sister and both are first seen pounding millet; this scene thus recalls the sequence on the Baya whilst also moving beyond it to establish familial relations. The camera first presents Kaddé's naked torso before rising to her face; thus a portrait is offered but one emphatically framed by an exotic physicality. Such a framing of the portrait seems of a piece with the relatively early stage of development that the Sara are made to represent in the film's arc.

The next introduction is of the man who will be Kaddé's suitor, Djimta. The two meet on the banks of a river where the sisters have come to wash their millet; the subsistence activity becomes the setting for a social interaction. In turn, this will permit the presentation of social reproduction. Scenes of courtship are followed by marriage negotiations, which Djimta conducts with the aid of a friend. The latter is required as an intermediary, an intertitle establishes, because custom prohibits the suitor from speaking directly to his prospective parents-in-law before the negotiations are concluded. Thus even whilst this sequence is acted, it is intended to convey an ethnographic specificity. Yet for all the specificity, the narrative also recalls the most conventional romances; the course of true love never did run smooth and at first the father is too demanding and negotiations are broken off. Kaddé is then shown being comforted by her sister. However, her distress is to be shortlived. Love will not be thwarted, and Djimta finds the means to meet the bride-price set by the father.

Once social relations have been established, the trajectory of the film is through further stages of civilisation. The camera shows boats on the Chari and Logone rivers, re-establishing the mode of the travelogue. The journey into the country of the Massa is then marked by a shift from the "primitive" huts of the Sara to clay constructions. The camera now also records a simple mill, and granaries. The presentation is of a more complex agricultural system and a more developed division of labour; the more sophisticated architecture is presented as an index of a higher degree of civilisation. This is underlined in the next sequence, on the Moundang. In their settlements masonry is used rather than mere clay and moreover this architecture is used for the construction of large ritual and social spaces. Now an intertitle states: "Moundang dancers form a sort religious confraternity which gathers at every new moon for ritual celebrations."[214] This ritual is recorded in detail, to form the longest dance sequence in the film. It is closed by an emphatic intertitle: "The tribes we have seen so far are animists… In the north of Cameroon, the Fula grouped in a number of sultanates have been Islamicised for several centuries."[215] This introduces a visit to the most important sultanate, and the palace of Reï-Bouba. The camera now records court spectacle. There is incessant activity but the situation is not analogous to that of a European court; a further intertitle reminds viewers that the economy is not developed: "Timber, livestock and harvest, all belong to the sultan."[216]

The final sequence is set in the port of Douala. After the journey to the interior there is a return to an outpost of European civilisation and, with it, the agitations of European life. Children play outside the missionary school; here a shift between religions is implicit. Then the camera shows the docks and so reprises the opening of the film. And there is a departure to match the arrival.

However, the departure does not mirror the arrival. It is not a simple return but a progress. The arc of the journey follows the arc of civilisation: from fetishists to muslims to Christians, from village to court and finally to the city developed as an international port.[217] These two trajectories are completed in different ways by the European, with Christianity and with commercial infrastructure. What is suggested is that the colonial presence will accelerate the development already implicit in the progress from the Baya to the Fula. The film, then, provides a narrative which is much less fraught than that to be found in Gide's journal, one fitting more readily with the colonial imaginary and its progress to individual freedom of conscience in a Christian framework and individual freedom to possess and exploit. However, there is perhaps a final ambiguity. The closing shot, of departure, shows the sea under "a black bank of clouds", to recall the words of Gide's dedicatee at the close of *Heart of Darkness*.[218] The waters are "sombre under an overcast sky" and the darkness at the end of the novella returns the reader to Marlow's comment at the beginning, when he observes that London has also "been one of the dark places of the earth".[219] The return to the metropole is not necessarily a return to a beacon of enlightenment.

Missionary perceptions

That the metropole might be a source of corruption was made clear enough to Marc Allégret through the missionaries' scandalised response to his work. The apprentice filmmaker went to some effort to edit his footage into a conventional narrative yet this did not mean that the film was readily received. A first, private projection of the complete film took place on 19 March 1927 but the most controversial screening was to be in early June, at the headquarters of the Société des Missions Évangéliques, where Élie Allégret served as a director.[220] After the screening both Daniel Couve, another director, and André Muller, the treasurer of the Société, wrote to Marc to denounce what they held to be the "unhealthy" and even salacious character of the film, which they believed to be particularly evident in the footage of dancing.[221]

Perhaps Marc should have anticipated difficulties, given that his situation was a knotted tangle of the social and the sexual; there were the close relations of Allégrets senior and junior with Gide, but also Couve's working relationship with Élie as a co-director, and even Couve's relationship with Gide, as the pastor who had been formally responsible for the latter's religious instruction. These relations were cathected strongly enough to generate much animosity and anxiety. Such anxieties were not restricted to the missionaries' private concerns about the nature of the relationship between Marc and Gide; they spilled over into public preoccupations with the status of the missionary project and how it was perceived. All of this marked the missionaries' reception of the film, and, in turn, conditioned Marc and Gide's own responses.

The letters of Couve and Muller may be judged to be part of a single campaign, ultimately issuing from the same authority, but the two authors offer their own inflections. Marc addresses this in his replies, which acknowledge the shared nature of the correspondence whilst also meeting the specific charges of each missionary. In his reply to Muller of 22 June, Marc made an argument similar to Gide's concerning the intelligence of the "whites" and the appearance of "blacks":

> I have tried to reach a rather stubborn audience, which has persisted in seeing negros simply as monkeys. Up until now 'documentaries' have pandered to this in showing the most grotesque and repulsive side of things. I wanted to show what had surprised me most during our journey, which is to say the beauty of the natives, something so pure and natural that it did not seem — and still does not seem — to be in any way indecent.[222]

Marc presents himself as countering both wilful misperceptions of the blacks and the mechanisms which reproduced such perceptions. The argument concerns French audiences and who and what are best positioned to confront their prejudices. For Marc, the task of representing the beauty and humanity of those he encountered was part of the broader rallying in which Gide was then involved; for this reason he had not wanted to produce a film for "Sunday-school children".[223] He would measure his success by the public won to his cause and "the awakening of their sympathy in front of these tableaux of simplicity and innocence".[224]

In contrast, for the missionaries the prejudices of the French public were inextricably bound up with Gide's reputation. Couve begins his letter of 23 June by stating frankly (as he sees it) that: "Everything that bears the name of André Gide is extremely suspect."[225] The film only served to confirm these suspicions. Couve, like Muller, was especially exercised by the footage of dances which "detailed all that which in fact demands to be veiled".[226] The brief letter concludes with reference to Gide: "As your father has known for a long time, my great and burning regret is that you yourself are complicit with all that is corrupt in his work."[227] This is a sweeping condemnation but probably the principal work preoccupying Couve was *Corydon*, Gide's dialogues on homosexuality, which had finally been commercially published in 1924. There were of course other candidates for Couve's reprobation, including *Si le grain ne meurt*, which finally went on sale in October 1926, and which contains amongst other things an unflattering vignette of Couve's father.

In replying to Couve, as in his response to Muller, Marc bluntly refused to recognise the indecent as other than a matter of European perception, and, implicitly also refused to recognise Gide as a source of corruption: "As for 'that which in fact demands to be veiled'", it is rather a question of "what you yourself would like to see veiled".[228] This riposte rehearses Marc's defence of *Corydon* to his father, where he argued that Gide was courageous in confronting truths rather than cloaking them.[229] Marc also rehearsed a point he had made to Muller, insisting that the utility of his film, and its articulation with Gide's campaign, would lie in its address to a broad audience rather than one of specialists.

Neither treasurer nor co-director were to be persuaded. Couve returned to the question of the audience in a letter of 28 June, insisting that the problem with Allégret's film was that, precisely because it was aimed at those without specialist knowledge, it courted misunderstanding; the indigenous populations are made to appear more sensual than they are, and this, for the uninformed, creates "an unhealthy impression".[230] On 1 July, Muller also returned to the "unhealthy spectacle".[231] He responded to the claim that the filmmaker was seeking to counter misleading documentaries by asserting that, in any case, Allégret's film was not properly documentary in character and that parts of it were presented in such a way as to offer "exhibitions which were corrupt and corrupting".[232]

> In Africa, in its natural setting, all of this has a quite different aspect to that which it assumes on the screen. This I grant quite freely. But you are far too familiar with Parisian audiences, and know full well that their reactions will differ from those of us who have experience of the colonies.[233]

Whatever the circumstances in Africa, the broad public, in its ignorance, was considered likely to draw at least unfortunate and probably unsavoury conclusions. The two missionaries saw Allégret as being aware of this and as pandering to base instincts. Gide remains the figure presiding over this corruption.[234]

Gide and Allégret, however, persisted in a public defence of their work. On the occasion of a screening in Brussels in May 1928, Gide delivered a lecture on the film. Here he drew an explicit distinction between Allégret's work and those films which dwelt only on the grotesque and repellent.[235] Rather, following Allégret, Gide argued that the filmmaker's task was to render attitudes and gestures comprehensible by "presenting them in the most favourable light" and in this manner awaken sympathy.[236] This is what one would expect from the author who can rejoice when a heart beats in sympathy. However, at this point Gide represses the fact that he was also the author incapable of sustaining reciprocity in the Congo. Instead, he asserts: "I think that in each race, and even in each being, there is some possibility for beauty, that a sensitive and sympathetic gaze may discern."[237] He was obviously inviting such attention from the film's audience.

> Here, as in every work of art, it is a matter of freeing the main contours from a great entanglement of things. The task for the cameraman is to simplify. It seems to me that it is best if his actions are governed by a desire to reveal the beauty of things, to make them more legible, so to speak.[238]

Evidently, the film was not to address that "great entanglement of all colonial problems" which had previously exercised the author.[239] Instead, simplicity was to be preferred as the best way to solicit the "sensitive and sympathetic gaze". Gide than goes on to state that this gaze is the achievement and property of civilisation. Inverting the arguments of the missionaries, Gide here presents civilisation as the matrix of sympathy rather than as a wellspring of all that is corrupt and corrupting.

This is what the African journey has revealed to the writer. So Gide returns to a staple of travelwriting: the discovery of the self in the other. He declares: "It is in encountering the other that each of us is able to better understand their own country."[240] This reflective act is itself an achievement.

> One of the most striking things — and one of the most difficult to grasp for the civilised European — is the great difficulty that (...) primitive peoples have in separating themselve as individuals from their clans, their tribes and their races.[241]

And from this Gide draws a conclusion: "we are obliged to recognise that there can only be a gradual victory over the formless and unshaped. Yet it is with such differentiation that civilisation begins."[242] Thus Gide's own epiphany in the Congo is magnified; his individual achievement, his "notion of differentiation", is multiplied to become a foundation of the civilised. In this manner,

Gide's reflections come to confirm and underline the narrative arc traced in Allégret's film.

There is a profound ambivalence here. Gide's disavowal of the other could not be complete. What is repressed returns, as the other cannot be entirely reduced to the same. Gide frames this fraught process as "a gradual victory" and in doing so dissimulates his own extreme reactions to the African encounter.

As an exegesis of Allégret's filmmaking, Gide's lecture stands as a rebuttal of the charges levelled by the missionaries. Yet his exegesis does not move in any substantial way beyond the apothegm he meditated at the Sambry trial. Here, once again, with the conquest of the unformed, Gide understands the African as a relatively passive object, formed in the perception of Europeans. And so here Gide is no longer fully a witness. He might be present to reflect on his own epiphany but, as such, has retreated into his interiority. He is not questioned and is not seen.

Civilisation, portraiture and contingency

As Gide was preparing his Brussels lecture he was also collaborating with Allégret on the illustrated edition of *Voyage au Congo*.[243] If the Brussels lecture was a defence of the film following the principles set out in Allégret's correspondence with the missionaries, then it seems reasonable to suggest that similar principles governed the selection of images for the illustrated edition. Mere exoticism was to be refused. Yet this did not mean that human physicality was to be excised from the visual record, for that would be to acquiesce before the missionaries' objections. It is in this sense that the photographs are as much the product of Paris as of Bangui and Fort-Archambault.

In their responses to criticism of the film, both Gide and Allégret had placed an accent on sympathy and humanity. There is a European mode for configuring this: it is the portrait. With this mode, the likeness of an individual is presented to invite the response of imagined interaction.[244] One interiority meets another and the viewer's response to the likeness is a response of "*like* subjectivity".[245] Yet Gide had difficulty in discerning African interiority and entertaining reciprocity. Too frequently, he could perceive only a lack of differentiation.

Given this difficulty it is perhaps unsurprising that there is some ambivalence in the selection of portrait photographs for the illustrated edition. Images of Gide are present, of course, and so are images of figures such as the Sultans of Binder and Reï-Bouba [Fig. 2.10]. However, by virtue of their social status these figures have already been individuated and the role of the camera is merely to reproduce this status. Other kinds of portrait are included; there is, of course, the group portrait of visitors at the entrance of the hut, with its informality of interaction [Fig. 2.8]. Yet this was not to become a model to be placed alongside the ethnographic one established by the photograph of the chief's daughter and her servant [Fig. 2.5].

Portraiture, like civilisation, requires differentiation; both are achieved only at a cost. This much is established in the illustrated edition through an extended sequence, where photographs are not isolated but follow each other in a regular fashion, with an alternation of an image and a single page of text. I want to draw together some of the arguments of this chapter through an analysis of this sequence, as it holds an important place in the overall organisation of the illustrated volume. By the time these illustrations were assembled Allégret had not only edited his film — and so become habituated to thinking in sequences — he had also been forced to defend his own approach to the act of representation. He had been obliged to situate his actions in relation to those of the missionaries. His photographs remained shadowed by his father's and he remained resistant to this. The extended photographic sequence reveals this in a particular way.

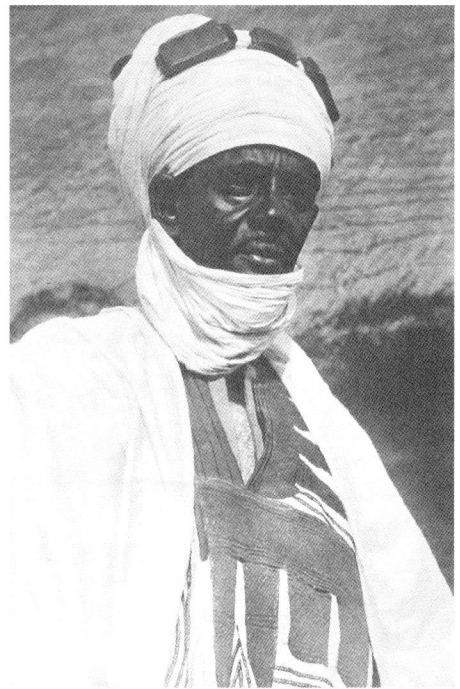

Figure 2.10. Marc Allégret, 'The Sultan of Binder', illustration at p. 228 in André Gide, *Voyage au Congo*, Paris: Gallimard, 1929.

The sequence belongs with the account of Fort-Archambault and Fort-Lamy and has 11 images, with the final image in the sequence — of Gide — standing as a coda. It begins with a photograph of inhabitants almost dwarfed by their habitat, with two separate groups of small figures shown standing by the banks of a river, beneath a great canopy of foliage [Fig. 2.11]. The sequence then unfolds with what are by now quite familiar types of image: boys at the river bank; a pair of children with a pestle and mortar for pounding manioc; another couple resting.

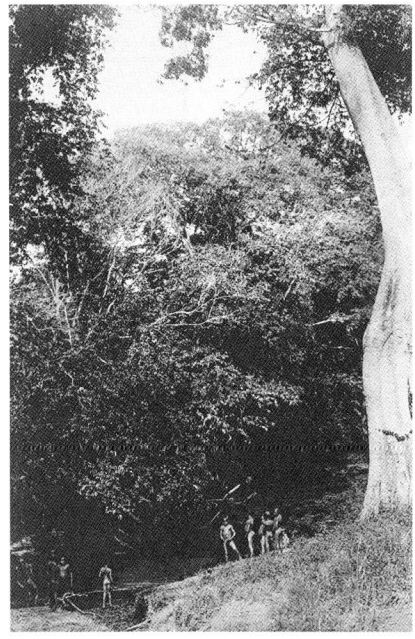

Figure 2.11. Marc Allégret, 'The banks of the Bobo', illustration at p. 116 in André Gide, *Voyage au Congo*, Paris: Gallimard, 1929.

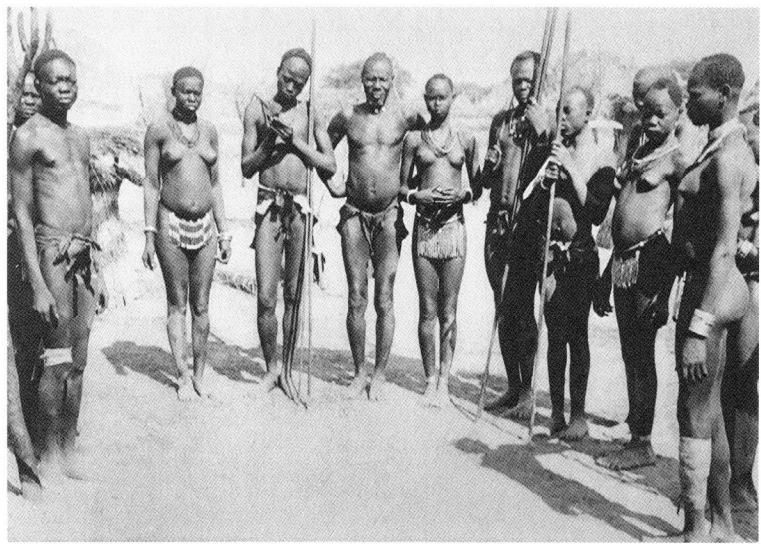

Figure 2.12. 'Our film actors (Fort-Archambault)', illustration at p. 126 in André Gide, *Voyage au Congo*, Paris: Gallimard, 1929.

There then follows an image of a game of pushball, a team game played with a giant, patchworked ball, an event which is also featured in the film. Conforming readily enough to conventions — whether of the landscape with staffage or the ethnographic survey — these photographs are unremarkable. However, the next image shifts the sequence to a different register.

This photograph shows a quite large group of figures and is captioned: 'Our film actors (Fort-Archambault)' [Fig. 2.12]. The viewer is thus presented not simply with members of a specified indigenous population, but with those about to assume roles and become protagonists in the drama of the Sara courtship. They are about to perform the paradox of "acting naturally". There is then something curious about the status of the figures, and this may be discerned even without reference to the caption. The image shows an assembly; people have been gathered before the camera but the gathering is neither spontaneous nor formal. The figure at the centre of the composition is the man who will play Kaddé's father, and Mariom stands to his left; these two both face the camera and adopt quite formal poses. However, others present are shown in profile and others again are unresponsive or indifferent. The latter are not necessarily marginal figures; for example, the man immediately to the right of the "father" seems to be intent only on examining his fingernails. So this photograph does not have the unforced sociability of that taken at the entrance to the hut but nor does it have the orderly air of the image of the Gabon catechists. The actors are waiting, gathered "on location". The image is a production shot and not a film still; it shows performers but not performance.

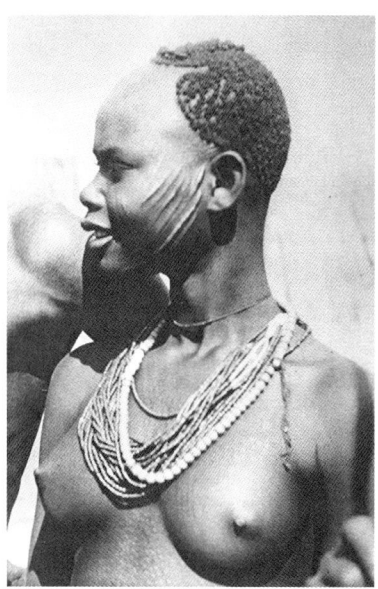

What does it mean to be a performer in this context? Whilst actors, the individuals remain members of a community — the "location" is theirs — and they are gathered to perform their ethnographic specificity. The next image in the sequence, closely related to the preceding, suggests as much [Fig. 2.13]. This is captioned as an image of Kaddé, and so maintains Mariom's fictional identity. Here she is

Figure 2.13. 'Kaddé', illustration at p. 128 in André Gide, *Voyage au Congo*, Paris: Gallimard, 1929.

presented in profile, her framing with naked torso recalling her first presentation in the film. The photograph was probably taken immediately after that showing the group of performers; the height, pose and proximity of the man to her right match the "father's" and the vertical shadow cast on her left shoulder in the first image is still present. All that seems to have happened is that the photographer has moved closer and to the right and Mariom has similarly turned to face right; the result, though, reveals a distinctive coiffure and prominent scarification, the sorts of sign Perrier had invited his collaborators to record. The image obeys the conventions of ethnographic survey, as is confirmed by its use in a popular form of the survey published in *The Illustrated London News*. There the photograph is captioned: "With hair partly shaven and deep scars on her cheek, the design indicating the tribe to which she belongs: a Sara-Madjingaye belle."[246] So in some contexs the photograph could signify specificity readily enough. However, in the context of the extended sequence this signifying becomes a little more troubled. Here identity itself will be called into question.

The next image in the sequence is entitled "Woman from Barguirmi (Boïngar)" [Fig. 2.14]. A woman is shown almost in profile and in a half-length view and in these respects her image is comparable to the preceding one of Mariom. Both women are turned from the viewer so that interaction is suspended. Yet in contrast to all preceding images of women in the volume, the woman from Barguirmi is clothed. Whilst her clothing is perhaps not entirely what missionaries such as Couve and Muller would wish for, it is at least a more modest attire than Mariom's.[247] In keeping with this dress — and again in contrast to Mariom — the woman from Barguirmi has downcast eyes and a more demure demeanour. But what is the viewer to make of this demeanour? Is it part of a performance, to be understood in relation to that of "Kaddé"?

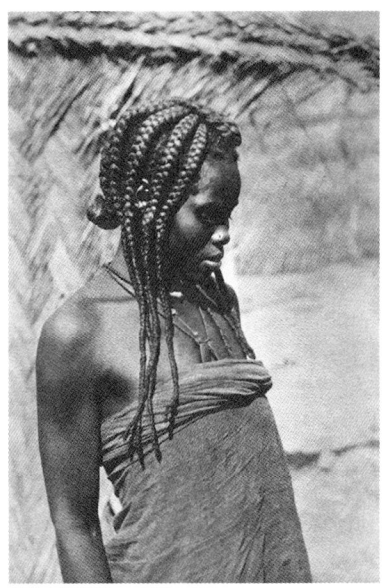

Figure 2.14. 'Woman from Barguirmi (Boïngar)', illustration at p. 131 in André Gide, *Voyage au Congo*, Paris: Gallimard, 1929.

These questions are suggested by the juxtaposition of the photographs, the rapid transition from one to the other with the turning of a page. Yet if such questions are implicit in the contrast between Mariom and the woman from Barguirmi, they are made more explicit in the next pairing of images, the final pairing in the sequence. Questions are prompted more forcefully here because the final pairing is of images of the same woman. The first photograph is captioned "Young Girl from Fort-Lamy (Arab-Sara half-caste)" [Fig. 2.15]. This "Young Girl" acknowledges the camera, and in a cheerful fashion. Yet the figure does not conform to conventions in the manner of the image of Mariom and nor is she defined by an activity, labour, or a clearly established context. Indeed, the background seems almost wilfully confused although enough can be made out to establish that there is a backdrop and that this is a posed photograph.[248] The young woman is neither quite naked nor fully clothed; thus this image is not submitted to the principles operative in the immediately preceding illustrations.

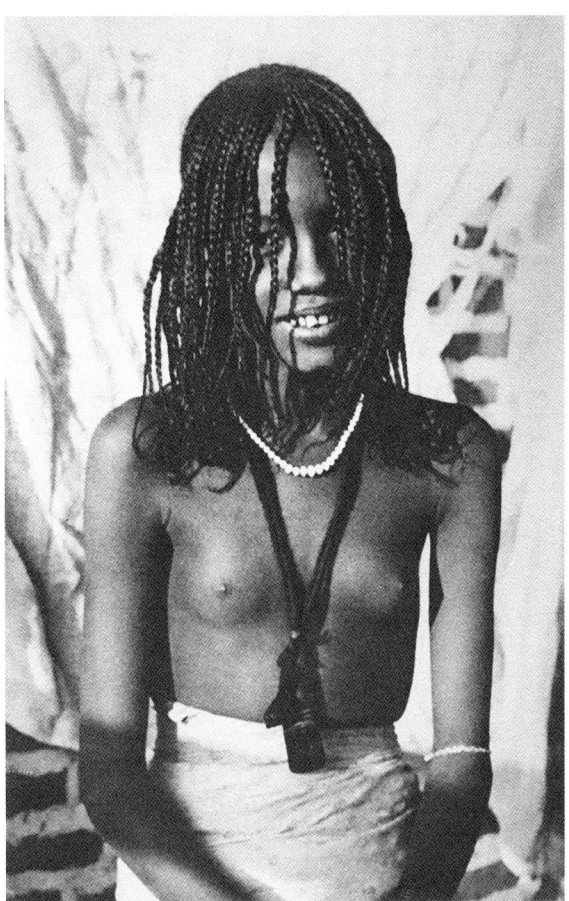

Figure 2.15. 'Young Girl from Fort-Lamy (Arab-Sara half-caste)', illustration at p. 132 in André Gide, *Voyage au Congo*, Paris: Gallimard, 1929.

The final image in the sequence offers a further complexity [Fig. 2.16]. Here the relation of figure to frame invokes the portrait format and the young woman is now wearing a print dress and has downcast eyes. There is then a further transition from an unclothed to a clothed body, recapitulating that from Mariom to the woman of Barguirmi, and there is a similar movement from a smiling figure to a more reserved one. Yet because in this final pairing the transitions involve a single person, they appear more directly as a staging, rather than as arising simply from a juxtaposition of images. Thus, taken together, these four images of women have different degrees of legibility and generate a sense that in various ways — and perhaps more or less willingly — these women have been asked to perform roles.

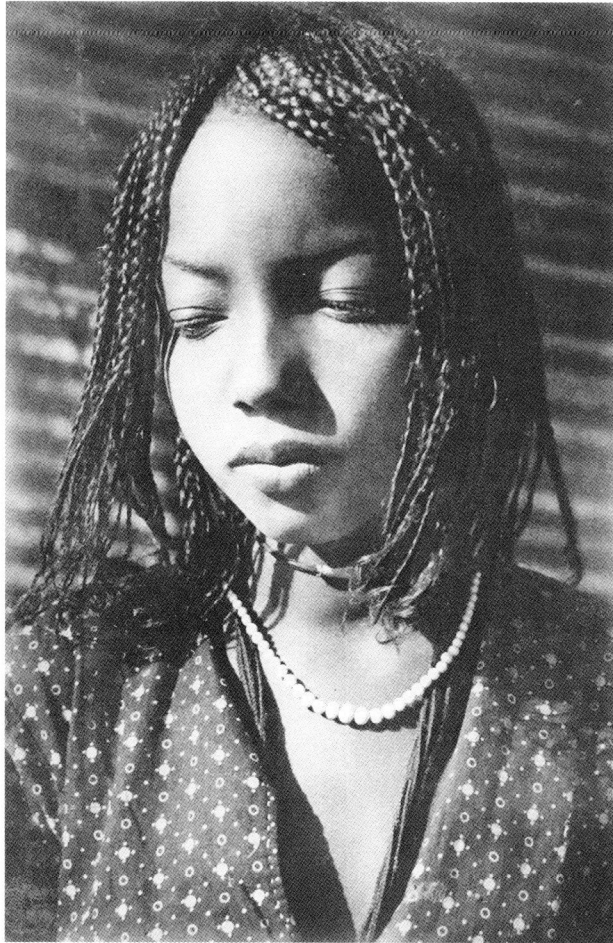

Figure 2.16. 'Young Girl from Fort-Lamy (Arab-Sara half-caste)', illustration at p. 135 in André Gide, *Voyage au Congo*, Paris: Gallimard, 1929.

The caption to the photograph of the young woman identifies her as an "Arab-Sara half-caste" and this signals what Allégret would have understood as a joining of different ethnic identities. If Mariom — particularly when designated "Kaddé" — could represent a Sara "type" this is not quite the case for the "half-caste". In her first photograph she has a pendant around her neck with an amulet of the sort which often contained a fragment of the Quran. In her second photograph, her dress not only covers her but also conceals the amulet. So the transitions between the photographs may involve a staging of conversion. As much is suggested by the partial catalogue of photographs Allégret compiled on his return to France. This comprises 17 loose, typed sheets organised by place and subject, following the itinerary of the journey. The photographs of the young woman are included on sheet nine, for Fort-Lamy.

Boulboule: bust, seated
    « «   «   standing
Boulboule: head resting on hand.
      « « : Madonna
      « « : hair over face
      « « : fogged exposure
      « « : nude
   id. 2 examples
   id. 2 examples[249]

The first title on the list corresponds to the first image of the woman in the illustrated edition and the fourth title, "Madonna", designates the second. Clearly, Allégret considered this image of the young woman with downcast eyes to stand in relation to a category of Christian iconography. If the sequence of four images of women is read as moving from the pagan to the Christian then it becomes a recapitulation of the arc of Allégret's film.

The practice of using clothing to establish degrees of civilisation was very widespread in the colonial period. It might be enforced or it might be part of the process of conversion encouraged by missionaries. A certain Biblical authority for the need for clothing could be derived from the description in Genesis of Adam and Eve's reaction on eating of the fruit of the Tree of Knowledge: "And the eyes of them both were opened, and they knew that they were naked; and they sewed fig leaves together, and made themselves aprons." (Genesis 3: 7) There are numerous stagings of similar transitions. In one missionary postcard, for example, a semi-clothed "Honest Martha" stands in contrast to her fully clothed sister,

Mary, as described in the Gospel of Luke (10: 38–42) [Fig. 2.17]. The contrast is between what Allégret had described as "simplicity and innocence" and the civilised state.[250] Implicitly, Mary has been brought to a knowledge of her fallen state and also to an understanding of her need for redemption though Christ. Attaining this knowledge was usually the result of considerable preparation, on the part of both missionaries and converts. Yet this process was telescoped in Allégret's film by the movement between different "tribes", which compressed a longer history of encounters between the more and less civilised. The illustrated edition presents a different scenario as Boulboule makes a swift transition from (partially) naked to clothed, and, implicitly, a transition from one belief system to another. Indeed, here the former transition stands for the latter; Boulboule seems to have undergone less a spiritual conversion and more a change of physical appearance.

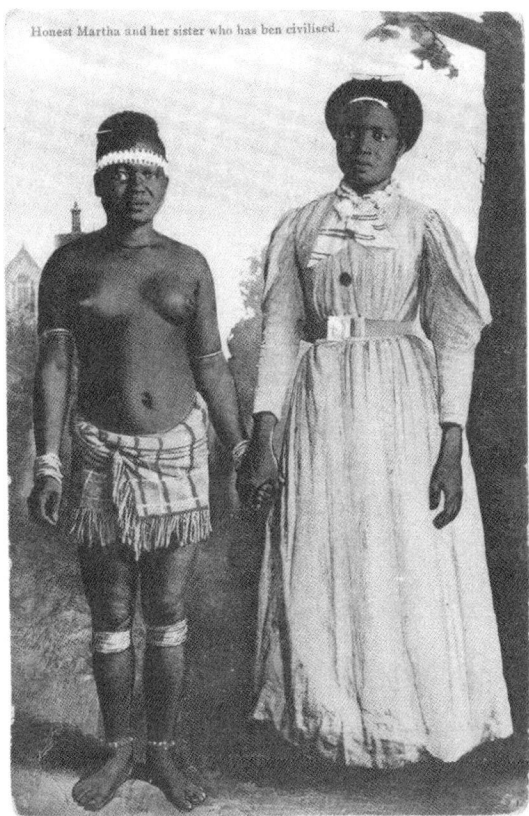

Figure 2.17. Anon. 'Honest Martha and her sister who has ben civilised', hand-coloured photograph reproduced as postcard, c. 1912.

Boulboule is presented as Martha and then, with the turning of a page, assumes the mantle of Mary. One could say that here there is an iteration of Marc's riposte to Couve: instead of that which demands to be veiled, it is rather a question of "what you yourself would like to see veiled".[251] For in donning her print dress Boulboule has in effect brought herself into at least outward conformity with the missionaries' sense of propriety. As a result, the image would not be one to provoke concern over how African bodies might be misperceived in Paris. Yet this propriety could create its own anxiety, one derived from uncertainty over the meanings which could be attributed to matters of appearance. And this in turn was related to anxieties about the missionary project.

Protestants such as those of the Société des Missions Évangéliques had come relatively late to missionising as the doctrine of predestination interpreted strictly meant that the Saved are already known to God and therefore attempts to convert were redundant.[252] One may only persevere in faith, hope and charity; the Saved cannot be descried because individuals do not display external signs of grace. Ultimately, then, human vision cannot establish anything from the status of a figure as clothed. Only God has knowledge of the saved and thus images of Martha and her sister have a troubling ambiguity; the sister has been civilised but it cannot be clear that she is, indeed, among the Saved. So are the activities of the missionaries pointless, or, worse, corrupting? Should Martha be left in her "simplicity and innocence"? These are the questions which arise from Allégret's photographs and his presentation of them. Here Boulboule's agency is unclear, and this is also the result of editings and elisions.

In Allégret's photographic catalogue the entry following those dedicated to Boulboule is: "Hamra, young Arab girl".[253] Allégret recorded in his personal journal that Hamra and Boulboule were amongst those with whom he had sexual relations.[254] There is a brief note in the journal concerning his introduction to Boulboule:

> After lunch Adoum brought me a rather young girl, although with a very pretty face. In order to raise the price, he thought it necessary to say that she was the daughter of a marabout. I was putting her in the bathtub when Hamra arrived to take the measure of her rival. But we got things worked out.[255]

So Allégret was perfectly capable of exploiting his privileged status in Africa, as were so many other Europeans. He was hardly reflective about his use of prostitutes. Yet these events are recorded in his private journal and of course form no part of Gide's account; they were no more meant to come to light than were the liasons of the administrator Sambry with the wives of militiamen. Despite his riposte to Couve, and his denunciation of veiling, Marc was quite prepared to dissemble his own exercises of power.

Dissembling is also present in the suite of images of women, where the final image of Boulboule as "Madonna" approaches the status of a portrait, in the relation of figure to frame and in the presentation of the reflective and reserved person. The image is the likeness of an individual presented to invite the response of imagined interaction. In this it is distinct from the range of female types presented earlier in the sequence in the illustrated edition. Nevertheless, whilst it is distinct from the more sexualised images in the sequence, the "Madonna" image remains defined by the sequence. And it also remains part of another sequence, that of images of Boulboule which Allégret catalogued but did not publish, and which includes three eroticised nude photographs. In his editing of the first sequence and in his suppression of the second there are two related performances. In the editing, Boulboule is given a role as "civilised"; and then, in the suppression, Allégret gives himself a similar role, for his entanglements are not to be represented. Civilisation may be an even slower conquest than Gide had allowed.

So if there is ambivalence in Gide's reaction to the African encounter, there is a similar ambivalence in Allégret's responses. His suite of images of women stages the civilising process and offers different roles for the "innocent" and the "civilised". This may be understood as a reflection on the paradoxes of the missionising project, with its conflicting desires to preserve innocence and to inculcate knowledge. Allégret is happy enough to unfold some of this conflict in the illustrated volume, yet the full extent of his own complicity is not to be disclosed.

Finally, the image of Boulboule dressed may be compared with that with which this chapter began, that of the two explorers taking tea. Both images may be described as performances and both may also be described as collaborations. If such descriptions draw the images together they also serve to underline the divergence between these photographs. Gide performs his own script under his own direction; Boulboule does not. And this is not simply due to the distinction between a self-portrait and a portrait. Portraiture requires differentiation and for Gide this is a prerogative; he distinguishes himself from others and does not direct himself as others do. In contrast, Boulboule's differentiation is a product of her place in Allégret's sequence, a product of the distinction between her image and that of other women. Thus her image is structured by patriarchy; she does not have the relative autonomy of Gide or the Sultan of Reï-Bouba. Her performance is directed and Allégret, of course, is the director; it is his staging which brings

Boulboule forward to the proscenium. Yet this did not involve crossing a threshold. If Boulboule's image may be compared to that of the two explorers, it cannot be so readily compared with Girodet's portrait of Belley. Bouboule has not acceded to representation in the fullest sense. Her image may approach the status of a portrait but is not quite secure in that status. Hers is a contingent portrait.

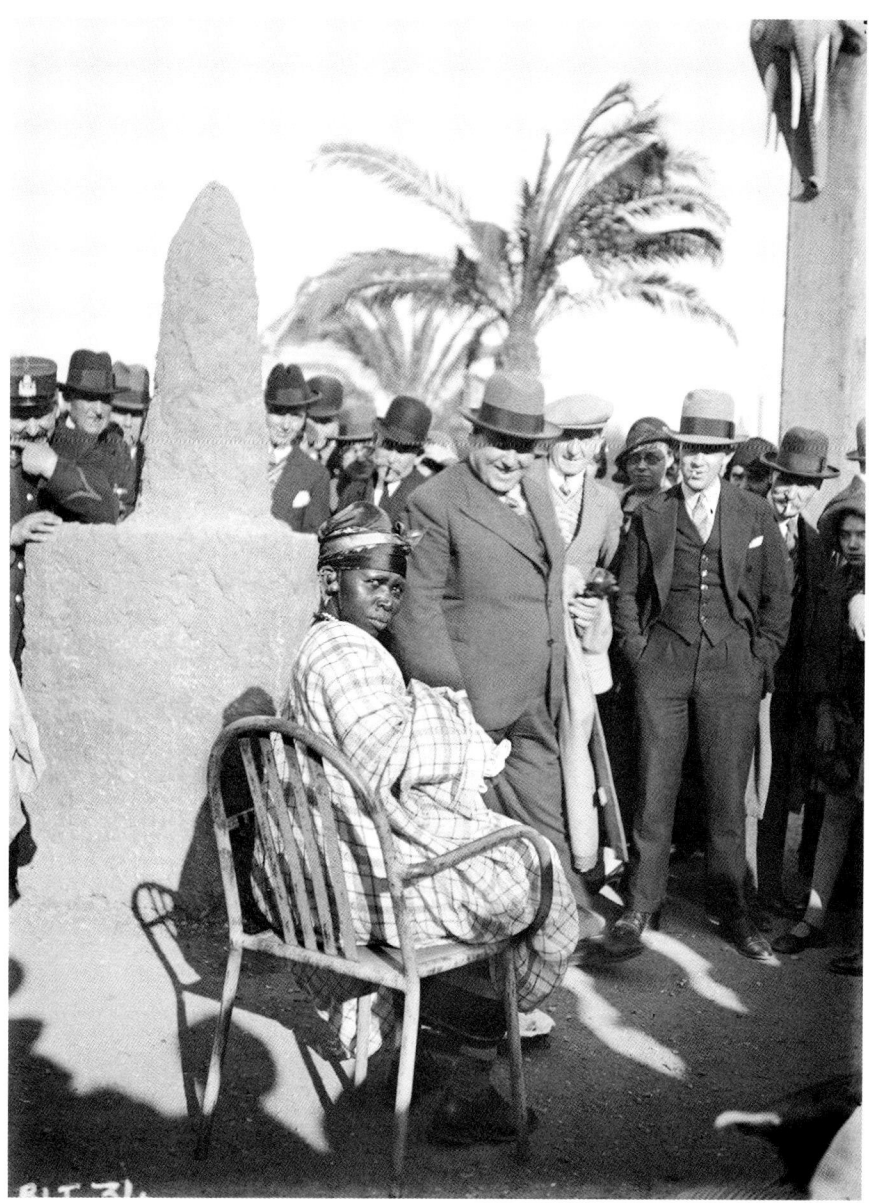

Figure 3.1. Joseph Blanchet, 'A Sudanese woman surrounded by a crowd', photographic print, 1931.

3. Staging, actors and audiences

The *Exposition coloniale internationale* in Paris

Joseph Blanchet, a rather obscure figure, took a number of photographs at the *Exposition coloniale* of 1931. Of the 69 which have been preserved, one is distinctive for its focus on an individual; this image shows a woman seated on a metal chair, turned somewhat awkwardly but nevertheless looking steadily at the photographer [Fig. 3.1]. The woman is seated next to a small roughcast obelisk on a large plinth, indicating that she is somewhere in the vicinity of the Pavillon d'Afrique Occidentale Française (A.O.F.). Whilst the rest of Blanchet's photographs of the exhibition may very readily be categorised as views of pavilions and precincts, this photograph is much closer to a snapshot; within the sequence it is anomalous. The awkwardness of the woman's pose suggests that the scene is not prepared for the camera in the manner of Blanchet's other compositions, which are happily parasitic on the configurations created by different aspects of the exhibition's architecture. If the scene with the woman seems chanced on rather than rehearsed, it is nevertheless similar to the other photographs in already being a spectacle; a quite considerable crowd has gathered and the shadows in the foreground show that the photographer's viewpoint is shared by others, who effectively encircle the woman. Evidently, the "gawping mob" of 1889 has not yet dispersed.[1] Despite encirclement, the woman is not the crowd's sole focus of attention. Some figures look in the direction of the photographer and while some are smiling others are not. Gazes and responses are various. Thus, at several levels, acts of looking and the act of photographing are made part of the image. In this, the photograph could be said to thematise a dynamic of the *Exposition coloniale*, the fleeting yet sometimes fraught relationship between visitors to the exhibition and those exhibited.

That the spectacle of the exhibition might create its own tensions was the cause of considerable anxiety for the event's organisers. They took pains to police the behaviour of all present, the visitors as much as those exhibited. The ironies of this were not lost on the exhibition's detractors:

> Read all about it in the papers:
> *Photographers and natives*
> 'The General Commission of the Exhibition has been made aware of several incidents which have occurred involving amateur photographers and natives of the French colonies in Africa, principally the negroes of A.O.F., who, refusing to be photographed, have even met photographers with threats of violence.
> In order to avoid further such incidents, the General Commission recommends to photographers to take sensible precautions when approaching the natives.'
> Just as when hunting big game in the bush.
> But these incidents can easily be avoided if one follows colonial practices.
> Don't they have truncheons at the Exhibition?[2]

The irony pursued here is that while the hunter after images is equated with the hunter after big game, the former may not have recourse to the instruments of the latter. The commentator is prepared to entertain the question: if the *Exposition* brings the colonies to the metropole, what precludes a similar importing of brutal colonial practices? Such a question up-ends the structure of the civilising mission, and begins to address what was entailed in the French rescuing of those "arrested" in their development.[3]

The proper maintenance of a functioning colonial structure was one of the tasks undertaken by the organisers of the exhibition. Demonstrating the need for such a structure could proceed through its own moments of carnival. So, in a rather predictable comedy of inversion, *Le Journal de l'Exposition coloniale* for June 1931 announced an "Exhibition of the whites amongst the blacks", to be held in 1934. Allegedly, this event had been decided at a secret cabinet meeting, and the details were soon to be published in the *Journal officiel*: "It's a done deal: the Metropole is going to show its natives under the shade of the palm-trees at the gates of Timbuktu."[4] There would be the usual types of display and entertainment, including a stand for Peugeot and performances by Mistinguett. The latter was the performer most frequently compared with Josephine Baker, the Queen of the *Exposition coloniale*, and so her invitation to Timbuktu would not come as a surprise.[5] Needless to say, transport would be courtesy of the engineers at Citroën, veterans of the trans-Saharan *Croisière noire*.

What is at stake here is the principle of comparison which would measure the achievements of European civilisation — and above all the achievements of its technology — against the putatively limited progress of the colonies. However, on the front page of the same issue of the journal, Maréchal Hubert Lyautey, the Commissaire général de l'Exposition, offered an important clarification of this: "Colonising is not simply a matter of building docks, factories and railways, it also involves winning the sympathy of the savage hearts of those in the deserts and savannah."[6] The comparison, then, was not only a matter of infrastructure; it also had its human dimensions, as Albert Sarraut had taken pains to establish. And Lyautey also echoed Sarraut in emphasising the need for further work. "While showing the immense tasks already accomplished by the colonising nations, the Exhibition will also show how much more remains to be done."[7] Just how much there was to be done was what was underlined in the imagined comedy of contrast between Paris and Timbuktu. This is already revealed in the very structure of the comedy, for the inversion is incomplete, with Pierre Laval's cabinet being held to have deliberated the decision to exhibit, and not any comparable body in Timbuktu. This registers an absence of agency; those in Timbuktu cannot be imagined to command the resources of Lyautey and Laval. Agency and its absence: these are, in various ways, the subjects of the present chapter. For the *Exposition coloniale* was above all a celebration of agency and part of Lyautey's role was to figure this, and to build quite literally on his reputation as a man of action. In what follows, I shall examine the form Lyautey gave to the *Exposition coloniale*, and then turn to those opposing the project. This will once again be an exploration of limits, of the difficulties of thinking beyond the colonial imaginary. This chapter is, then, best understood as a broken hinge, connecting incommensurable elements, within itself, and within the present book. But the principal subject of the chapter is the *Exposition* held in Paris in 1931, and I begin, quite literally, with the foundations of the exhibition.

Lyautey's project

The project for a French international colonial exhibition was much meditated and much delayed. An exhibition was first anticipated in 1912 but then postponed; the First World War created further delays but planning was resumed in 1919. Of course, the colonial imaginary had undergone a transformation during the war years and plans had to be adapted accordingly.[8] After even more delays, at the end of July 1927 Lyautey assumed control of planning for the exhibition.

The first substantial manifestation of his work was the laying of the foundation stone for the Musée Permanent des Colonies, on 5 November 1928. The inauguration of this — the intended relic of the exhibition — was also the inauguration of work at the chosen site at Vincennes, at the eastern edge of Paris. On this occasion Lyautey gave a speech that served as a touchstone for his supporters and so may serve as an introduction to his conception of his task. After the conventional expressions of gratitude, he recalled the context in which the planning for the exhibition had been resumed:

> In resolving to mount this Exhibition, in the aftermath of a period of murder and fratricide which has covered the world in ruins, what the government wanted was a striking demonstration that our civilisation has other fields of action than the battlefield, and that the nations of the twentieth century are able to compete fairly and openly in works of peace and progress (...) The colonial endeavour — which has so often been unrecognised, misrepresented or thwarted — is in fact the most charitable and constructive work of all.[9]

These words were well suited to the occasion, and to the orator. Through them, Lyautey exploited his reputation as the pacifier of Morocco and Madagascar, that is, as a man of action and an able constructor.[10] He could claim with confidence: "What sets Colonial Conquest apart is that it *gets things done*."[11] Yet this dynamism needs to be tempered and Lyautey had a clear view of how to do this when establishing relations with the natives: "we must always take care to adapt ourselves to their laws, traditions, customs and beliefs — to *understand them*".[12] This may recall Louis XIV's instructions to La Pérouse. Yet when taken in the context of Lyautey's speech as a whole the injunction most closely resembles the words of Sarraut when acknowledging that "the races we protect have a human wealth, a moral and social value", which was to be respected even whilst being developed and transformed.[13]

How was the development to be accomplished? And how could it be represented? To answer these questions it is necessary to distinguish between the different orders of presentation within the exhibition. The ideal schema is established in the seven volumes of the *Rapport général*, which appeared between 1932 and 1934 under the direction of Lyautey's secretary, Marcel Olivier. This report was an idealisation of a complex series of negotiations and compromises; it was a rationalisation and in this resembles one of Lyautey's speeches, albeit one writ very large.[14] Examining this retrospective projection is useful, for in its very abstraction it allows one to grasp more readily the structure of the exhibition and the relations of its protagonists.

The first volume of the *Rapport général*, entitled *Conception et organisation*, has five parts. It opens, conventionally enough, with the history of the project from 1912 to 1931. There follows a section on administration, setting out the role of the Commissariat général. The third section concerns general regulations and classifications and the fourth financial organisation. The final section then addresses the organisation of the commissariats for the various French colonial possessions and for the participating foreign powers.[15] The second volume of the *Rapport* is titled *Construction* and the third *Exploitation technique*. This latter volume deals with prosaic matters of coordination and works up to the business of ticketing. Thus the first three volumes deal with the process of bringing the exhibition into being and conclude with the admission of the visitors.

Conception, design, construction, admission: this seems a logical enough ordering. It is the logic of the *Exposition* as conceived by its organisers. Yet the volumes of the report need not have taken this form, nor dwelt at this length on matters of preparation. The report for the *Exposition universelle* of 1889 — to return to that example — ran to ten volumes but only one of these is concerned with the preparation of the exhibition.[16] As a blunt comparison this may not be particularly instructive and, at most, it indicates a shift of emphasis. However, this shift takes on a greater significance if one compares the roles of the French state in 1889 and 1931.

The task of the exhibition of 1889 was effectively that of the Great Exhibition of 1851, the presentation of the progress, or "point of development" of "the industry of all nations".[17] Measuring the progress of industry in 1889 required both the probity of the jurist and the patience of the cataloguer; the resulting report was to display these qualities in the proportional and synoptic treatment given to the exhibitors, to the various makers of watches, turbines and rifles. In essence, the *Exposition universelle* of 1889 was a medium for capital with the French state as willing mediator. The *Exposition coloniale* of 1931 had a different task and the state a different role to play, or, rather, different *roles*. For in 1931 the French state was both organiser and exhibitor. Lyautey was Commissaire général but the exhibitors responsible for the various sections and pavilions were the governors of the different colonial territories, with their own budgets and their own interests. Of course, that the organisers and exhibitors were ultimately in the same employ did not mean that business was conducted smoothly. One might find, for example, Governor Bonamy, as Commissaire des Territoires Africaine sous Mandat à l'Exposition Coloniale, pursuing a correspondence with Lyautey to complain

about the lack of progress in the construction of the main pavilion for his regions.[18] And so on. Yet the purpose of the final *Rapport général* was not to record
acrimony but to document the collaboration between organisers and exhibitors.
If, in this documentation, the report did not differ markedly from its predecessor
of 1889, where it did differ was in the presentation of the relationship between
collaborators and audience.

In 1931 agents of the state were called on to play different roles and so the record of the *Exposition coloniale* could not be limited to documenting their respec-
tive performances, for performances need audiences. The agents of the French
state require their citizens. Such, after all, is the structure of the Republican
imaginary. There are to be exchanges between leaders and led and all classes are
"to act for themselves".[19] Citizens have their part to play even as they compose an
audience. The fourth volume of the *Rapport général* acknowledges as much. This,
the central volume in the sequence, is entitled *Vie d'exposition*; it continues the
narrative of the earlier volumes in detailing the visitor's experience, from the initial advertising of the event through to the process of welcoming and orientating.
The labours of the organisers and exhibitors bear fruit if the visitor is conducted
effectively through the *Exposition* and is thereby inducted into the colonial project.
Dedicating a volume to this experience marks a departure from reports such as
that of 1889. Yet this is eminently reasonable. The French state was much more
than a mediator in 1931; the *Exposition coloniale* had multiplied and enhanced its
roles and French citizens were the only meaningful audience for its performances. In 1931 it was the state which exhibited itself.

The first four volumes of the *Rapport général* are concerned with the French
protagonists in the exhibition. It is only once these have been characterised that
there is a presentation of the different colonial possessions of France (and her
rivals). This is the order of priorities. The final volumes of the report form their
own sequence and, within this, the account of each colonial possession has the
same logic. In each case, the fundamentals of geography and history are followed by an account of raw materials and possibilities for development. There
then follows a discussion of how all this is presented at the exhibition.[20] Thus in
the *Rapport général* as a whole there is an iteration, an account of the *Exploitation
technique* for the *Exposition coloniale* is followed by an account of exploitation for
each colony. Such are achievements of the state.

Lyautey and Sarraut might well have been in agreement that "association" —
as opposed to "assimilation" — was the preferred colonial model, but the *Rapport
général* indicates clearly enough that those associating were not to be understood
to be on equal terms.[21] At the opening ceremony Paul Reynaud, then minister for

the colonies, could protest that "the natives" were "our partners", yet the exhibition was above all a French production, a series of iterations of the "mise en valeur".[22] It was a French organisation at work, getting things done. What, then, were the roles ascribed to the indigenous populations present at the exhibition?

Time, portrait, patriarchy

Within the logic of the *Exposition coloniale*, the agency of the indigenous populations lay in the past. The temple of Angkor Wat — to take the example of the exhibition monument most favoured by commentators — was a great achievement but an ancient one. Moreover, what was displayed at Vincennes was not this achievement itself but the ability of the French to recreate it. This mode of display makes the colonial exhibitions structurally distinct from the universal exhibitions. The latter were occasions for competition, for showing "the works of industry of all nations", conversely, the colonial exhibitions presented the distance between industrialised nations and their colonies. If this was implicit in the structure of the *Rapport général*, it was made explicit in the popular guide, *Le Livre d'or de l'exposition coloniale*. As an "informed guide", it offers a model of interpretation for the visitor to follow.[23] In the *Livre d'or* different possessions are presented, roughly in the order of their acquisition. Each territory is presented as a colony, and then as a colony at the exposition, reimagined in its development. Again, what is on display is the process of bringing into being the colony as colony, as ordered and shaped by the coloniser.

In the *Livre d'or* as elsewhere, Algeria is the guiding example; it is presented as none other than an "immense 'laboratory of colonisation'".[24] Accordingly, the first feature in the book is: 'L'Algérie métropole second', and this is followed by 'L'Algérie à Vincennes'.[25] As Algeria is the old colony, the work of progress has largely been accomplished and there is less contrast with the exotic. The next territory to feature, Tunisia, has a slightly different configuration. Here there will be two forms of development, one more directly economic and the other "human", conforming, more or less, with the pillars of Ferry's policy and Sarraut's. Thus the French efforts in Tunisia are "productive" but also the result of careful "stewardship".[26] This project of development is, then, also the realisation of Fanon's "two frames of reference" in which "inferiority comes into being through the other".[27]

Accompanying these texts are illustrations which negotiate the modernisation of each colony and its transformation into an image of France. Some of the traditional charms of the colony are to be preserved and these are duly illustrated (and

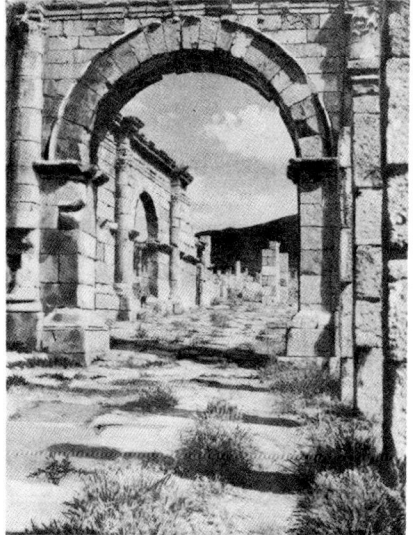

Djemila. — Arc sur le Grand Cardo.

Figure 3.2. Anon. 'Djemila', illustration, p. 37 in Fédération Française des Anciens Coloniaux, *Le Livre d'or de l'exposition coloniale internationale de 1931*, Paris: Librairie ancienne Honoré Campion, 1931.

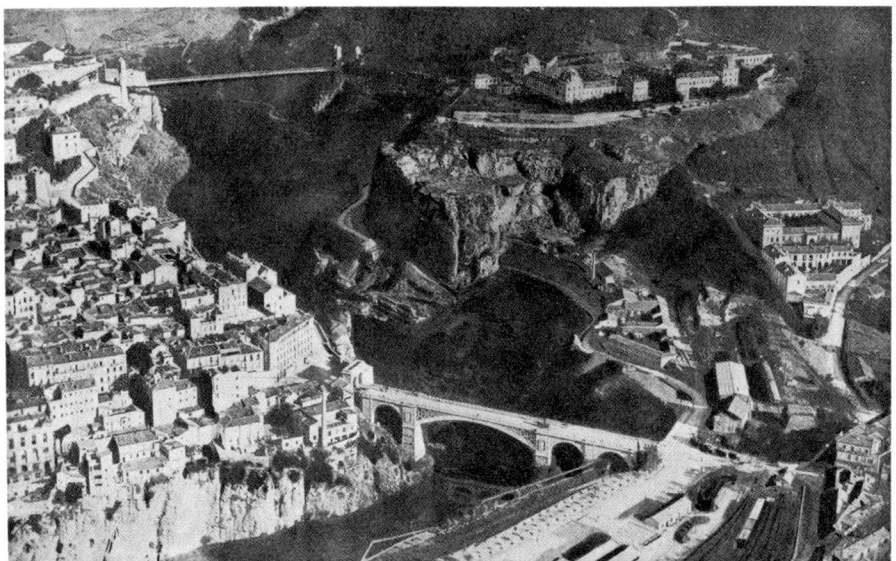

Algérie. — Constantine survolée.

Figure 3.3. Anon. 'Algeria', illustration, p. 38 in Fédération Française des Anciens Coloniaux, *Le Livre d'or de l'exposition coloniale internationale de 1931*, Paris: Librairie ancienne Honoré Campion, 1931.

these aspects of the colonies were those chosen for reproduction in Vincennes). Yet the architecture of the colonies tends to be earth-bound [Fig. 3.2]. It may have its grandeur, and in its antiquity may tacitly be acknowledged as a precedent for French examples, but even such recognition confirms the status of the buildings as monuments to a past glory. In contrast, the future is represented by the colonisers' initiatives, by the modern infrastructure and modern building techniques. Illustrations show bridges thrown across ravines and difficult terrain made readily accessible [Fig. 3.3]. Bridges, with their obvious symbolism, were much favoured by the book's designers, for now architecture is no longer earth-bound. Neither is its picturing; liberal use is made of aerial photography (at this date still a novel form, although not a neutral one, dependent as it was on a technology which also helped to ensure military superiority).

Needless to say, this work of modernisation is superintended. The section of the *Livre d'or* dedicated to French participation contains no less than 47 photographic portraits of the various governors, secretaries and directors taking part. Pride of place is, of course, given to Lyautey, with a portrait courtesy of the important French photographic studio, Manuel Frères [Fig. 3.4]. Other notable figures are associated with their territories. So, to follow the order of the *Livre d'or*, after the various introductions, the first feature on Algeria is adorned by a portrait of M. Peyrouton, Secrétaire général du Gouvernement général de l'Algérie. A portrait of M. Manceron, Résident général en Tunisie, accompanies the account of the Tunisian economy. The next territory to be presented, Morocco, had a different political status and required a different kind of portraiture. The Treaty of Fez of 1912 (orchestrated by Lyautey) had established Morocco as a French protectorate, preserving the sovereignty of the Sultan yet installing a Commissaire Résident général to act as intermediary between the Sultan and other foreign powers.

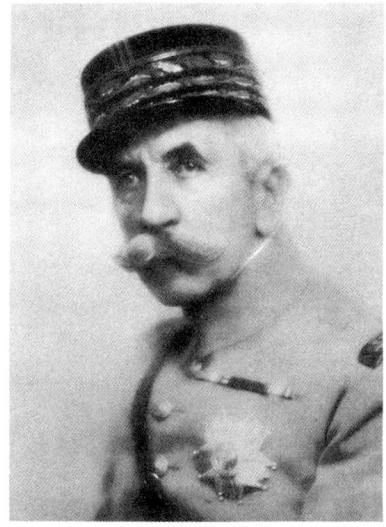

Figure 3.4. Studio G. L. Manuel Frères, 'Monsieur le Maréchal Lyautey', illustration, p. 6 in Fédération Française des Anciens Coloniaux, *Le Livre d'or de l'exposition coloniale internationale de 1931*, Paris: Librairie ancienne Honoré Campion, 1931.

Accordingly, whilst the text on Morocco was written by the Résident général, Lucien Saint, it is the Sultan, Mohammed ibn Yūsof, who is presented first, in a photograph again by Manuel Frères [Fig. 3.5]. A portrait of Saint, from the same studio, follows a few pages later [Fig. 3.6].

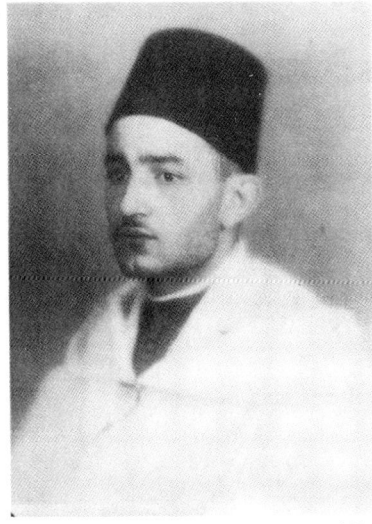

S. M. LE SULTAN DU MAROC

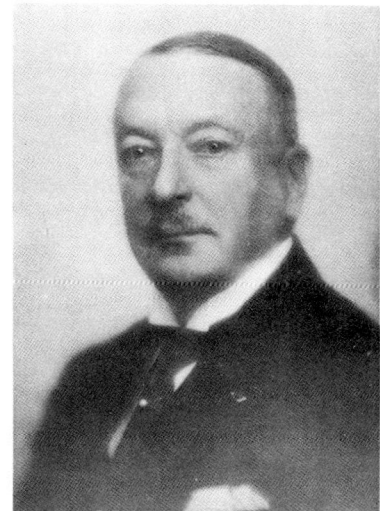

M. LUCIEN SAINT, Gouverneur général du Maroc.

Figure 3.5. Studio G. L. Manuel Frères, 'Mohammed ibn Yūsof, Sultan of Morocco', illustration, p. 50 in Fédération Française des Anciens Coloniaux, *Le Livre d'or de l'exposition coloniale internationale de 1931*, Paris: Librairie ancienne Honoré Campion, 1931.

Figure 3.6. Studio G. L. Manuel Frères, 'Lucien Saint', illustration, p. 53 in Fédération Française des Anciens Coloniaux, *Le Livre d'or de l'exposition coloniale internationale de 1931*, Paris: Librairie ancienne Honoré Campion, 1931.

These are portraits of presiding figures. Patently, they are images of patriarchy and as ubiquitous. Similar images are to be found as frontispieces, in magazines, and — perhaps above all — in newsprint. Manuel Frères specialised in catering to the latter. Founded in 1900 as Studio Henri Manuel, its success as a portrait practice encouraged Manuel to exploit the ductility of the photograph and in particular the growth in newspaper illustrations; in 1910 he created a press service to commercialise his extensive archive of negatives.[28] Whilst the older Reutlinger studio was slower to respond to developments in the press and declined after the First World War, in 1919 Manuel and his brothers Lucien and Gaston founded the company Manuel Frères, and at the peak of its success in 1925 the company occupied all five floors of 27 rue du Faubourg-Montmartre.[29] In the interwar period, those in charge of the archive of Manuel Frères were on hand to provide the appropriate images of "national" figures, making their own contribution to the cohesion of the nation state.[30] They provided 21 of the portraits in the *Livre d'or*. A portrait by Manuel Frères might well be the result of a private transaction, but such commissions were often made in anticipation of the image crossing the threshold into the public sphere. Reproduction in a newspaper might be the first in a series of transformations of the portrait. Frequency of reproduction might adumbrate translation into other media, consecration through a variant in oil on canvas, and even the apotheosis of the public statue (with its inevitable crowning of pigeonshit). Lyautey's portrait progressed through these stages, including many photographs, by Manuel Frères and others.

Under the Third Republic these stages of the portrait could mark the progress through public life of *les grands Français* in service to the state. Yet in the context of the *Exposition coloniale* it was difficult to articulate the relationship of *les grands Français* to *la plus grande France*. As much is clear from the front matter of the *Livre d'or*. In his capacity as minister for the colonies, Reynaud wrote a brief introduction to the book, which opens with a generous acknowledgement of the work of those such as Peyrouton, Manceron and Saint, those who were exemplary in "forging the links between the past and the future" of the colonies.[31] This is the work of modernisation on display in Vincennes, and it was Reynaud's wish that this work would reveal to French visitors that they were "citizens of a Greater France", one reaching across the globe. However, Reynaud also has to distinguish between metropolitan France and the France of overseas, and, implicitly, between citizens and others. In his foreword, Olivier has to make a similar negotiation. He begins by celebrating France as "a nation with 100 million inhabitants" yet such a unity of nation and population was precisely what was difficult to maintain.[32] Olivier acknowledges that 60 million of the inhabitants live beyond the borders of the mother country and so inhabit a France which is not, somehow, France. Ambiguities persist and the colonial imaginary remained the framework for their management; thus Reynaud and Olivier alike would insist on the benefits and hence "the legitimacy of colonisation".[33] The *Livre d'or* was to record all of this and so it was important that those preparing its documentation were authoritative; Olivier follows Reynaud in praising figures such as Peyrouton and Manceron, and in recognising them as "authentic colonials".[34] Their service to France and their role in public life are not in question and as such they are exemplary. The presence of their portraits in the *Livre d'or* confirms their status. Nevertheless, this confirmation also participates in a larger economy of images.

The portraits within the *Livre d'or* were defined in part by their function as public, and commemorative images. For Reynaud the very act of working towards a future implied commemoration, insofar as the work should be recognised and continued by a grateful younger generation. By virtue of this, the portraits also served to entrench two frames of reference within the publication. These images commemorated those dedicated to the making of a Greater France but the subjects depicted were defined in relation to their objects, the colonial others as yet unmade, as yet unable to assume identities as French. In effect, the portraits figure metropolitan authority and colonial subservience. Within the *Livre d'or* the portrait of Manceron, for example, is set to work against a photograph of an anonymous "Moorish woman from Sfax" on the opposite page [Figs 3.7 and 3.8]. Manceron is decorated, displaying the recognition already offered to him by the state. The anonymous woman is decorative, with a complete native costume and a place within what seems a courtyard setting with palms and other paraphernalia, including a hookah. Both photographs are highly conventional; officer and odalisque assume established roles. Different aspects of patriarchy brush against each other here; they are distinct yet ultimately cannot be separated. On the one side is that metropolitan authority which is to oversee the development of a Greater France and on the other a fantasised figure of an oriental sensuality.

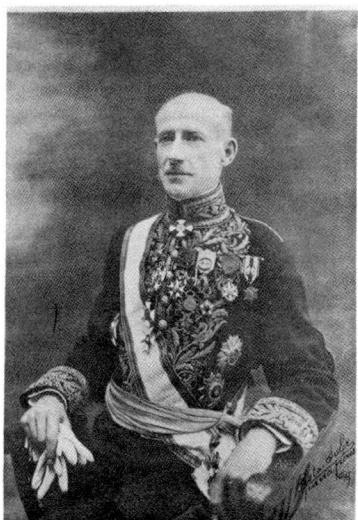

M. MANCERON. — Résident Général en Tunisie.

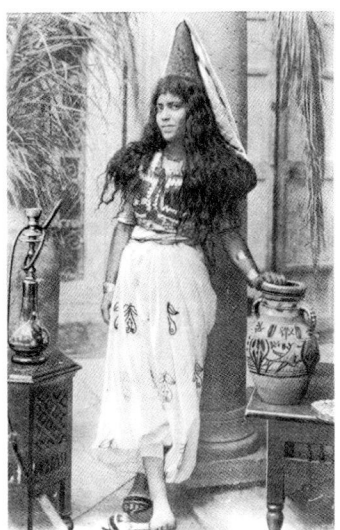

Manuscrque de Sfax.

Figure 3.7. Photo-Solex [?], 'M. Manceron', illustration, p. 42 in Fédération Française des Anciens Coloniaux, *Le Livre d'or de l'exposition coloniale internationale de 1931*, Paris: Librairie ancienne Honoré Campion, 1931.

Figure 3.8. Anon. 'Moorish woman from Sfax', illustration, p. 42 in Fédération Française des Anciens Coloniaux, *Le Livre d'or de l'exposition coloniale internationale de 1931*, Paris: Librairie ancienne Honoré Campion, 1931.

In turn, these images took their place in a further hierarchy, above the photographs on later pages, photographs of equatorial Africa, of the banks of the
Logone and the regions of Oubangui-Chari. Thus the structure of the *Rapport
général* is given pictorial form in the *Livre d'or*. The publications abound with signifiers of "the primitive" and "the colonised" yet the people represented — and
transported — are to be acted upon, improved, educated, reformed, convert-
ed. Their own acts are only of limited interest; they are always preliminary to
European actions. They are signifiers but the colonisers are the signified.

That French civilisation is the stake of the *Exposition coloniale* is indicated
clearly enough by the anxiety noted earlier, regarding the appropriate behaviour
of visitors. In the official guide to the exhibition André Demaison was clear:
"there will be no pandering to the base instincts of a vulgar audience".[35] Yet he
promptly reminded himself that such clarifications were hardly necessary. After
all, "Maréchal Lyautey, and with him Gouverneur général Olivier and all their
collaborators, regard you, dear Visitor, as a man of good taste."[36] Nevertheless,
men of discernment would hardly object to sage advice, if offered with the best
of intentions and the greatest solicitude:

> When encountering indigenous displays, do not laugh at the people and
> things which at first you do not understand. The thoughtless laughter of
> a few Frenchmen has made more foreign enemies than cruel defeats and
> vindictive treaties (...) Let a properly elevated French gallantry accompany
> your visit![37]

A true gentleman is considerate and understands his responsibility to protect
those weaker than himself. Demaison sees this as the appropriate response to
colonial display. The state communicates and French citizens — enfranchised
males — are to be worthy interlocutors. Such was the object in view; it organised
the exhibition and also structured opposition to the colonial project.

Structures of resistance and the limits of opposition

In 1923, when Sarraut came to publish his project for a new colonial policy, he had
used the occasion of the *Exposition nationale coloniale* in Marseille to make his own
work punctual. Repeating this in 1931, he opened his book *Grandeur et servitude coloniales* with reference to the Parisian exhibition. His refrain was also familiar. Moral
progress remained the goal, for both colonised and colonising. In Sarraut's view,
the French sense of "the Rights of Man" is such that "the French coloniser feels

himself to be guided at all times by a legal and moral code, one which constitutes a tradition that it is his duty to maintain".[38] This tradition was indeed tenacious, as can be seen from the debates on colonialism at the annual conference of the Ligue française pour la défense des Droits de l'Homme et du Citoyen.

Lyautey's speech inaugurating the Parisian exhibition was given on 6 May 1931; a little over two weeks later, at the Ligue's conference, further speeches were given which presented colonialism in a very different light. Here the signal contribution was made by Félicien Challaye. A veteran of Savorgnan de Brazza's tour of the Congo of 1905, which had led to sharply critical reports of the concessionary regime, Challaye had continued to campaign and had been in correspondence with Gide after the latter's return from Africa.[39] At the Ligue's conference he submitted the following order of the day, derived in part from President Wilson's Fourteen Points:

> The Congrès de la Ligue des Droits de l'Homme et du Citoyen, considering:
> That colonial regimes violate the right to self-determination;
> That they involve countless violations of the rights of individual;
> (...) Condemns in principle the current capitalist system of colonisation.[40]

In his speech in support of this motion, Challaye passed in review the reports of the Socialist Maurice Viollette, and the Radical Albert Bayet. From Viollette he retained the proposition: "the pretext of civilising is merely hypocrisy".[41] He then turned to Bayet's report:

> Bayet writes 'Henceforth, colonisation must have as its goal moral and intellectual elevation, economic development and emancipation...'
>
> 'Must have as its goal!'... It has always held up this goal, or at least this has always been claimed. This has always been the refrain when we have wanted to colonise: it has always been the principle we have invoked: to bring to others our civilisation! Under this pretext we have established our regimes of oppression and exploitation.[42]

Freedom remained cast to the horizon. And thus Challaye concludes of Bayet's motion: "It is inspired by an idealism which I know to be perfectly sincere but which today is co-opted to support the colonial regime."[43] Taking the reports together he makes it plain that idealism is open to hypocritical abuse. In Challaye's view there could be only one conclusion: "If you refuse to condemn colonisation in principle, our league will have to change its title and become the league for the defence of the rights of *the white man and the French citizen*."[44]

As one might expect, Violette's defence of his position rested with the achievements of France in promulgating the principles of the *Declaration of the Rights of Man*; this alone, he claimed, could be the "legitimation" of colonialism, with an echo of Sarraut's own defence.[45] Yet there were also echoes of Blum's arguments. The history of France constituted at least one defence of colonisation, as did the imagining of futures for the territories should French protection be withdrawn. For what could be expected of the colonies? "Challaye, do you really want to abandon them to themselves?"[46] Thus Violette was led to defend the making of men. "Citizens, I will speak plainly: at present it is still impossible to find in the colonies the men who are able to carry forward the work begun by "the white race".[47] Here Violette drew on the full temporality of the colonial imaginary. His argument would carry the day; at the vote, Challaye's motion received 643 votes and the opposing motion of the central committee 1523.

Challaye's motion failed because his opponents in the Ligue could find an alternative within the structure of the imaginary, in the model of a democratic colonialism. The anti-colonial campaign mounted by the French Communists in 1931 rejected this model altogether. The Communist aim was clear: "to incite indigenous revolt against French imperial rule and to support the struggle for complete independence".[48] The *Exposition coloniale* thus became the occasion for "a vast campaign of agitation, not only in the colonies, but also and above all among those colonised people settled in France and among the mass of French workers".[49] As part of this campaign the Parti communiste francais (PCF) also planned an anti-exhibition. The idea seems to have come from Willi Münzenberg's Anti-Imperialist League in Berlin and the first plan was for an exhibition in that city. However, the project for a Parisian display was quickly established.[50] An informant report by 'Joé' of 20 June 1931 noted: "Everything will be done to imitate the Vincennes colonial exhibition but so as to counter its message."[51] A two-page visitors' guide offers some indication of what was involved in this. Where the *Exposition coloniale* shows liberation, the anti-exposition reveals oppression. Indeed, the unveiling of the truth concealed at Vincennes is a dominant metaphor. The title of the anti-exhibition was: *La Vérité sur les colonies*.[52] And where the temporality of Vincennes shows everywhere progress, the anti-exposition reveals European decadence. This was perhaps clearest in the display of "European fetishes", sculptures turned out on the rue Sainte-Sulpice for Catholic churches. Christian worship is not placed at the end of an arc of development but is repositioned as another form of animism. There is an inversion of hierarchy, something rather familiar within the avant garde by this date. Yet this inversion preserves relations, even whilst reassigning values.[53] And so in the anti-exhibition, as at Vincennes, the French viewer remains the principal subject addressed.

At least some members of the PCF seem to have recognised the limitations of this approach and attempted to address different audiences. On such attempt was noted in a surveillance report of 14 July 1931 detailing the circulation of tracts in the compound behind the temple of Angkor Wat which was "reserved for militia, colonial troops and Indo-Chinese exhibitors".[54] This tract was one of the very rare documents to address those transported to the exhibition, 200 of whom were in this particular compound. The tract begins by setting out the French programme of exploitation being pursued in the colonies and emphasises that this is a programme from which the indigenous workers and peasants will derive no profit. The tract then moves from the colony to the metropole.

> Before your departure, the French colonisers made you a number of charming promises. But, on arriving in France, you have realised that your situation is more wretched than that of a herd of cattle. Your accommodation is no better than a stable and your food hardly fit for pigs.[55]

This trajectory from colony to metropole is akin to that of the *Livre d'or*, however, in that publication there was an ascent to a new level of civilisation, whilst here, once again, there is an inversion.

> In bringing you to the colonial exhibition, the French have treated you like exotic animals, presented for the amusement of the crowds like a troop of monkeys or orangoutangs at the zoo.[56]

The tract is blunt in presenting the spectacle of the exhibition as a further exploitation, matching that exacted in the colonies. Here is another confrontation of limits. What does it mean to be told of your exploitation? What does it mean to be compared, repeatedly, to an animal? Clearly, the comparison is intended as a flat rejection of the project of making men. It is also a call to resist and here, at least, an alternative is presented, an agency and another identity imagined. The tract continues directly: "Right now the workers and peasants of our country, already aware of their dignity, are rising up against those who would exploit them."[57] A sense of dignity is a precondition for action.

Shame

In the rhetorical scheme of the Communists, the antithesis of dignity is shame; the tribune for this rhetoric was *Monde*, a journal founded in 1928 by Henri Barbusse. This journal's critical coverage of the *Exposition coloniale* began shortly after it opened, with a relatively long piece by Georges Altman. He begins:

> Two young Malagasy women, their slender bodies wrapped in white robes, sit on suitcases, waiting. No doubt they have just arrived. They look steadily at the huge flight of steps in front of them, which ascends the fiery red pavilion dedicated to Madagascar. The fifty-metre high tower surmounted with the sculpted heads of horned cattle lowers over the Tananarive restaurant... where Alsatian women (!) with traditional costumes and coiffures are serving the local wine. The two Malagasy women in white watch them...[58]

In this description the women are not straightforwardly part of their setting; they are not the staffage appearing in the photographs produced for the organisers of the exhibition. They are seated on their baggage, as if newly arrived backstage rather than already performing. They are not yet part of a spectacle. Instead the author watches them as they watch. It is the bedecked Alsatians who have become the spectacle, outlandish as they seem in their present context. Altman's account is highly unusual in moving towards this alternative perspective. His description continues:

> these two women are impassive and only their eyes move, eyes which are now those of emigrants the world over, of those who have been transplanted; eyes which are questioning, fearful, frightened... A first sight, then, at the entrance to this Exhibition, a sight which will be repeated almost everywhere in this vast enclosure: one waits.[59]

Altman acknowledges the women's quiet resistance to a performing role. They have been transplanted and if Altman imagines them within a category of experience he does not share, he does not speak for them. His next lines are also unusual. The "first sight" of the exhibition seems, initially, to be Altman's but an ambiguity is introduced when the sight is described as "repeated". Is it Altman's experience or the women's? Ambiguity is sustained in the final clause which, again, could refer to the author or to the women, who were introduced sitting, waiting. This stasis is important. It is made a counter to Lyautey's celebration of colonialism as progress, of colonial conquest as that which "gets things done" (a description Altman quotes).[60] Yet if Altman's perspective is brought towards that of the exhibited, he does not occupy their position. "Those who watch do not laugh; gravely, with averted eyes, a word is exchanged and then there is a short laugh, but its meaning is unclear."[61] Altman acknowledges the limits of his comprehension. This is part of a refusal of the logic of the exhibition, a rejection of one form of spectatorship.

In a later text published in *Monde*, Altman draws out a contrast between the attitude of those exhibited and the vulgar European spectators. He has not found himself amongst those visitors described — or imagined — by Demaison in the official guide.

> A sound, always the same sound, of a monotonous drone, draws your attention to the centre of a laughing crowd. There is much laughter at the Exhibition. One goes there to laugh. An old black man dances, filing away with a curved bow at a strange violin, playing to the gallery.[62]

This scene is of the type which the organisers of the exhibition were supposed to eschew, precisely because it was a stimulus to vulgarity in the crowd:

> Coins rain down from all sides (...) *Mirci, la dame, mirci, moissié, mirci, mirci, ci bono, ci bono*, a plaintive ballad of poverty that amuses those gathered round. Also watching in the crowd there is tall militiaman wearing khaki and a red fez; when the old man pauses the soldier speaks to him in dialect, quickly rapping out his words. The crowd falls silent and listens whilst for a moment the two are off in their own world. Then the militiaman shrugs his shoulders, seemingly frustrated. He strides off and the old man takes up his song (...) And the crowd, finding him back as they like him, resume their laughter.[63]

Here the literal intervention of the militiaman is also a metaphorical one, where the comic performance is suspended. For a moment another world is opened, and again it is one which is not readily comprehended. The old man ceases, for a moment, to be a performer and enters a dialogue to which the visitors are not party. It may be that the soldier has asked the older man not to abase himself for money but this has to remain conjecture and that is the point: the soldier's view is not that of the visitors. In any case, the interruption is brief and a norm is re-established. However, the interruption has had its effect; the reader of Altman's account is placed at a distance from the norm, estranged from it. The scene is not now the old man's performance but instead the attitude of these viewers.

What is discovered here is shame, and as Jean-Paul Sartre recognised, shame has a specific structure:

> [A]lthough certain complex forms derived from shame can appear on the reflective plane, shame is not originally a phenomenon of reflection. In fact no matter what results one can obtain in solitude by the religious *practice* of shame, it is in its primary structure shame *before somebody*.[64]

Altman has attempted to install this structure, to encourage the visitors to see themselves. "Shame is by nature *recognition*. I recognize that I *am* as the Other sees me." [65] The recognition, in Sartre's account, takes place in private, when the philosopher imagines himself discovered spying through a keyhole.[66] Altman wants such a private situation to become public, and not just in the sense of taking place in the public spaces of Vincennes, but also in the sense of transforming the collective perception which the *Exposition coloniale* was designed to inculcate. Lyautey and Olivier intended the exhibition to reveal the great work of French civilisation in the colonies. For Altman the *mise-en-scène* of the exhibition was to be challenged by shifting attention from the colonial performance to the metropolitan audience. In this way "the prextext" of civilising could be denounced as "hypocrisy".[67] This was to become a trope of the rather circumscribed literature of resistance.

Consequently, in another text in *Monde*, Léon Werth also begins with a description of an audience:

> A small, respectable crowd: they would not talk to a negro with that insolent tone which a colonial adopts when speaking to a man or a beast, thereby dishonouring himself. They only smile an indulgent, superior smile. If the negro runs an errand, they will give him a few coins. They have no doubts; they are civilised. The colonies produce mahogany and rubber. The negros eat coconuts and wear loincloths or are decked out with shells. Their mission on earth is to serve as attractions at the colonial exhibitions. Perhaps one day we will manage to civilise them.[68]

This is a refinement of the situation described by Altman; here it is not even a matter of vulgarity, for the members of this public are "respectable". Yet this becomes part of an assumed superiority. It is an embodiment of inequality, and as such made to figure the colonial project. Werth concludes by moving back out to this larger world:

> Overseas, oppression and slaughter. But the crowds can still smile at the dance of an old negro. And so it was during the war, when the pretty nurses smiled at the soldiers' stories. The colonial exhibition is like the home front. Here there is nothing of the realities of the front.
> But those who have seen these realities (...) will, when meeting a native, never quite be able to conquer their shame at being white.[69]

This juxtaposition of different experiences will recall Gide's desire to see "behind the scenes" and learn what is hidden there.[70] And like Gide, Werth had spent time in the French colonies.[71] The knowledge acquired there is the source of shame, unmasterable under the indigenous gaze.

Roger Parry's third space

Only one photographer seems to have explored anything of these structure of shame and it may not be a coincidence that this was someone both versed in technologies of the *mise-en-scène* and with direct experience of the French colonies. That photographer was Roger Parry. Initially trained at the École des Arts appliqués à l'Industrie, in 1923 Parry had advanced to the École nationale supérieure des Arts décoratifs. In 1928 he met Maurice Tabard and began working as his darkroom assistant. After Tabard became director of the studio Deberny-Peignot in June 1929, Parry followed him there. In the summer of 1930 Parry then travelled the western coast of Africa with Fabian Loris (although unfortunately almost all of the photographs he took in Africa were accidentally destroyed). On his return to France, Parry established himself as an independent photographer.[72]

The majority of photographs Parry took of the *Exposition coloniale* conform readily enough to the model adopted by Blanchet in being architectural views following the visual cues of the architects. The familiar landmarks appear: the tower of the Malagasy Pavilion, the distinctive profile of the imitation Angkor Wat and so on. These photographs of the exhibition are conventional. However, three images seem to make a studied exception; these are photographs taken in one of the housing compounds [Figs 3.9, 3.10 and 3.11]. While three photographs cannot be held to constitute a sustained body of work, these three are nevertheless more than isolated records of chanced-upon scenes. They share features and rehearse configurations. These photographs differ from the conventional views but are not snapshots in the manner of Blanchet's image of the seated woman.

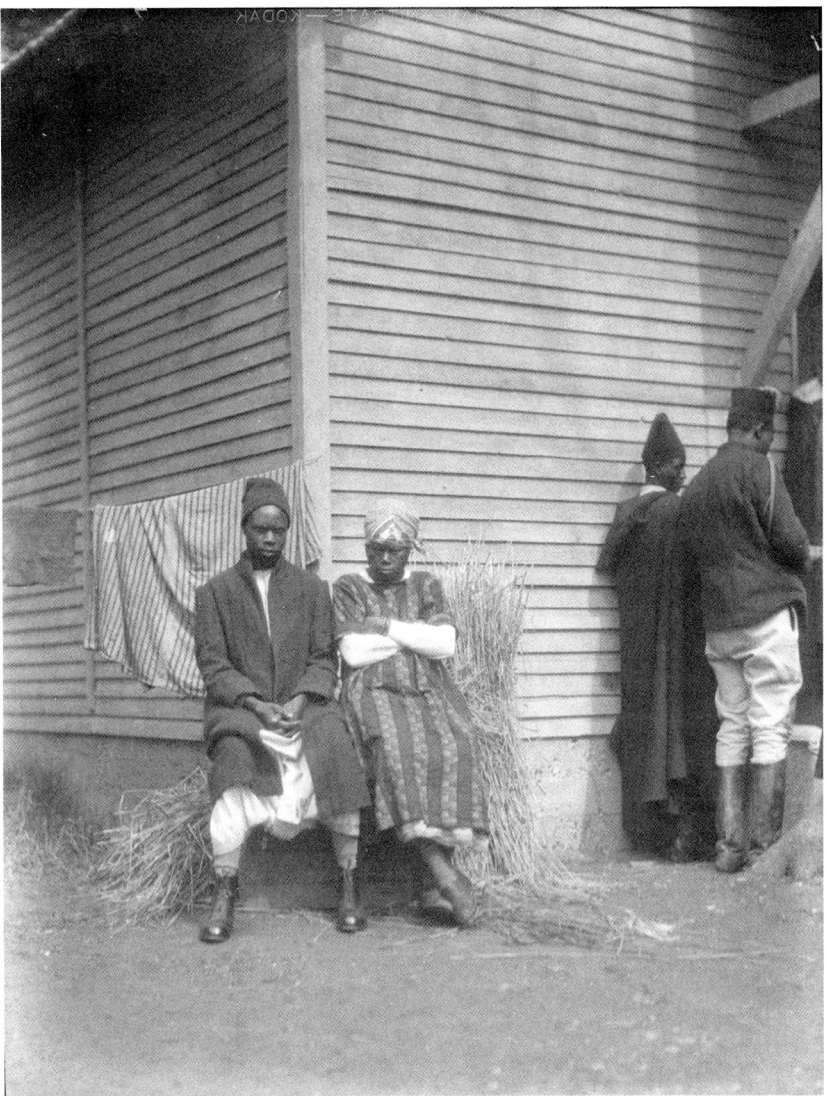

Figure 3.9. Roger Parry, 'Seated man and woman', photographic print, 1931.

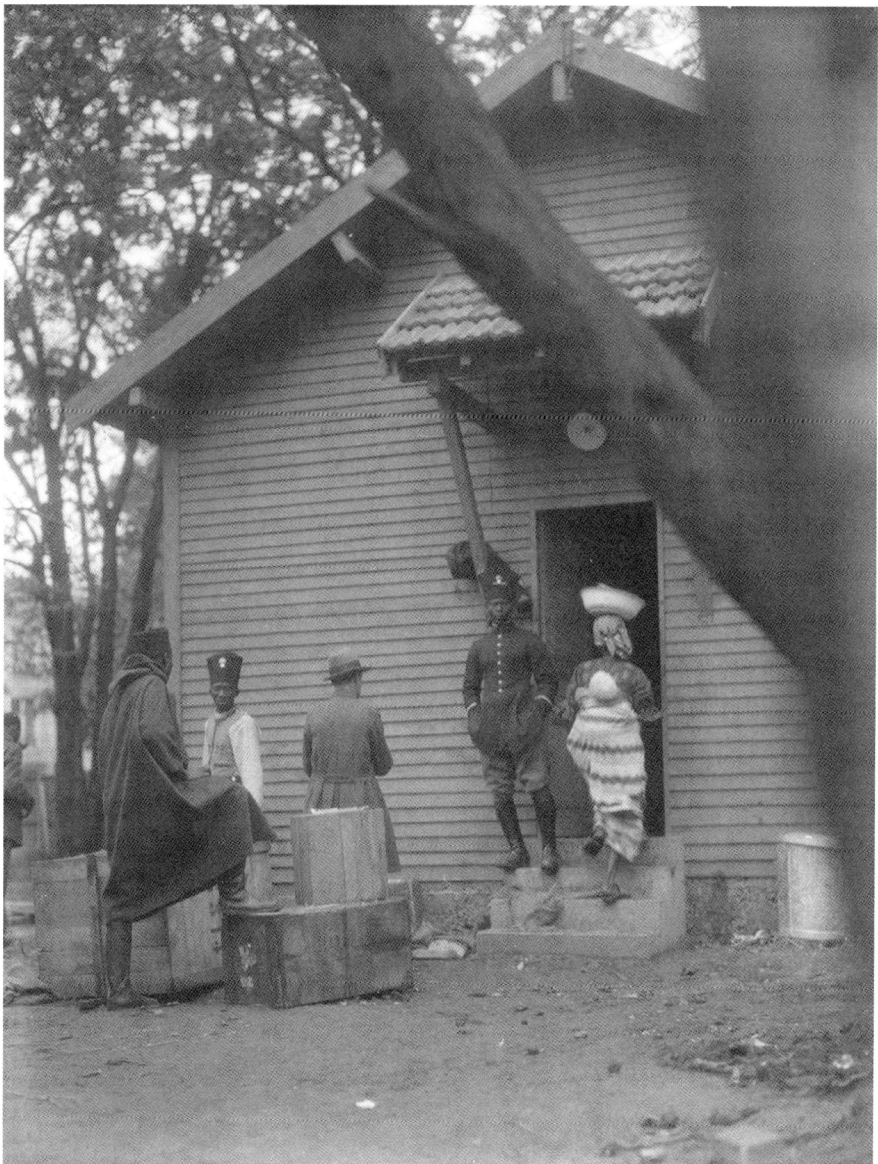

Figure 3.10. Roger Parry, 'Figures in front of a building', photographic print, 1931.

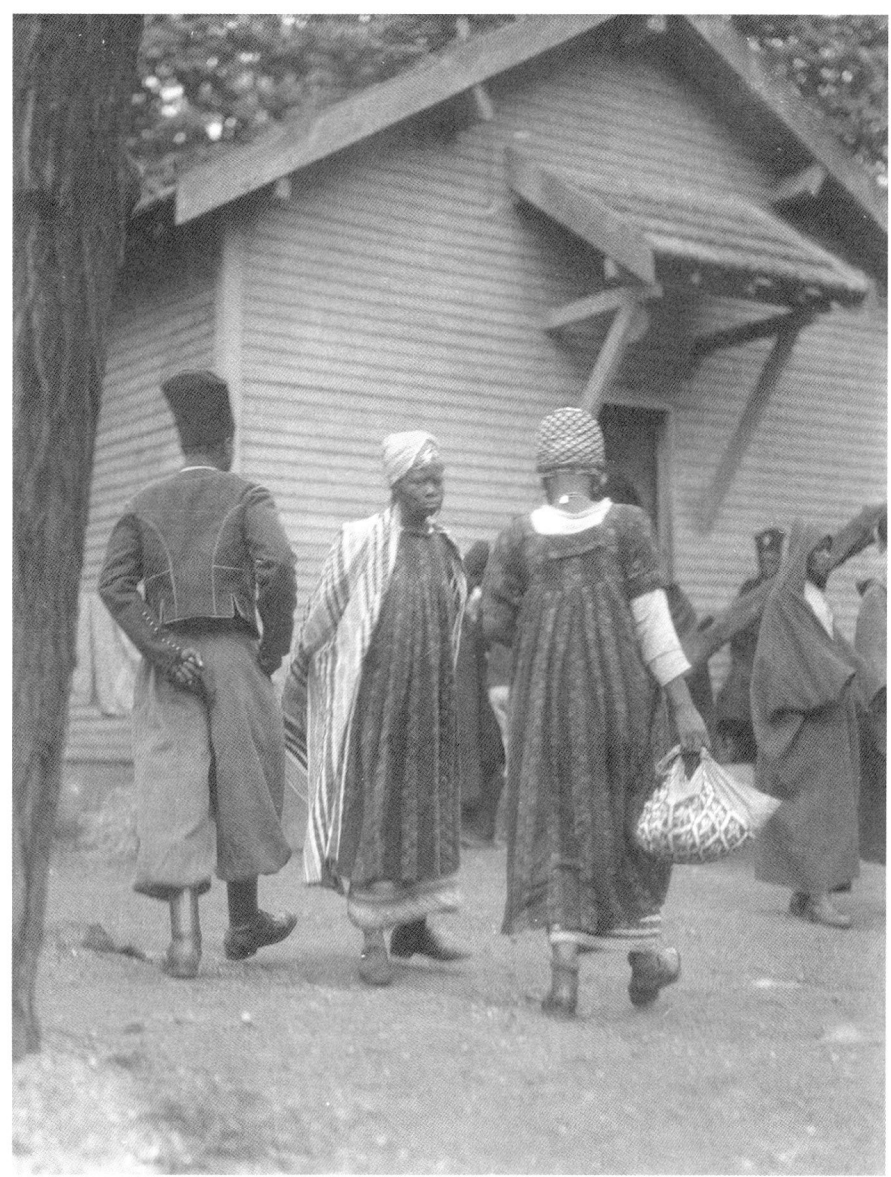

Figure 3.11. Roger Parry, 'Walking figures in front of a building', photographic print, 1931.

If Parry's photographs of the pavilions record the staging of the exhibition the photographs of the compound are an attempt to picture something else, although this is something which is not quite "behind the scenes". Certainly, the building shown is unremarkable and is clearly not part of exhibition's public presentation. In each view of it there are a number of figures, with some orientated towards the photographer and others away from him (and that they are images of people at all marks them out from Parry's largely deserted architectural studies of the pavilions). These are not populous crowd scenes, nor are they portrait studies of individuals. The figures are not posed but some nevertheless respond to the presence of the photographer and so the photographs cannot be described as candid. Thus in various ways the photographs resist easy categorisation. Such resistance has sometimes been made a novelty — a striking discrepancy — and, in turn, this is sometimes judged as revelatory. But this does not seem to be the case here. This is why describing these photographs as picturing what is "behind the scenes" is misleading, insofar as common usage suggests such picturing to be revelatory. Indeed, it is difficult to imagine what might be revealed here. The figures photographed are moving in different directions and are not interacting, and so the resulting images are not "scenes" in the sense of showing incidents or events. The figures may be more or less active but there are not unifying actions. The photographs are devoid of narrative.

Precedents for this type of image may be found in the superimposed prints made by Tabard. As the latter's erstwhile assistant, Parry had an intimate, practical knowledge of this process, which he demonstrated in his work with Loris for an edition of Léon-Paul Fargue's *Banalité*.[73] These images were novelties, with discrepancy and disjuncture posed as revelatory. To the extent that these works were within the ambit of Surrealism, the different elements of superimposed prints could be understood as the more or less disparate realities brought together in André Breton's formulation of the Surrealist image.[74] Parry's photographs of the compound do not create such sparks; nothing leaps from one terminal to the other.

Instead, some sense of the photographs might be gained from turning round the metaphor of viewing "behind the scenes", and returning some emphasis to the role of the witness. I have tried to show that viewing was — for some commentators at least — rendered problematic at the exhibition and this seems to be what Parry was exploring (albeit in a tentative way). His images are a little like Allégret's photograph of the visitors to the hut, in that they are experiments in looking. Yet whereas Allégret's photograph was an image of Gide beginning to see, and to bear witness, this is not the case for Parry's work. And this seems to be because "witnessing" could not be a valorised mode in the context of the

Exposition coloniale. Instead, in Parry's three photographs there is a refusal to "reveal", to "indicate". It is in this sense that Parry could be held to photograph a third space, one which is neither the performed spectacle nor the revelation of something which the performance conceals, as was the ambition of *La Vérité sur les colonies*. Parry, like Werth, would not content himself with the role of "gawper". Yet Parry also seems to have understood that the type of investigation that Gide had pursued in Pacha's subdivision was not possible in Paris. The exhibition would not yield material for a testimony. And this is why it is easier to describe what Parry's three photographs are not; they are a sum of refusals. The space Parry photographs is perhaps closest to that described by Altman; the figures in Parry's space are not playing roles, they are between scenes, between activities. They are waiting. In the sum of refusals an ambiguity is sustained rather than resolved.

Such photographs can be accounted for within the rather informal photographic practices of the period. Most of those attempting to make a living by photography worked as freelancers and understood that they had to be prepared to turn their viewfinders in a variety of directions.[75] This seems to have been the case for Parry's visit to the *Exposition coloniale*. Here the number of exposures tells its own story: 29 for the pavilions and installations, and three for the housing compound.[76] Yet the photographs of the compound remain distinctive and are perhaps best understood as a critical reflection on Parry's other images of the exhibition. Here Parry is watching himself look, considering what it might mean to make a photograph without a motive or a motif. Such, paradoxically, might constitute a resistance to the logic of the exhibition. Yet the critical stance adopted here is maintained only for the time needed to make a few exposures and the moment of reflection is curtailed.

The means to circulate such critical reflections were equally restricted. *Monde* carried occasional illustrations but not photographs and whilst the PCF had launched a photojournal in 1928 — which from the outset had attacked the hypocrisies of French colonialism — this had folded by the autumn of 1929.[77] There would be a renewed engagement with photography when the journal was relaunched in January 1932, yet this was of course too late to provide coverage of the *Exposition coloniale*. At this moment the PCF was renewing its cultural policy and also created the Association des écrivains et artistes révolutionnaires, and in due course Parry would become one of the relatively few photographers to belong to this group. Yet none of even this restricted number of photographers could be held to have their practice fully determined by their affiliation.[78] The critical stance would remain just one amongst others. Parry's third space would remain marginal in almost every respect.

The burden of civilisation

If it was difficult to find other than marginal spaces from which to view the *Exposition coloniale* critically, such spaces did exist. One emerged, fleetingly, at the centre of the exhibition project; it briefly enabled an alternative response to the question of making men.

A Congrès International et Intercolonial de la Société Indigène was held in early October 1931 under the auspices of the *Exposition coloniale*, when the latter had nearly run its course. The organisers described their objectives in a defensive tone: a specialist study of indigenous societies, they proposed, was desirable but it would be unfortunate if this study appeared as "as a mere appendix to the economic problem", thereby seeming to betray an inclination to "underestimate the properly human value of indigenous peoples".[79] This unstable combination of economic and human values again recalls Sarraut's project and indeed the former minister of the colonies was president of the conference's organising committee. Lyautey himself restated the problem, in comments made following Sarraut's introduction: "at present we tend to be obsessed by economic questions and concentrate on markets and business and so we have lost sight of something: man".[80]

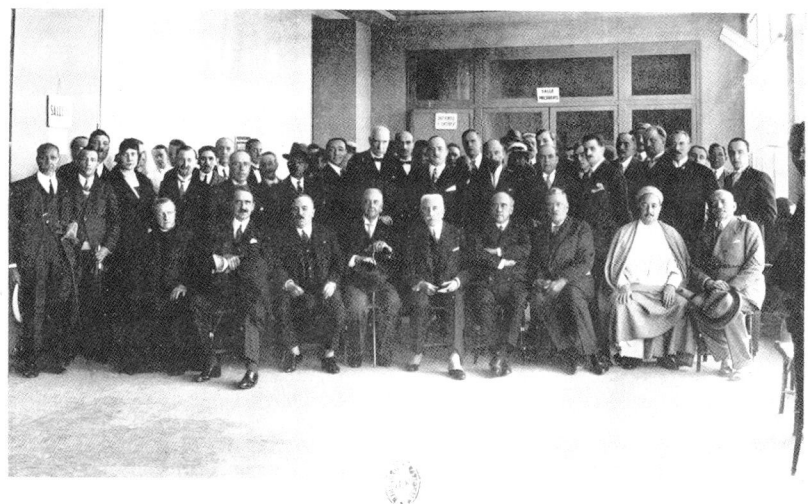

Figure 3.12. Anon. 'Delegates of the Congrès International et Intercolonial de la Société Indigène at the Cité d'Information', frontispiece in *Congrès International et Intercolonial de la Société Indigène*, Paris: École coloniale, 1931.

As was appropriate for such an occasion, delegates came from a wide variety of backgrounds and each had their own expertise, or at least some measure of authority. Yet despite this diversity the central debates at the conference may be summarised readily enough, unfolding as they did from Lyautey's contention. "Man" was indeed becoming visible in the colonies, yet in a distinct fashion. There was progress towards individualism yet recognition of this was mixed with anxieties concerning what was destroyed in the process. What did it mean, after all, to make in one's own image? None other than Élie Allégret was responsible for addressing this problem in the general report. He was charged with considering whether social and familial arrangements were compatible with the spirit of individualism which was posited as the natural tendency of Western civilisation.[81]

Allégret was not alone in addressing these questions. Strikingly, African voices were to be heard at the conference. Paul Hazoumé, from Benin, also gave a report on social and familial conditions. His conclusion was simple yet challenging. He reminded his audience "that indigenous histories rest on religious beliefs" and then levelled this charge: "the sad fact is that European nations have added to these histories only a thoroughly materialist conception of life".[82] This was an effective challenge because it directly addressed the problem Lyautey raised in his introductory remarks. What were the true benefits of civilisation? Hazoumé's remarks were embraced by the missionaries present and, in a later debate, Allégret directly rehearsed his words. Maurice Leenhardt also turned to them when he was called on to summarise the task of forming mentalities.

> Hazoumé has got to the heart of the matter, when after sketching his rather bleak picture, he demands: 'Show us your ideal.' Our ideal is not defined by Reason, it is something far greater than that: it is to win men to us not as subjects but as brothers. We want to win a moral victory.[83]

The anonymous photographer whose job it was to document the conference seems to have understood at least some of the implications of this. Photographs were taken at both of the conference venues, at the exhibition itself, in the Cité des Informations, and at the École coloniale. The two images were reproduced as a pair of frontispieces for the second volume of conference proceedings. The first shows the gathering at the Cité, the point of orientation for visitors to the exhibition [Fig. 3.12]. The photograph at this venue is a quite conventional group portrait, although in order to comply with convention and include all delegates the photographer has had to retreat to a distance and the resulting composition is rather awkward, with a broad empty space in the foreground. Lyautey is seated almost at the centre of the group; his spats are clean despite the often-bewailed mud at the exhibition site, created by crowds and the damp summer. The image in some respects resembles a graduation photograph, and this is appropriate enough if one understands Lyautey as a master surrounded by colleagues and students. The group portrait also resembles a graduation photograph in showing those who have reached a specific level of attainment. Some, like Sarraut — seated at Lyautey's left hand — have authority conferred by considerable colonial experience. Others have authority conferred by their status as designated representatives of indigenous groups. The latter have successfully been made men. They are the beneficiaries of civilisation. These individuals have made the journey from the colony to the metropole; they have crossed physical boundaries and symbolic thresholds and, in showing their presence at the Cité, the photograph records this.

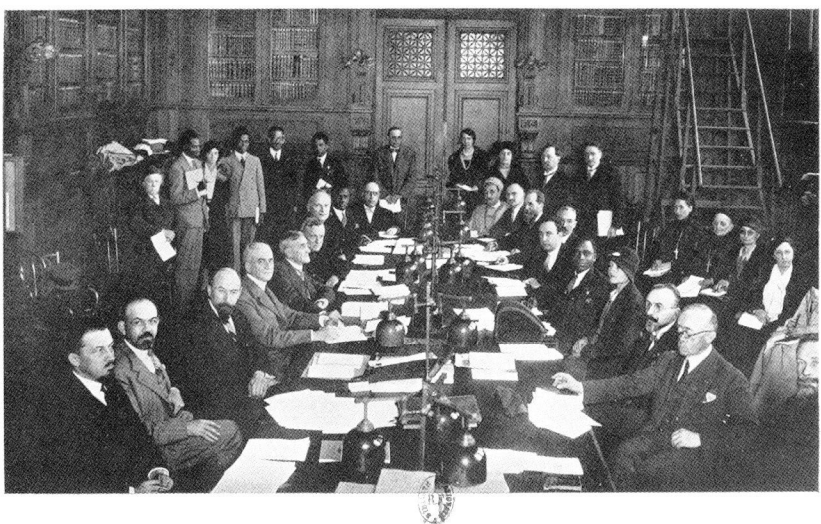

Figure 3.13. Anon. 'Delegates of the Congrès International et Intercolonial de la Société Indigène in the library of the École coloniale', frontispiece in *Congrès International et Intercolonial de la Société Indigène*, Paris: École coloniale, 1931.

The second photograph, taken in the library of the École, is rather different [Fig. 3.13]. The library was a privileged space for the organisation and reproduction of colonial knowledge and as such it was one of the spaces in which students mentally prepared for the work of winning men as brothers. In photographing this space, the photographer may have gained an elevated position by perching on a library ladder similar to that visible in the background to the right. The result is a composition structured by the long library table. Poses are a little more informal and there is plenty of clutter on the table. Rather than marshalling as at the Cité, here the photographer has interrupted the to-and-fro of scholarly debate. The character of this debate is perhaps the reason for the curious editorial decision to include a pair of frontispieces. These images show not just delegates convened and the conference in session; they also show "the ideal". The first photograph shows the men won as brothers, and the second shows this fraternity sealed by scholarly exchange. (This "fraternity" is extended to the women present, although it is perhaps significant that the only woman seated at the main table is the stenographer.) The "brothers" from the colonies have won the right to debate. The indigenous representatives are shown acceding to at least a level of representation.

The two photographs are composed to affirm two different aspects of the colonial imaginary, patriarchy and fraternity. Such a combination makes the photographs more than simple iterations of the imagery of the *Livre d'or*. The delegates are not merely types and they perform their own roles; in the context of their participation in the conference, they are individuals, differentiated as such. Some, like Hazoumé, could challenge the colonial lobby. Nevertheless, it was the case that the differentiation took place within the confines of the École coloniale and the *Exposition coloniale*. The stage remained that set by the French state. So I turn now to consider a different space, and different types of performance.

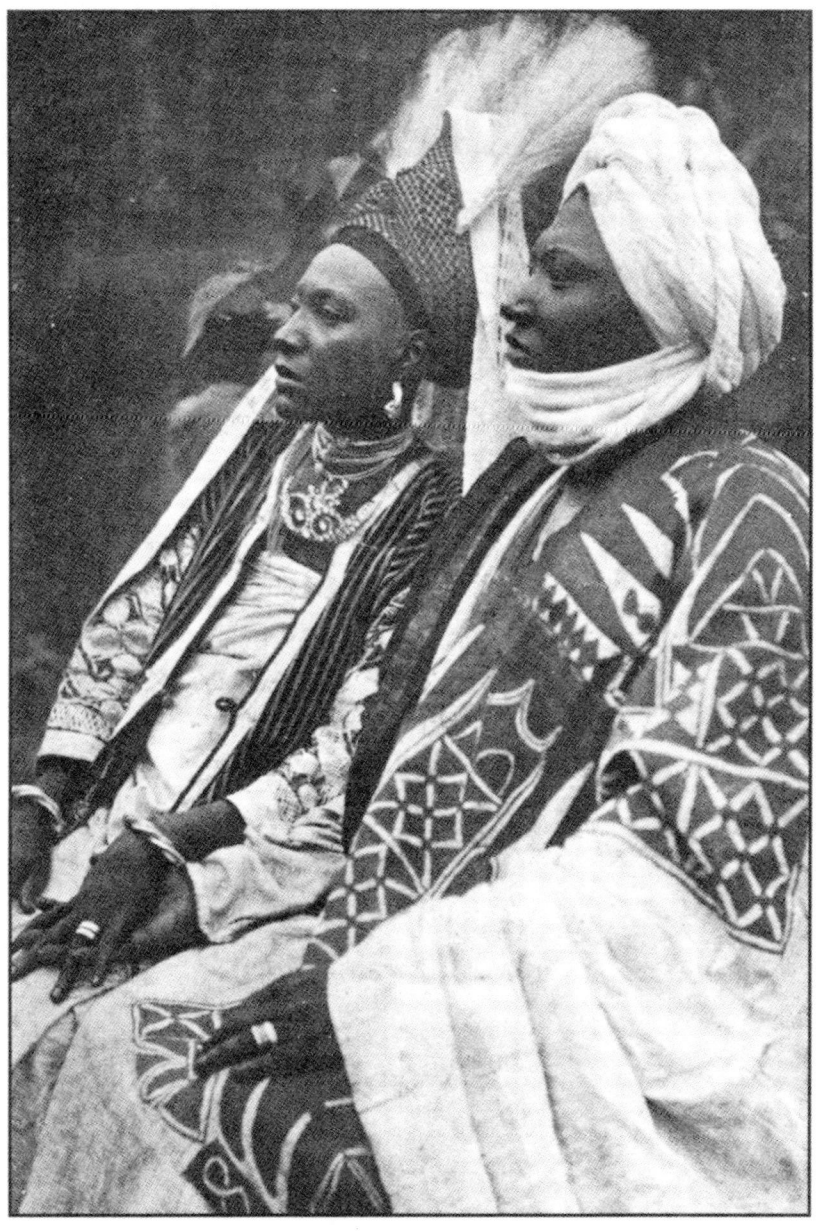

Figure 4.1. King Ibrahim Njoya, 'King Njoya of Bamum with one of his wives', illustration, p. 4 in *Der evangelischer Heidenbote*, 86: 1, January 1913.

4. Performance, appropriation and dispossession

King Ibrahim Njoya and Mosé Yeyap in the Cameroon Grassfields

In 1912, King Njoya of the Bamum orchestrated a self-portrait with a favoured wife [Fig. 4.1]. Njoya shows himself in profile, seated next to Ndayie, in a composition which was arrived at in collaboration with Anna Rein-Wuhrmann of the Basler Mission. The self-portrait seems to have excited interest in missionary circles, as it was soon published in *Der evangelische Heidenbote*. Here it was given the following extended caption:

> King Njoya of Bamum with one of his wives. (The King's own photograph.) King Njoya of Bamum is also an illustration of African 'royal wretchedness'. He belongs among those pitiful chiefs who, despite having turned to Christianity, cannot be baptised, because they must live in polygyny in keeping with popular custom.[1]

The caption offers a particular coding of the photograph, one quite in keeping with the missionising project. Like all captions, it makes salient certain features of the image at the expense of others and viewers in Fumban, the capital of the Bamum Kingdom, might well have been struck by various aspects of the portrait which the caption-writer neglects. They would have recognised that Njoya is wearing a type of Hausa dress, and thereby making some acknowledgement of the influence of Islamic traders from north of his kingdom. Conversely, they also would have understood that Njoya's costume is decorated with symbols of the Bamum and so acknowledges the skills of local weavers and dyers. And what might have seemed to readers of *Der evangelischer Heidenbote* a literally touching detail, that of Ndayie's fingers overlaying Njoya's hand, would have elicited a different response in Fumban. For the king was not to be touched.[2] Thus the photograph records a breach of court etiquette.[3] However, registering such a failure of observance involves an assumption, namely that in the making of the photograph ceremonial conventions were to be maintained. Yet what were the protocols in this unusual situation of a royal photographic collaboration? This seemingly trivial question is important because it broaches the larger issue of how technologies of representation support or challenge social relations.

This is a particularly complex issue in the case of Njoya's photograph. The self-portrait is a particular kind of performance: it is at once a fashioning of an appearance and of an artefact. It is a presentation of self and also a display of skill. In turn, this exercise of skills involves a command of resources and it is here that the issue begins to become complex. Njoya's resources include *inter alia* the weavers and dyers of the royal household and Rein-Wuhrmann's camera and her access to the means for developing and printing. Thus whilst some of Njoya's resources are local other are not; photography in Fumban in 1912 may fairly be described as an alien technology and for precisely this reason it was a valuable resource. However, understanding how it was valued and how it was used by Njoya cannot be disentangled from his other acts of representation and self-representation, acts which were part and parcel of his duties as King of the Bamum.

Extraversion and representation

The interlacing of fingers may be appropriate in one context yet not in another; what may be an affecting sign of intimacy may also be a transgression. Njoya's self-portrait has, then, a certain instability, an equivocation, betraying a conflict between one set of customs and an imposed civilisation. What is at stake here is a negotiation at once with different categories of personhood and different procedures of representation. These are, of course, bound together in the self-portrait precisely as the simultaneous fashioning of an appearance and an artefact. Yet if Njoya's self-portrait as accepted as *his* performance, then personhood and procedure are not merely imposed; in important respects equivocation belongs *to* the portrait and is part of Njoya's fashioning.

Developing this argument entails a rethinking of the "alien", of what is involved in the combining of new procedures with existing ones. It is not the case that agents and representations are stable in "traditional" contexts until disrupted by the forces of history. Artefacts are mutable and so are agents, who may refashion themselves to respond to particular circumstances. And whilst circumstances changed radically in the Cameroon Grassfields during the colonial period, it remained the case that existing practices could be adapted to respond to the contingencies and ambiguities of the colonial encounter. Perhaps the scholar who has been the most vigorous in pursuing the implications of this is Jean-François Bayart, who rejects any definition that "maintains that a 'culture' is composed of a stable, closed corpus of representations, beliefs or symbols".[4] For Bayart, such definitions succumb to "the logic of cultural closure" which is "inherent in the invention of tradition".[5] The alternative he proposes is an acknowledgement and analysis of extraversion, of those tactics which consist "in espousing foreign cultural elements and putting them in the service of autochthonous objectives".[6] He argues that "situations of domination, in particular colonial domination, open an immense field" for such tactics.[7] In what follows, I hope to show that this was indeed the case for the Bamum Kingdom during the reign of King Njoya, and that various practices of extraversion were developed both within and against the colonial imaginary.

Divergent interpretations of Njoya's self-portrait in Basel and Fumban should not be judged simply a matter of incommensurate audiences and knowledges, for that risks its own kind of cultural closure. Doubtless there were different contexts of reception in Switzerland and the Grassfields but these contexts need to be understood as fluid rather than given and stable. Bayart points toward this fluidity and argues that practices of extraversion are practices of mobilisation, involving the more or less fraught exploitation of existing resources. It follows that a resource is best understood as something potential: the value of the term lies in the way that it suggests the *possibility* of mobilisation. And there are very many possibilities; the investigation of resources should embrace not only objects, be they tools or weapons, but also traditions and innovations, old and new ways of making and responding. Procedures of representation are of course amongst such resources. As I argued in my first chapter, representation is a condition artefacts may arrive at. Rather than being an essential property, it is something to be mobilised. Understanding representation, then, is understanding the circumstances in which its mobilisation becomes both possible and desirable. Conversely, it is also involves understanding that artefacts and agents may be divested of their representational roles. This may involve violence.

In Fumban, around 1912, portraiture was a resource. It was not straightforwardly part of the Bamum repertoire, however nor was it entirely alien because some of the categories of personhood which lent themselves to portrayal were firmly entrenched in the Grassfields. The pre-eminent example was the sacred person of the King and the protocols governing approaches to his person offer confirmation of this. Nevertheless, the person of the King and the status of the sovereign were compromised from the first colonial contact. In response, Njoya was to attempt various mobilisations in increasingly fraught negotiations with colonisers and with missionaries, including, in due course, Élie Allégret. These negotiations were themselves complicated because they were not simply a matter of a dialogue between colonised and colonising; a key protagonist in what became a campaign against Njoya was Mosé Yeyap, an early Bamum convert to Christianity, a first cousin of King, and, ultimately, one of his most determined opponents. His history is inextricably bound up with Njoya's.

Njoya's appropriations

Njoya was a son of King Nsangu and his designated heir, whilst Yeyap was a son of Njikam, Nsangu's half-brother. Njikam was, at least for his mother Ngoungoure, a pretender to the throne which was to be occupied by Njoya; it has been quite plausibly suggested that Yeyap's hostility to Njoya derived from the failure of his father's claim.[8] Yet the political weakness of Yeyap relative to Njoya was to be its own kind of strength, for it created paths of adaptation quite different to those open to Njoya as reigning monarch. This fundamental divergence in resources would assume its full significance during the colonial period, when Njoya and Yeyap were obliged to confront German, British and, finally, French cultural practices.

For the Bamum, the colonial period began on 6 July 1902, when a German military mission led by Captain Hans von Ramsay and one Lieutenant Sandrock arrived in Fumban. This force had already seen action to the north of the region and Sandrock had been involved in fighting, which had led to the death of the Lamido Oumarou of Banyo on 1 February.[9] Njoya had had cause to rely on Oumarou at the beginning of his reign; he had been helped by Oumarou's cavalry in 1894 when vanquishing a rival, Gbentkom, during a civil war.[10] Doubtless Njoya would have tried to follow the fortunes of his ally, and would have been aware of the progress of the German forces.

Later, Njoya wrote his own history of his first encounter with the Germans. Sometime before 1908 he began to draft what would become a lengthy and detailed history of the Bamum; here he meditated at length on the moment of colonial contact.

'Let's fight them, let's drive them out', said the Bamum. — No, said Njoya. He had seen in a dream what the Whites would do to the Bamum. 'If we make war on the Whites, the Bamum will be exterminated immediately. Only a few of you will survive, you will be wretched.' And Njoya himself took from the Bamum their arrows, spears and guns. The Whites arrived and did not make war on them. Thus did Njoya secure the fortunes of the Bamum.

— However the Whites inspired much fear. What was to be done? 'I will go amongst them, said Njoya, and I will learn their ways.'[11]

Here Njoya offers an account of placatory skills, which is particularly striking for running counter to the combative reputation on which the Bamum had prided themselves. The King would join to these paragraphs a catalogue of his military victories but this addition only serves to underline his acts of conciliation.[12] With the considerable benefit of hindsight, he presents the first contact with the Germans as making an epoch; the bellicose tendencies of the Bamum have now to be curtailed and new policies adopted. As a further conciliation, and in order to calm his population, Njoya sets out to acquaint himself with the customs of the whites. The consequences of this would be manifold, as Njoya reveals by completing his account of the arrival of the Germans with a list of his innovations:

> In the past the Bamum did not know writing: Njoya taught it to them. In the past the Bamum did not know weaving: Njoya showed them how to weave. In the past the Bamum did not know how to forge iron, they did not know how to dress nor how to ride: Njoya helped them with all these things.
>
> In the past the Bamum did not know how to dye white cloth black, nor how to make bricks to build houses. Njoya showed them these things[.][13]

These achievements are reiterated at several points in Njoya's history and are clearly meant to redound to his glory. The skills of his weavers and dyers are evident in the king's self-portrait of 1912. However, the character of these innovations requires some explanation. They should not be seen simply as examples of colonial mimicry but rather as a continuation of earlier practices of the Bamum.[14]

When Njoya first came to draft the history I have just cited, he drew together a set of oral traditions concerning the origin and expansion of his Kingdom.[15] The point of origin is established in the very first line of the text: "This book is the history of the Kings coming from Rifum."[16] The Kings of the Bamum were held to come from elsewhere, from amongst the Tikar, to the east of what would become the Bamum territory. The history of their kingdom is a history of migration and conquest, with the expansion carried through most forcefully under King Mbuembue in the first half of the nineteenth century. On acceding to the throne Mbuembue declared: "I will set the borders of my kingdom with blood and iron."[17] Thus the Bamum identified themselves as warriors: the signs of their martial prowess were found in the insignia they took from those they had defeated and bound in servitude. For the Bamum, Kings came from elsewhere and so did their regalia.[18] These important objects came to be the property of the secret societies active in the royal palace. Of these societies the most important were *Ngüri*, a society of princes, *Mbansié*, a society of retainers and *Mutngu*, the society responsible for matters of justice; the objects of *Ngüri* once belonged to the vanquished Tikar, those of *Mbansié* to the Koutie and those of *Mutngu* to the Pambelie.[19]

As this shows, appropriation was a sign of strength during the expansion of the Kingdom and Njoya's innovations should be considered in this light. The latter are examples of extraversion, yet during the early years of contact his practices were not yet tactics seized on the wing.[20] During the colonial period Njoya sought to allay the fears of the Bamum by adopting European symbols, forms and technologies (and using the medium of the book as a vessel for an oral, dynastic history is another instance of this, although here there are also important Islamic precedents). His appropriations would even extend to large architectural projects, including two palaces built using European methods. This continuation of earlier practices is nicely captured in an anecdote related by the artist Ernst Vollbehr, who travelled through the Bamum Kingdom in 1911. Vollbehr records a visit to Njoya's school (yet another of the King's innovations).[21] On this occasion, the tune of the German national anthem was struck up. However, Vollbehr's translator then informs him that the text sung was "Fumban, Fumban über alles" [Fumban, Fumban, above all].[22]

There was a comparable exploitation of portraiture. Images of the German Imperial family seem to have circulated in Fumban from the first years of colonial contact; a photograph taken in the capital in November 1905 shows images of Queen Luise and either Emperor Wilhelm II or Prince Heinrich, hanging over doorways to the palace [Fig. 4.2].[23] This placing is significant. It was a practice in the Grassfields to hang small apotropaic sculptures or other objects over such thresholds and there is evidence of this in a photograph of Njoya in a doorway, seated beneath medicines of this type.[24] Yet the use of these medicines seems to have ceased after 1903, when it is probable that they were replaced by portraits, as seen in the 1905 image.[25] Even if the portraits did not directly "replace" the medicines, the removal of the latter in favour of the former ensured there was no competition between these different types of powerful object. So the Imperial portraits could, in their own way, be held to be apotropaic. After all, they represented a distant but powerful group, the agents of which exercised authority — and deadly force — in the Grassfields. Avoiding the destruction of the Bamum was the result of Njoya's ability to negotiate with these agents. In turn, the Germans would acknowledge the significance of the Imperial image for the Bamum: after Njoya supported a campaign against the Nso Kingdom he was presented with a photograph of Wilhelm II.[26]

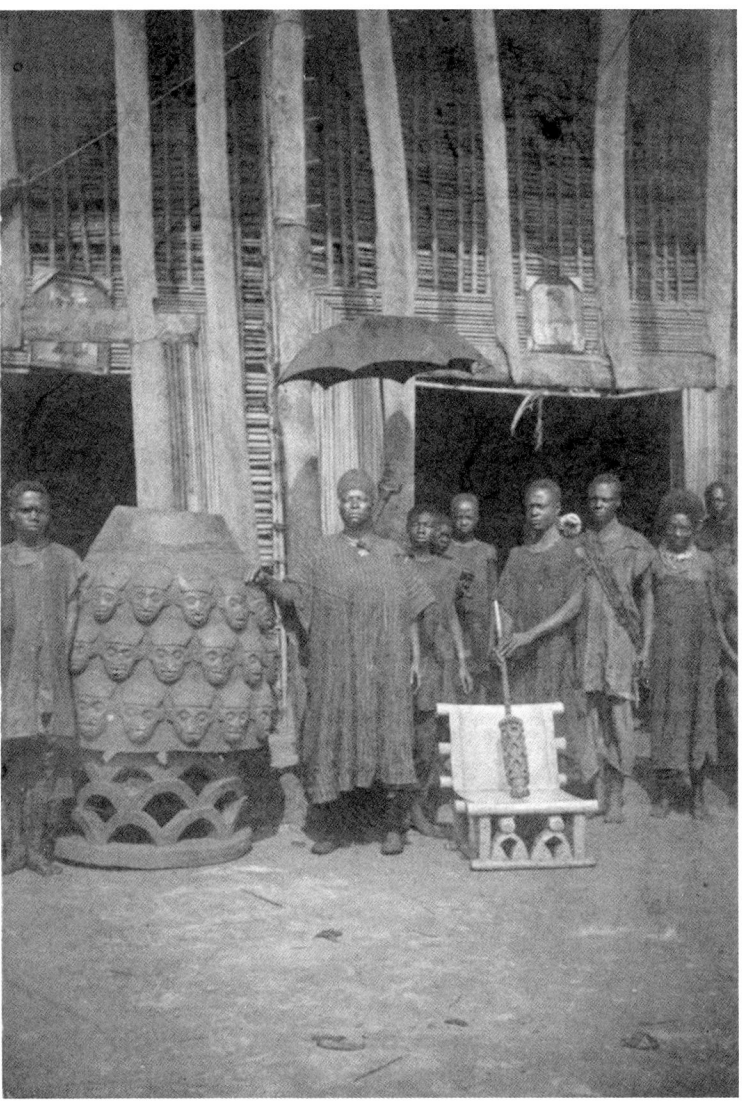

Figure 4.2. Martin Göhring, 'The Queen Mother in Bamum', photographic print, 1905.

Now, a portrait may be defined as a "site where someone speaks", a site for imagined interaction.[27] Besides, a portrait may be more or less tightly bound to a physical site and be efficacious in that context; the apotropaic use of Imperial images in Fumban offers one example of this. After 1902, Njoya had to navigate between this new imperial power and the older social and political organisation of the Bamum. The use of apotropaic portraits was an acknowledgement of the authority of the German Imperial house and also a recognition of the protection required by the Bamum royal household. This household was *the* privileged site; whilst Njoya's extraversions were espousals of "foreign cultural elements" they were put in the service of his own objectives, and these objectives were focussed on this site.

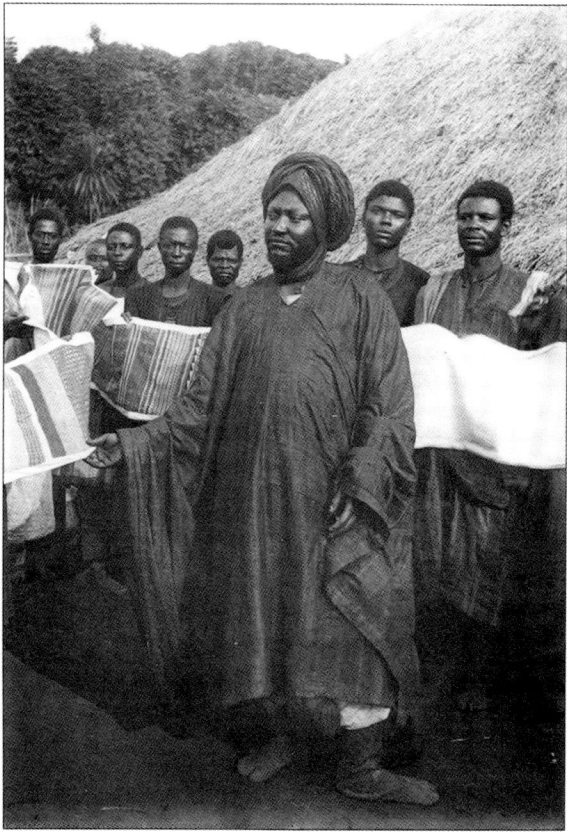

Figure 4.3. Marie-Pauline Thorbecke, 'King Njoya and his servants display a weaving sampler', photographic print, 1912.

The palace was the "village of the king" [*nžü mfon*]; the first village from which all others sprang.[28] The groups large and small comprising the Kingdom were established by a king for a son or retainer with the title *nži* and each group had its own "village" [*nžü*].[29] Thus the palace was the epicentre of political, economic and religious affairs; it served to organise the rule of the Kingdom and the authority of the King was located here. Against this background, it is not surprising that there are so many photographs showing Njoya within the precincts of the palace, or before it, or with its synecdoche, the throne.[30] It is equally unsurprising that there are a number of other photographs of the King with productions of the royal household. The images are diverse — and indeed were taken by different photographers for quite different purposes — yet there is a measure of unity in the diversity, in that the photographs display various aspects of the same phenomenon: royal authority [Fig. 4.3].[31] These displays could be so extravagant as to tax — perhaps deliberately — the capacities of European technology; early in 1908 Njoya showed Bernhard Ankermann a royal costume for the festival of *Nja* which could only be photographed using two cameras [Fig. 4.4].[32] In these portraits of Njoya with the Bamum he is shown with his innovations, and as showing them: "Njoya showed them these things".[33]

There is evidence that this involution of display was effective. At least, there is a similar involution of reception, whereby the later occupiers of the region, the French, recognised the German recognition of Njoya. In one of the first full reports written after the region was transferred to French control, one Sous-Lieutenant Sartous moves from Njoya's innovations to his exemplary status, from his extraversions to his estimation by the earlier colonisers:

Njoya is an ingenious inventor and, with his deep love of his country, he has dedicated all his efforts to setting his people on the path to progress. He is always present as an example to his people, with European manners, living in a house built using our methods and means, and, on his plantations, making experiments with our agriculture techniques.

There is much to be said for this interesting figure, a fervent admirer of white civilisation. Due to his intelligence, dedication and courtesy, the Germans considered him to be one of the foremost native chiefs. He was highly decorated. A photograph shows him in full military dress, with a white cuirass and epaulettes, displaying the number 48 above two crossed marshall's batons. One imagines he was given an honorary rank in the German army.[34]

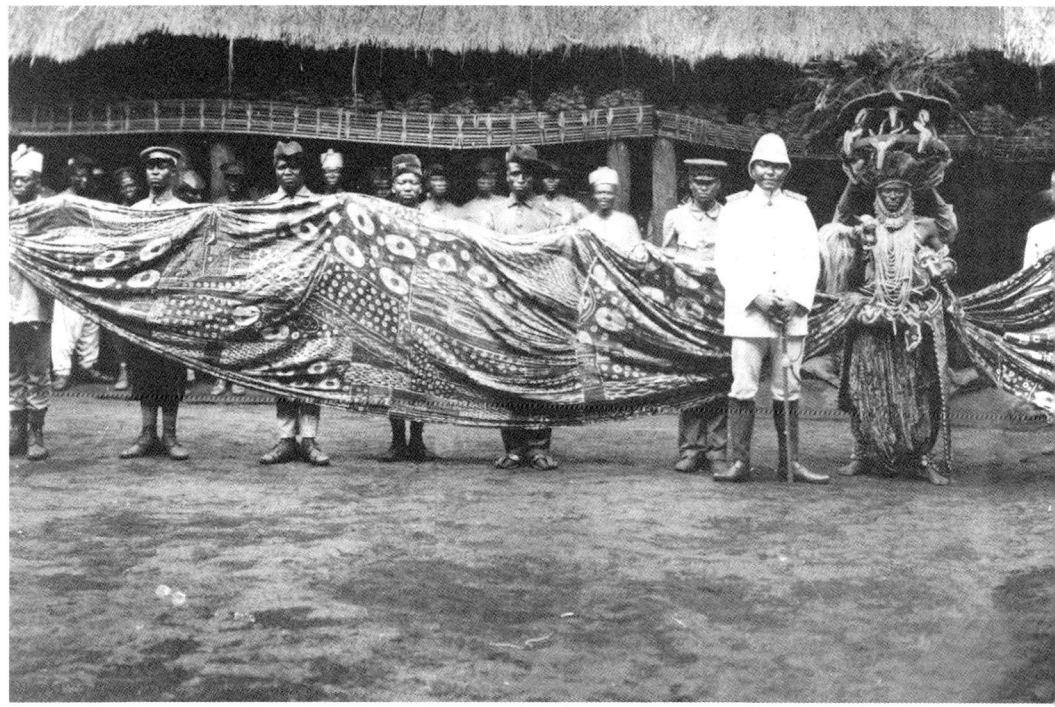

The French were duly impressed by these German honours and, conversely, to the extent that the colonisers confirmed the status of Njoya, his status was confirmed for the Bamum.

This estimation of Njoya was enabled by both the antecedent practices of extraversion amongst the Bamum and by the German method of administration adopted in Cameroon. For the Germans avoided interfering with the political structures of the Bamum Kingdom.[35] Moreover, the German military station was at some remove from Fumban, being located at Bamenda, more than fifty miles from the Bamum capital. Thus, whilst Njoya could hardly have claimed to have conquered the Germans, from the Bamum perspective his appropriations could be interpreted as signs of the continued strength of the Kingdom.[36] Yet such strength could only be exercised in certain ways. It was curtailed by the nature of the colonial encounter, which of course differed profoundly from the earlier

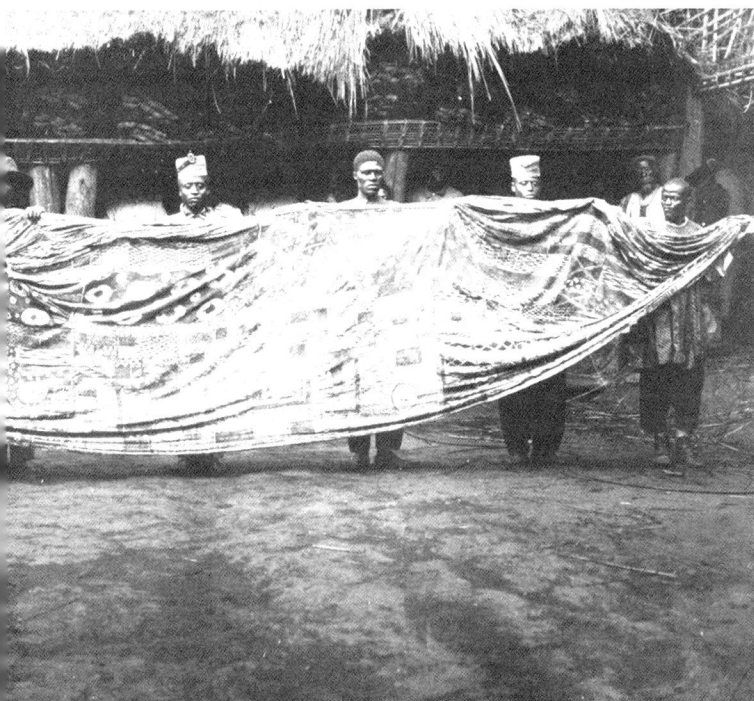

Figure 4.4. Benhard Ankermann, 'A Royal costume for the Nja festival. Njoya poses in a German officer's uniform', composite from two prints, 1908.

histories of Bamum conquest. To take the most prominent example, Njoya could embark on the creation of a palace using European construction methods, and so present himself in the image of a European monarch. Yet at the same time Njoya's actions were also guided by consideration for his own subjects. Thus the King's building project did not mean that he attempted to transform his relations with his wives, offspring and retainers. Nor did it mean that Njoya was prepared to abandon the places of sacrifice and libation in the old palace, or his role as high priest in the cult of ancestors.[37] For if Njoya was to maintain his position he was obliged to preserve a range of social and religious structures. However imaginative, his appropriations could not be allowed to compromise his relationship with his own population. For these reasons, the King's innovations may be characterised, paradoxically, as conservative. Mosé Yeyap's responses to Njoya's actions also involved tactics of extraversion but directed to quite different ends.

The making of Yeap

In 1906 Yeap was sent by his family to the mission school at Njissé, where he won the favour of Martin Göhring who, like Rein-Wuhrmann, was a member of the Basler Mission.[38] Yeap soon became fluent in German, a language Njoya never acquired.[39] On Christmas Day 1909, as a result of the proselytising of the Basler Mission, Yeap was amongst the first Bamum to be baptised. Thus he quickly came to embrace the resources of a European language and a European faith. These resources were to be mobilised most effectively in the period after the First World War, as a result of the political transformations wrought by that conflict.

Before 1914, when Njoya could comfortably maintain his status, the Bamum Christians were tolerated and Njoya even sent some of his many children to the mission school.[40] However, his attitude was to change after the outbreak of war and the German retreat from Cameroon in 1915. The Kingdom now came under British control. With the German missionaries gone, Njoya began a persecution of the Bamum Christians. This persecution only ceased with the arrival of a new missionary, Élie Allégret, in July 1917.[41] By this date Cameroon had been transferred to French administration and Allégret arrived in Fumban wearing a French officer's uniform; thus his mission was explicitly linked to colonial authority.[42] Now under French suzerainty, Njoya was obliged to ensure freedom of conscience in the Bamum Kingdom.[43] This was to be the first of a series of compromises exacted by the new administration.

Yeap's status relative to Njoya was now transformed. A struggle between Njoya and the French authorities began to unfold, passing from a reduction of King's household, to the curtailing of his political power and then the destruction of his authority. This was a prelude to the King's eventual exile in 1931. Whilst Njoya was to have his power increasingly circumscribed, Yeap's star was ascendant; already at some point before December 1919 he moved from the role of an informal intermediary to that of official interpreter for the French.[44]

Yeap became an exemplary figure. An educated Christian, he was recognised by Allégret as one of those men "capable of collaborating in the moral and economic development of the country".[45] He was a member of the picked race and was represented as such; one group portrait of his family was made into a postcard for circulation by the Société des Missions Évangéliques de Paris [Fig. 4.5].[46] Yeap stands, embracing his children and sheltering his wife. This patriarchal role and this ideal "Christian family in Fumban" stood in contrast to the polygyny of the royal household deplored by *Der evangelischer Heidenbote*.

As Yeyap's influence increased, the royal household was progressively undermined. In 1920 Njoya was obliged to dismiss 1,127 retainers.[47] This was intended to be a slowly unfolded project; the reduction was to be calculated and gradual as the administrators in Cameroon were aware that a swift and brutal transition was in itself dangerous.[48] Then, in November 1922, the administration of the region was reorganised, with the creation of a new *circonscription* which permitted the French to place the King under closer surveillance.[49] These developments only increased the enmity between Njoya and Yeyap.

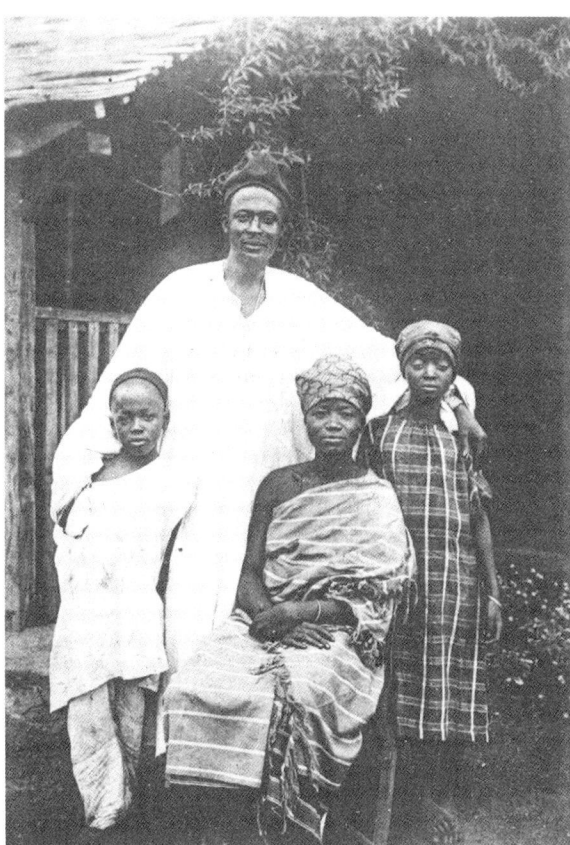

Figure 4.5. Anna Rein-Wuhrmann [?], 'Christian Family in Fumban', postcard, undated.

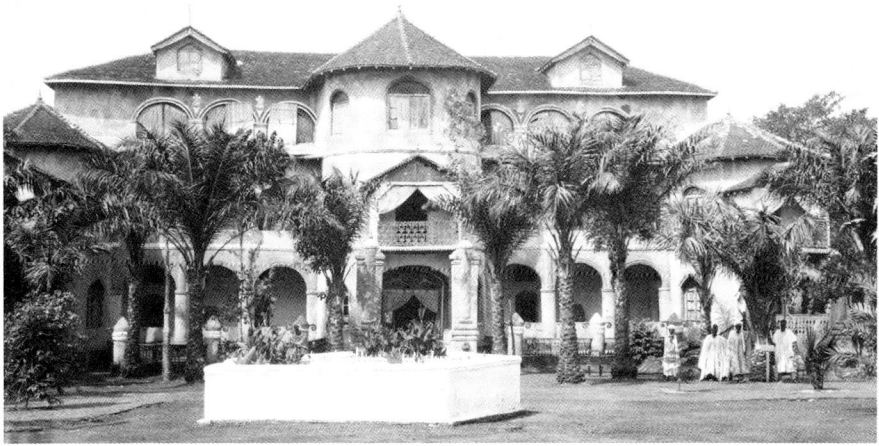

Figure 4.6. George Schwab, 'Njoya's palace of modern buildings', photographic print, 1929.

The palace and the museum

As the French colonial administration in Cameroon developed a strategy for the containment of Njoya, the scope for his practices of extraversion became more restricted. These had been centred on the preservation of the palace and its structures for the rule of the Kingdom but as the household was undermined so this strategic base was eroded. As a consequence, Njoya was reduced to those tactics which may only insinuate themselves "into the other's place".[50]

Yeyap had his part to play in the execution of the French strategy. This would involve his own innovations, including in 1920 the founding of that most modern of institutions: the museum.[51] Whilst Yeyap's museum drew on European precedents it also exploited a situation created in part by Njoya. The King's response to the new regime had followed from his earlier appropriations and, in 1917, as the French asserted their authority in Fumban, Njoya began work on another new palace [Fig. 4.6]. This, his last major project, was to result in a structure even grander than that built before the war, one which would not be completed until 1922.[52] The construction and decoration of the palace drew on the range of skills which Njoya had fostered in his workshops before the war; at the beginning of the project a team of eight artisans was created to coordinate the division of labour.[53] However, while Njoya's energies remained concentrated on the palace, the work of Bamum artisans was beginning to circulate in new ways. In 1918 an exhibition of their products was held in the distant city of Douala, the largest port in Cameroon.[54] It was this combination of intensified artisanal activity and new markets which Yeyap took to be propitious for the founding of the first museum in Fumban.

In many ways, the museum was a rival to the palace even though it was initially installed in a humble fashion in a mud hut. As one would expect of an effective rival, the museum shared certain features with its competitor whilst also seeking to distinguish itself. Museum and palace were alike in being centres of production and display yet they were distinct in important respects. Njoya could innovate with architectural styles but did so to create a new version of his established seat of power. The palace was an example of royal magnificence and stood at the end of the "tradition" in which favoured forms and materials were subjects of royal monopoly.[55] Njoya's new palace was designed to secure a network of relations through patronage, in order to preserve an increasingly fragile authority. Whilst Yeyap's museum was also a means of displaying the skills of the Bamum, in this case the skills were not to be exercised in the service of the sovereign; Yeyap's display had the self-avowed purpose of educating artisans and stimulating production. Doubtless some French observers would have appreciated that the transformation effected here — from palace to site of instruction — was also that which had taken place in the Louvre after 1789. Yeyap, indeed, could be understood as a "revolutionary".[56] The difference between the palace and the museum was, then, a difference in the deployment of resources. In this respect, the rivalry of palace and museum assumed the form of an inverted relationship. The palace was a site for innovations with the purpose of conserving authority; the museum was a site for conservation with the purpose of developing innovations.

Yeyap and Njoya's rivalry was precipitated into conflict on 12 May 1924, when an anonymous letter was delivered to Léopold Veauver, the chief of the subdivision in Fumban; this letter detailed a number of complaints against Yeyap. On 14 May, Veauver went to the marketplace and issued a proclamation to the effect that any complaints against the interpreter were to be lodged formally. However, members of Njoya's entourage persisted in demanding Yeyap's immediate dismissal. Gaston Ripert, the chief of the *circonscription*, was now called to Fumban; in the meantime Njoya's entourage began to gather supporters in the capital.

When Ripert arrived he flatly refused to examine the case against Yeyap in the presence of an armed mob. He informed Njoya that if the King's supporters did not return to their villages they would be dispersed by force. Thus the conspiracy against Yeyap came to dress Njoya's power against that of the French administration. Who would be the victor in such a trial of strength was entirely predictable. Eventually, on 21 May, the crowd did begin to disperse and the ringleaders were arrested; this was the beginning of the end of Njoya's reign.[57]

For his part, Ripert took this opportunity to enact a previously formulated policy and suppress the tribute which the King commanded. This act sealed Njoya's fate for it destroyed the economy of collective redistribution centred on the palace. Hitherto, the King and the Bamum chiefs had renewed their relations of obligation through the payment of tribute during the principal festival in the Bamum calendar, the *Nguon*. Now they were forced to abandon this festival.[58] The older political structure was replaced with a system of regional chiefs, nominated by Yeyap.[59] From the perspective of the French administration the suppression of the tribute lifted a burden from the population and so was one further step towards the prosperity promised by French civilisation.[60] Ripert thus enacted at a local level the economic policy for Cameroon established by the first French governor-general, Jules Carde. His policy precisely entailed the transformation of the indigenous economies through the introduction of private property and wage-labour.[61] In turn, this was part of a programme of moral education. When Carde succeeded to the position of governor-general, he acknowledged that he wanted to finish the work begun by the missionaries. As he understood it, his role was to take the native and to "make of him a 'man', in order to prepare him to be willing and able to act in the effectively in the station to which he was born".[62]

At this moment of transition for the Bamum Kingdom, Yeyap reorganised the artisans who had previously been employed by Njoya. Their workshops were relocated to an "artists' avenue" and a larger version of Yeyap's museum was constructed at the top of this thoroughfare.[63] In 1927 this new division of labour was brought more directly under colonial administration, with the founding of an artisans' school and the creation of a system of payment through indemnities.[64] All of this was a demonstration of what could be achieved by the making of men, at least in the French account:

> The creation of this avenue for artisans and the development of the different industries located there are the results of initiatives we owe to one of the leading figures of Fumban, a intelligent and distinguished individual who has shown great dedication to his country. Interpreter for the

Administration, he is valued by the chiefs and loved by the people. He is a Christian and an elder of the Church. An administrator said of him: If the Mission formed just one personality like this, it would be sufficient justification for its presence in this country.[65]

If Yeyap was exemplary in his devotions and his domestic arrangements, he was also exemplary in the performance of his public duties. Like Njoya, he was happy to be seen to be performing his role. For example, Yeyap could pose in front of his museum for a visitor such as the missionary Ernest Huguenin [Fig. 4.7]. He presents himself at the site of his own achievements. He is framed by artefacts and architecture (although Huguenin's photograph shows only one pillar to the right, that to the left having been cropped). This framing provided by the museum recalls that of the royal palace and by standing before the doorway Yeyap's position recalls that of figures — including the monarch — before the palace. Yeyap guards his own threshold.

Figure 4.7. Ernest Huguenin, 'Yeyap in front of his museum', photographic print, 1930.

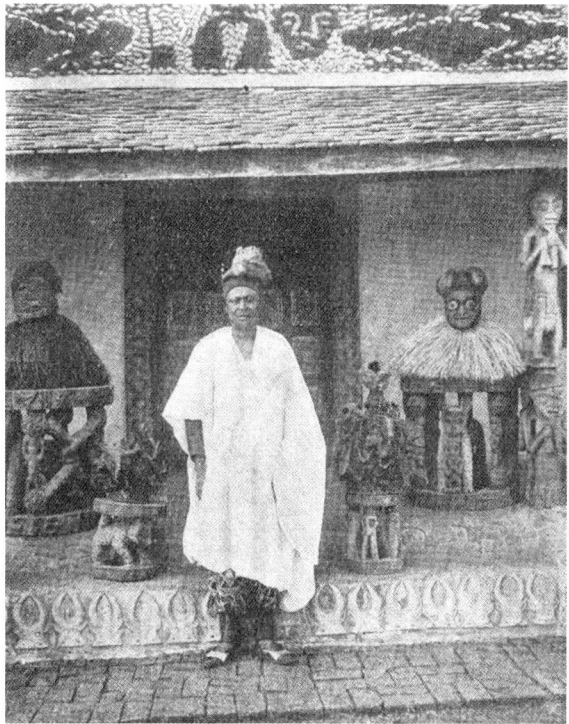

The photograph of Yeyap at the museum was taken by a missionary, as was the photograph used for the postcard of the family group. Yet in other respects the two images of Yeyap are quite different. This difference is of some importance. Despite the fact that the photograph of the family group was to circulate in public, it remains a "private" image of a family. Indeed, one might say that its currency was this privacy. For the missionaries, the image of the family must have represented a divinely ordained set of relations: "Wives, submit yourselves unto your own husbands, as unto the Lord. For the husband is the head of the wife, even as Christ is the head of the Church: and he is the saviour of the body" (Ephesisians, 5: 22–23). The photograph of Yeyap's family worked within a genre that was fully cognisant of such hierarchies. The picture of Yeyap before the museum is different but complementary. It is a portrait of a figure in an official role. Yeyap is in a public space, the street reorganised expressly for the commerce of artisans, and he stands before a public building, the museum created to encourage this commerce. Thus in the two missionary photographs Yeyap is portyrayed in distinct but compatible private and public roles. It was in the performance of these roles that he was exemplary: not in fulfilling one role or the other but in sustaining both. For in maintaining private and public roles, Yeyap was participating in a recognisably modern, European division.[66] The two portraits — in their divergence and complementarity — show what it is to be made a civilised man.

Exhibition, alienation and dispossession

The transition from the palace to the museum was also, in various ways, a transformation of the status of representation. As King, Njoya had represented in the sense of making visible what was invisible: royal authority. He had been peculiar in being able to represent, and for this reason the staging of his presence had to involve appropriate insignia and demeanour and an appropriate code of conduct for those in this entourage.[67] The palace was the privileged stage for such performances. Yet with Njoya's reduction and the creation of the system of regional chiefs, there was to be a new dispensation. Yeyap's private and public roles were together part of this dispensation, with Yeyap's persona thus quite at odds with that of the King.

In due course Yeyap's institution would assume the title of Musée des Arts et Traditions Bamoums; it was to mark off the past as a discrete period by making artefacts into representations of that past ("this is how it used to be done"). When serving as such examples, the artefacts were thereby separated from their primary functions (as, for example, insignia). The objects were given a new status when they were treated as relics of a defunct tradition, a tradition which Yeyap's artisans were now seeking to revive. Writing to another museum professional, Eugène Pittard of the Musée d'ethnographie de Genève, Yeyap presented his work in precisely these terms: "I have concerned myself above all with what is characteristic of our tribe. I have tried to renew that decorative work which our fathers took such delight in."[68] However, the renewal was not simply a matter of entering objects into the museum, it also involved the active suppression of their previous use. This, in turn, was to involve its own violence.

Sometime in February 1930, Charles Frey, another member of the Société des Missions Évangéliques, wrote a letter to his superiors in Paris. Destined for publication in the Société's journal, the letter was a contribution to that genre of missionary literature designed to maintain the support of patrons. Such texts detailed the trials of Christians amongst pagans, and were frequently shaped as narratives of redemption: successful conversions were presented as beacons in longer, darker histories of persecution. The occasion for Frey's letter was a signal event in what he saw as the campaign against paganism in Fumban: this was an exhibition of sacred objects organised by Yeyap and held on Christmas Day, 1929. Frey describes it in the following terms:

> That which until now had been carefully hidden from the sight of the uninitiated, that which the people had venerated in fear, that which had been one of the principal supports of the authority of the pagan chiefs, the jujus, emerged from their hiding-place and appeared before the people on the occasion of a great festival.[69]

Frey was happy to labour his point. The event was "a decisive moment" for the Bamum people "because it brought down one of the central pillars of the pagan social order; and this was achieved by members of the Christian community".[70] Thus the exhibition was held to be part of a shift in the balance of power within the Kingdom; the event was not just a defeat of paganism at the hands of Christians, it was also part of the larger campaign waged against Njoya.

There are three eye-witness accounts of the events of Christmas Day 1929 and each offers a different perspective. Frey draws out Yeyap's role in the perceived development of the Bamum. The second account is by Huguenin, and this is more immediate. Huguenin begins not with Yeyap's exhibition but with the ceremonies which followed it, the baptism of ninety catechumens before an assembled audience including Njoya. "The church being too small, divine worship had to take place at the [mission] station, under a shelter made of posts planted in the ground, covered with palm-leaves."[71] Having established the new dispensation, Huguenin then turns to the destruction of the old, with the "public presentation of certain masks and jujus".[72] He notes that on 28 December, and in honour of the visiting governor, Théodore Paul Marchand, there was a further "exhibition of all manner of Bamum work, an agricultural exhibition, and also more traditional dances with costumes and jujus".[73]

The significance of revealing these sacred objects lay in the character of their secrecy; most were musical instruments and their power derived from a twofold usage. These instruments were played when the secret societies convened. Two of the most important societies, *Mbansié* and *Ngüri*, convened at the same time on a weekly basis and the music they played, what was referred to as their "talking", was to attract the attention of the King.[74] The "talking" was intended to be heard far beyond the confines of the societies' quarters in the palace. Secrecy, here, was not a matter of the concealed identity of members but concerned the concealed nature of the proceedings of each society. Women, children and the uninitiated could hear the music of *Mbansié* and *Ngüri* but not see the means by which it was produced. Indeed, the Bamum ascribed the music to animals rather than men. Clearly, the distinction between performers and distant auditors was a distinction between initiated and uninitiated. The difference between immediate and mediated experience was established on initiation, for this seems to have involved not just sight of the instruments but a physical encounter with them; on initiation to *Mbansié* neophytes would have their forearms crossed like bound prisoners and their hands thrust into a double gong. This experience symbolised their powerlessness before *Mbansié*; henceforth the initiate was bound by the codes of the society and also thereby bound to the other members of the group. So for the members of the society the sight and sound of the instruments were integrated experiences, which were also the experience of the society's unity. Secrecy constituted solidarity. When the societies' instruments were displayed on Christmas Day in 1929, and again three days later, this solidarity was fractured, as was a social order.

The display was an emphatic reduction and it was not just that the display reduced the instruments to mundane objects. Previously, as Frey had noted, the uninitiated were prohibited from viewing the instruments.[75] Now the unpunished sight of the objects effectively deprived them of their function by demonstrating the dissolution of the power of the societies. In some respects, the removal of these objects from their customary protection may be seen as a new variant on the Bamum practice of appropriating the reserved objects of those vanquished.[76]

If the transition from palace to museum entailed a transition from function to representation, this was also enacted through the Christmas exhibitions.

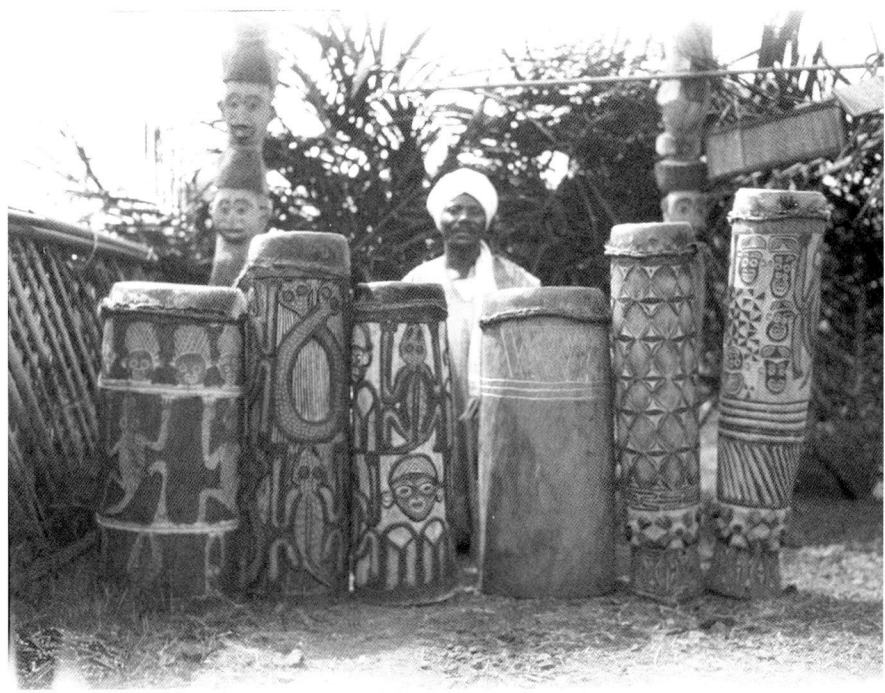

Figure 4.8. George Schwab, 'Man sitting behind a line of carved, decorative drums', photographic print, 1929.

These exhibitions were photographed by the third eye witness, George Schwab, an American missionary and amateur anthropologist. Schwab was visiting the Bamum as a field investigator for the Peabody Museum of Archaeology and Ethnology of Harvard University.[77] Accordingly, his photographs conform to a specific genre; their conceit is that they are merely transparent, not revelatory [Fig. 4.8].[78] For the revelation had taken place with Yeyap's exhibitions and Schwab's photographs were taken in order to acknowledge this; the objects had already been presented to view, the photographer's own work was ancillary. Instead, the objects are to be seen grouped, already settling into categories, approaching the status indicated by the captions which were to be added by Schwab in due course, and which themselves already approach the work of the museum catalogue. Such images are quite removed from those of Njoya with his throne or before his palace. The photographs, then, entrenched the objects as representations and, as such, anticipated the objects' next destination: the museum.[79] In Fumban, Schwab acquired a large number of objects for the Peabody Museum, supported by the J. T. Worthington Fund, and it is clear that Yeyap acted as his agent. Schwab's photograph of Yeyap is simply captioned: 'Our friend the interpreter who got us things' [Fig. 4.9]. Here, once again, Yeyap is seen to perform his public duties. And once again, here Yeyap's power is dressed against Njoya's.

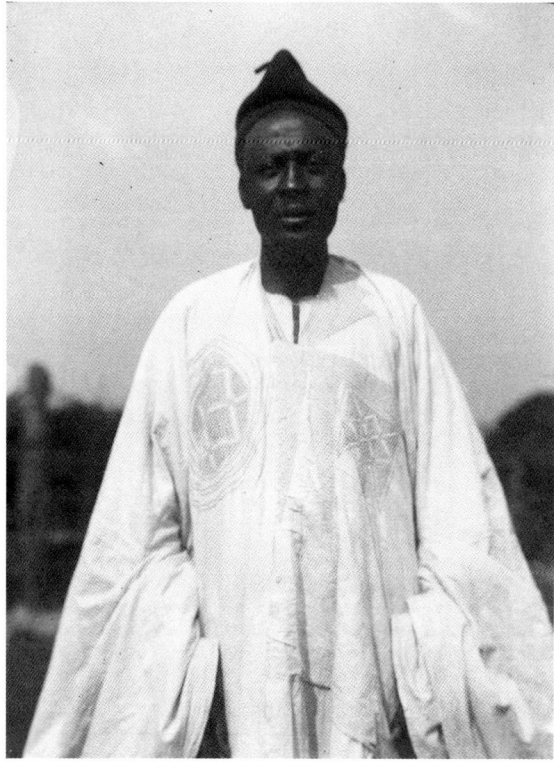

Figure 4.9. George Schwab, 'Our friend the interpreter who got us things', photographic print, 1929.

Yeyap's exhibitions were effective in suppressing the "pagan" social order but this success contained its own dangers. The French administration had been careful to avoid a sudden collapse of Bamum social structures, and so whilst Yeyap suppressed one order he had to attempt to construct another. If a visitor such as Hugeunin saw an old and new dispensation, "moments of complete paganism" and also baptisms, the foregathered Bamum may have seen something else.[80] For Yeyap coordinated matters not only for the benefit of the governor and the missionaries but also to address the Bamum population. The latter would not view events straightforwardly from the Christian perspective of the Europeans, Americans and catechumens. Accordingly, Yeyap's event drew on Bamum festivals and specifically on the *Nguon*. Aspects of this festival of solidarity were now to be transferred to the new solidarity of the growing Christian community. However, this was not entirely an imposition, as is made clear in Rein-Wuhrmann description of the *Nguon* in her book of 1925 on the Bamum:

> The children await this masquerade with the same impatience that our own children await Father Christmas (...) My pupils called the *Nguon* the Christmas of the Blacks, because it is also a festival of love, when the adults give the children presents.[81]

Yeyap's task was to reorganise this perception; the Bamum were to see the events of Christmas 1929 as a new *Nguon*. Thus several features of the earlier festival were recreated. The *Nguon* was normally preceded by a corvée in which the palace was renovated and, before the construction of the "European" palaces, this would involve the restoration of walls and roofs with palm-leaves and bark. Huguenin's description of a shelter "covered with palm-leaves" indicates that in 1929 this labour was transferred to the mission station before the celebration of the baptisms. So the community's obligations were redirected. For the *Nguon*, ninety representatives of the Bamum population brought tribute to the King to be redistributed.[82] In 1929 this gathering of representatives was replaced by that of the ninety catechumens. The tribute gathered in the original *Nguon* was now to be replaced by what Huguenin was pleased to describe as "an agricultural exhibition".[83]

Such similarities created some continuity between the "pagan" and "Christian" festivals whilst also marking some distinctions. Of course, where the earlier festival affirmed the authority of the King, the events in 1929 did the opposite. Earlier celebrations of the *Nguon* had been exemplary in uniting in the figure of the King different economic, political and religious roles.[84] This was what was now destroyed. Yet the attempt to construct a new, Christian order was only partially successful. On one side, something of "traditional" authority remained, and on the other, something of "paganism" was renewed.

This persistence of traditional forms of authority is not discussed in any of the texts produced by the eye witnesses; this would hardly have been to their purpose. Yet it was photographed. At the same time as photographing sacred objects,

Schwab also made an image of a man he described as a "sub-king" [Fig. 4.10]. In fact, this individual has usurped Njoya's throne and also the crown used for the *Nja* festival [see Fig. 4.4]. This photograph is the antithesis of those designed to convey Njoya's authority. Yet this does not mean that it is an overturning of earlier compositions. The more closely the new display conforms to the format of its predecessors, the more directly it serves in the arrogation of the King's authority. Someone else now speaks from Njoya's site and Schwab's photograph is in this respect an anti-portrait, an image of the king dispossessed.

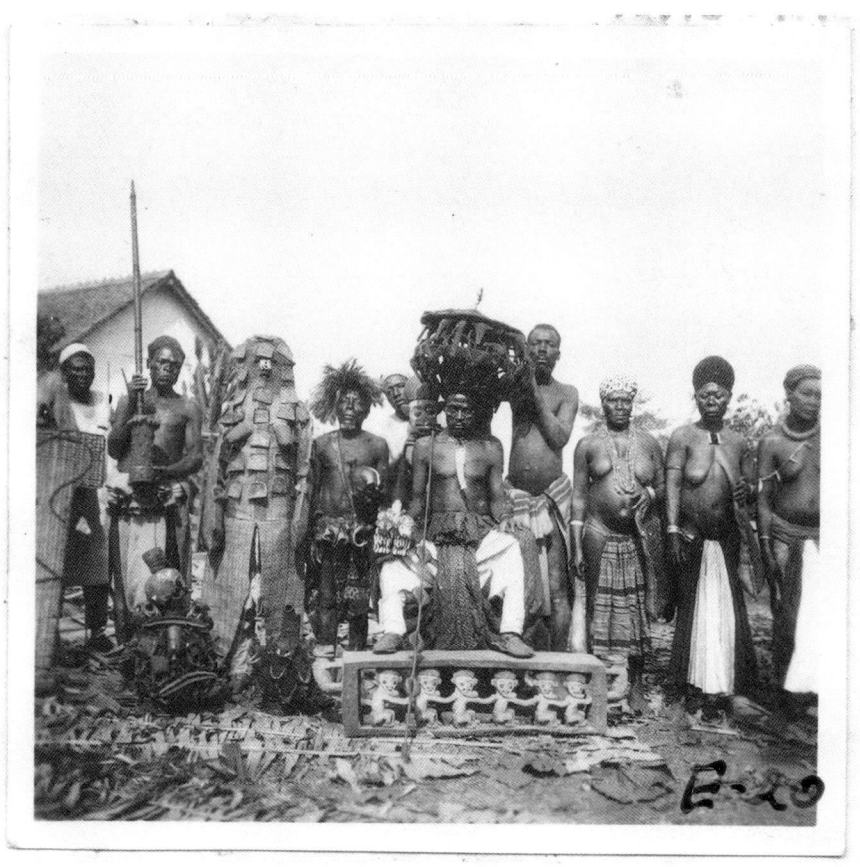

Figure 4.10. George Schwab, 'Sub-King on throne with attendants and crown', photographic print, 1929.

Whilst the photographed anonymous pretender to the throne does not seem to have maintained any grasp on power, the missionaries remained concerned about the nature and extent of their own influence. They were especially concerned about the persistence of paganism. This was because Yeyap's events separated out religious and political roles. On Christmas Day the key figures in the baptisms were Frey, Yeyap and Josué Muishe, who would become the first Bamum pastor; on 28 December the celebrations were in honour of the governor, Marchand. Thus there was in effect a separation of church and state. If in practice the missionaries and the administrators were collaborating on the same project, in Yeyap's organisation of events there was nevertheless a division of authority and arguably this division created its own threat to any new solidarity.

Frey registered as much in his review of the events of 1929. He noted that with the arrival of the colonisers, the power of the society responsible for justice, *Mutngu*, had been curtailed. "Since that time, the jujus have been less and less present; however, it is not without pride that the pagans say: 'The jujus no longer talk, but they are still alive.'"[85] Now Frey was able to declare: "Today the shroud of mystery has been rent; women and children quickly accustomed themselves to the sight of the jujus, something which had previously filled them with dread."[86] However, as a result:

> The Bamum people find themselves in a period of transition, and in order that they do not lose their way they must find some equivalent for their jujus because it is through these things that they have learnt the meaning of solidarity. Under the influence of civilisation, the collective property of the tribe has transformed itself into private property, and that is why a feeling of solidarity must be kept alive.
>
> Let it be that Christianity becomes for these people a new juju, one based not on fear but on love: the love of God, the love of one's neighbour.[87]

This is a precise summary of the civilising project and its vicissitudes. The very success of the operation of the market, which was supposed to facilitate the transition to a Christian community, was also taken to be a threat to that community. For every victory over the old paganism there had to be vigilance against the threat of what was dubbed "neopaganism", a threat imported by the colonisers in the form of the quest for personal profit.[88] Of course the missionaries sought to awaken individual consciences to salvation rather than create a sense of the personal profit to be derived from forms of economic exchange. Yet they feared that the suppression of one idolatry could lead to the creation of another and that their missionising could, in one respect, defeat itself.[89] Of course, much of this mapped with the concerns expressed at the 1931 Congrès International et Intercolonial de la Société Indigène. Allégret had already anticipated this in 1923 when he noted: "A new spirit of acquisitiveness has been awakened."[90]

Thus the creation of Yeyap's museum should be understood to produce a number of effects. It was an early, crucial stage in the reorganisation of the Bamum artisans, who were obliged to be increasingly responsive to market forces. Instead of working for the court and the secret societies, they were to become subject to abstract conditions of exchange, producing commodities. But whatever difficulties were created by the new economic order, after Christmas 1929 it was established as the dominant one. All artefacts were now to be subject to the same mechanisms of exchange. The museum and its conditions were secured.

For Njoya, the only path seemingly open was to submit to these conditions. After the public exhibition of the sacred objects, the King reacted by creating his own museum within the palace.[91] Even so, Njoya's museum should be seen less as a final appropriation of a European form than as a capitulation. For the very terms now differed from the earlier appropriations. Njoya's museum was not like his first European palace, to which a traditional social structure was partially relocated but not thereby transformed. His museum was, rather, an acknowledgement that that social order belonged to the past. In the view of the colonial authorities, the King's resources were reduced to a series of possessions for which he could act as curator.[92]

This acknowledgement of the new order was matched by an extension of the market for the arts of the Bamum. The issue of Cameroon's *Journal officiel* for 1 April 1930 carried the first full-page advertisement for the work of Yeyap's artisans. An advertisement is, by definition, an indication of a specific level of development of a market; its existence registers a distanced relationship between producer and consumer even whilst it seeks to mediate that relationship. In this sense the advertisement registered the final dissolution of the relations constituted by royal patronage. Materials previously reserved for the King and the palace were now accessible to anyone for the asking price. For example, a bead-decorated calabash could now be purchased for 100–200 francs.[93] Symbols became subject to similar conditions; the spider, the creature used in divination and hence representative of wisdom, had been a symbol reserved for royal usage but in due course it would become a trademark, stamped on all the artisans' commodities.[94] Yeyap's exhibitions had revealed the objects of the secret societies; Yeyap's advertisements indicate the extent to which the things of the palace and the arts of the Bamun were now reduced to the same condition of representation. The artefacts produced by the Bamum became a resource open to new forms of exploitation.[95] Now many of the resources deployed in the earlier portraits of Njoya ceased to be available to him.

The uses of the image of Njoya

What tactics remained to Njoya when the museum replaced the palace? After the events of May 1924, the King largely withdrew from public life and dedicated much of his energy to the completion of his history of the Bamum. The book is concerned with the achievements of the royal house and, above all, Njoya's achievements; in keeping with this, the reader is reminded at a number of points of the things that the Bamum did not have before his reign. He includes a narrative of his near-miraculous invention of an alphabet, so the very form of the written history is to be counted amongst Njoya's achievements.[96] In Njoya's history, his innovations are presented in the context of the royal lineage, in relation to the exploits and victories of his ancestors. Yet of the sixteen Bamum monarchs, eight are described as having "done nothing" and as having lived off the work of their forebears.[97] Success is defined here in relation to the other, to those outside the Kingdom, either those conquered, or those with whom the Bamum must negotiate, "the Whites". In essence, Njoya's history is the book of the Kings who come from afar and their achievements are defined as the controlling of things from afar. Now, this view might seem to be challenged by the arc of the book, which moves from a kinglist to a chronicle of administrators, for this arc acknowledges the transition of power from the Bamum to the colonial authorities. Yet the transition was neither straightforward nor complete: whilst the French authorities were in control at the moment when the manuscript was drafted, their actions are placed in a much longer history of conquests and challenges. And so Njoya's book may be understood as part of his final negotiation with the colonisers.

At some point between 1927 and 1930, the royal scribe and draftsman Ibrahim Njoya — the King's namesake — made a suite of 21 images to illustrate this history.[98] Executed using a combination of ink and pencil on paper, these drawings were produced with materials which had themselves come from afar. Their pictorial mode was also alien, as the drawings offer variants of a perspectival construction of space. Dutifully following the arc of Njoya's text, the drawings trace the history of the Bamum dynasty, moving from past to present to conclude with two portraits of Njoya [Figs 4.11 and 4.12]. These two images offer a summation of Njoya's tactics of extraversion; they show what remained to him.

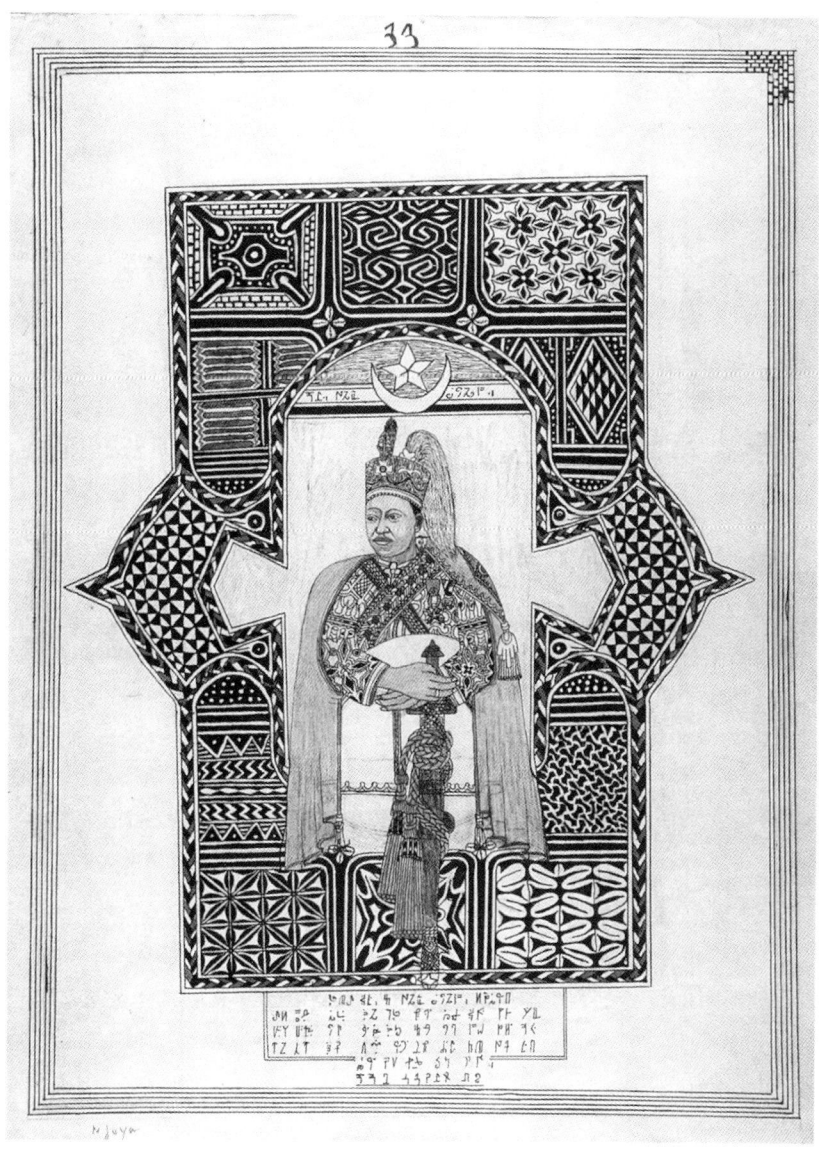

Figure 4.11. Ibrahim Njoya, 'King Njoya', ink and graphite on paper, 35×29 cm. 1927-1930.

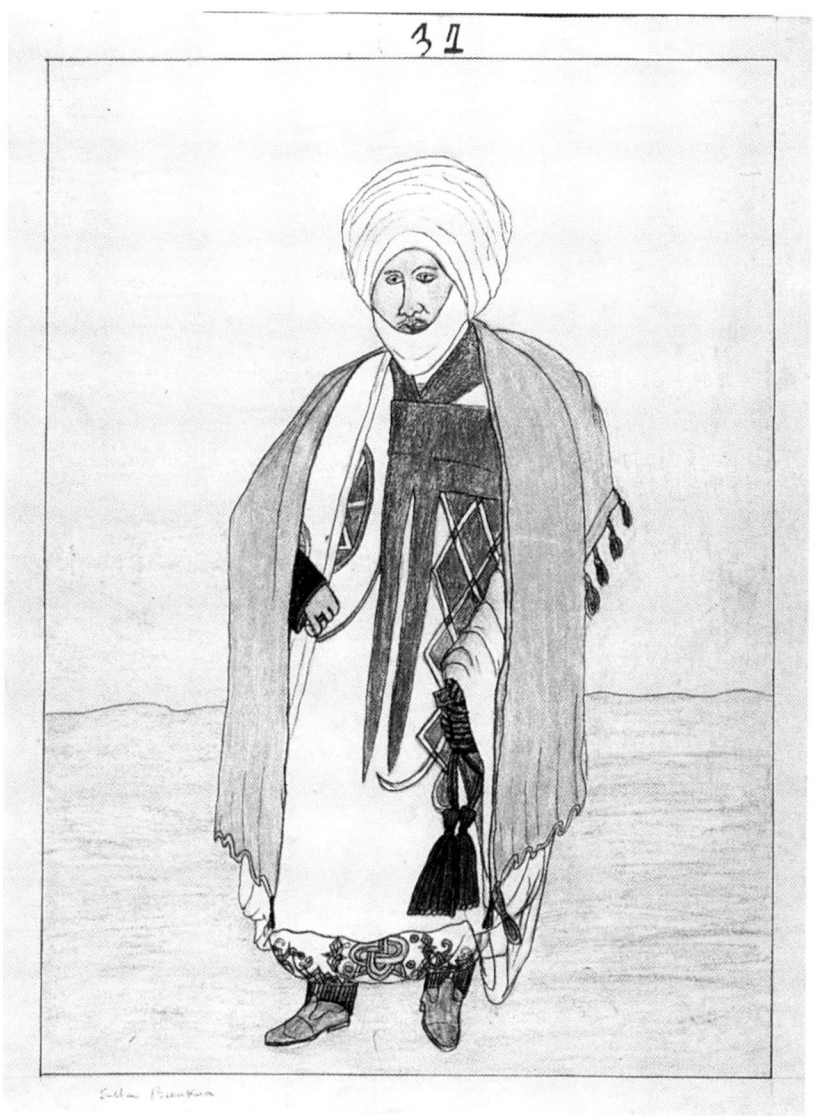

Figure 4.12. Ibrahim Njoya, 'King Njoya in Muslim dress', ink and graphite on paper, 35×29 cm. 1927-1930.

The images of Njoya have their own special place in the royal lineage, and they have to be understood in this context, yet they also need to be viewed in the framework of the suite as a whole. The suite has fourteen sheets of portraits beginning, of course, with the dynastic founder, Nshare. (Mbuembue is absent from the lineage but in all probability this sheet has been lost). These portraits are accompanied by seven other sheets. There is an image of the *Nguon* ceremony, and images of the meetings of the secret societies *Ngüri* and *Mbansié*. There is a map of Fumban and — on one sheet — a plan and elevation of the palace. There is also a view of Yeyap's museum and a further sheet is an assemblage of portraits of Yeyap and the most important of the new regional chiefs, including Njimouliom and Njikam, not coincidently Yeyap's relatives [Fig. 4.13].[99] These figures were direct rivals of Njoya and their images are accompanied by that of another of Njoya's most implacable enemies, Njinchara.[100]

The drawing of *Ngüri* shows a line-up of musicians [Fig. 4.14]. That of *Mbansié* is more complex, showing a view down onto a performance in a palace courtyard [Fig. 4.15]. Although one drawing is quite straightforward and the other more ambitious in its spatial construction, both are striking in existing at all. The very

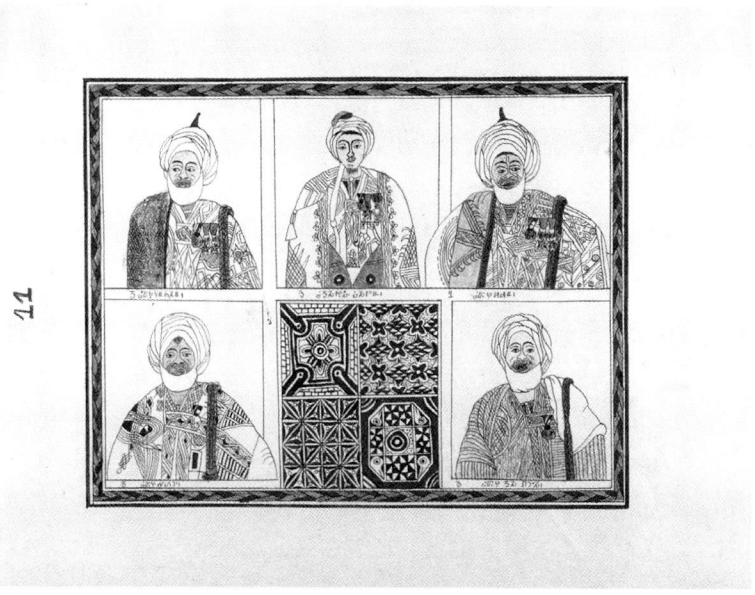

Figure 4.13. Ibrahim Njoya, 'Njimouliom, Mosé Yeyap, Njikam, Njinchara, Njimefire', ink and graphite on paper, 29×35 cm. 1927-1930.

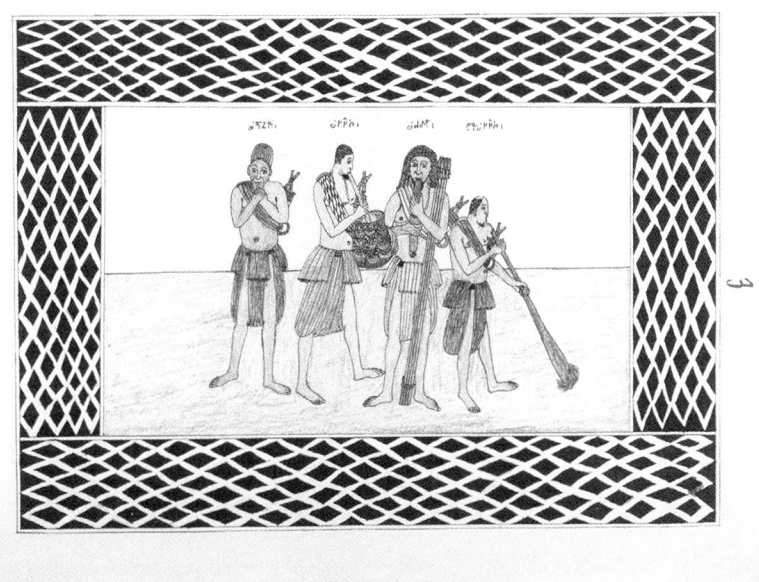

Figure 4.14. Ibrahim Njoya, 'Ngüri', ink and graphite on paper, 29×35 cm. 1927-1930.

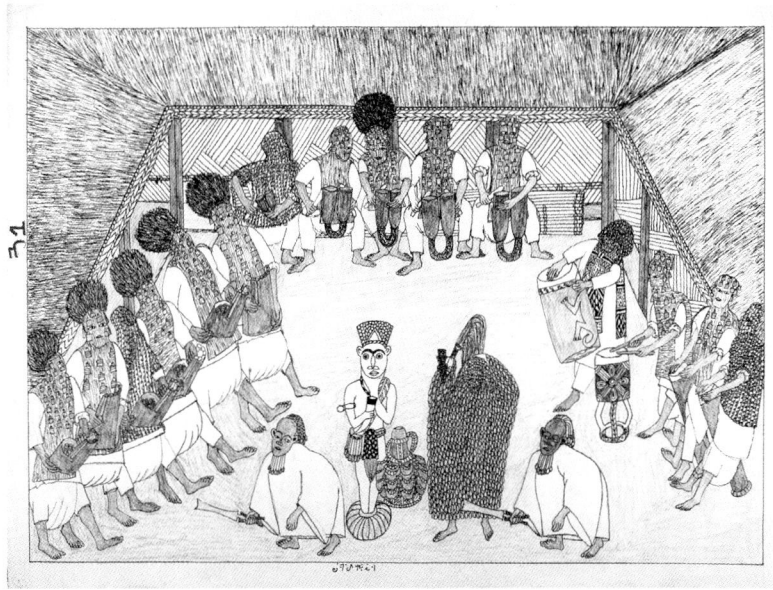

Figure 4.15. Ibrahim Njoya, 'Mbansié', ink and graphite on paper, 29×35 cm. 1927-1930.

possibility of these acts of representation is owed to a particular historical moment. Performances of *Ngüri* and *Mbansié* were emphatically not public displays; the meetings had been restricted to initiates and — because the two societies were rivals — members of one society could not attend the meetings of the other. Therefore, the artist has depicted two scenes which could not in principle be observed by any one viewer, much less offered to the view of others. Yet the principle I have just invoked was no longer operative by the time the images were produced. The drawings are not part of the distribution of authority which the palace effected because that structure of power was no longer in place; Yeyap and Ripert had seen to that. With the curtailing of the King's authority in 1924 the ceremonies of the societies ceased to take place. The images, then, are of the past, while they are produced using the materials of the colonial present: the paper, pencils and ink. In offering this particular combination of past and present, the drawings may be compared to Yeyap's museum. The museum and its conditions were indeed secured.

That the museum had replaced the palace is confirmed in the drawing of the palace's plan and elevation [Fig. 4.16]. The palace had been the "village of the king", the centre of the Kingdom. It had been the privileged site, one protected by modern forms of representation when Imperial portraits were hung above its thresholds. Now it was to be represented in a modern form which indicated its loss of centrality. The combining of plan and elevation in the drawing is an example of a quite elementary practice, and whilst the plan and elevation may be to different scales — as is the case here — the assumption underlying the practice is that there *is* a scale and that the different elements in such drawings are, ultimately, commensurate. That is to say, the elements are ordered through a larger scheme, a scheme for representing co-ordinate space. The use of this scheme has its own implications, because, as David Summers makes clear, the co-ordinate conception of space is opposed to older conceptions:

> The principal features of modern Western co-ordinate space are homogeneity, divisibility and infinity, relative to which more primordial spaces are qualitative, continuous and unified, and, as wholes, heterogenous with respect to one another.[101]

Co-ordinate space, homogenous and divisible, is an abstraction; the grid of this space is infinite and abstracted from any particular conditions. It is a space to be measured using arbitrary units such as the metre, and the drawing of the plan and elevation — conforming implicitly to such a scale — is thus a particular type

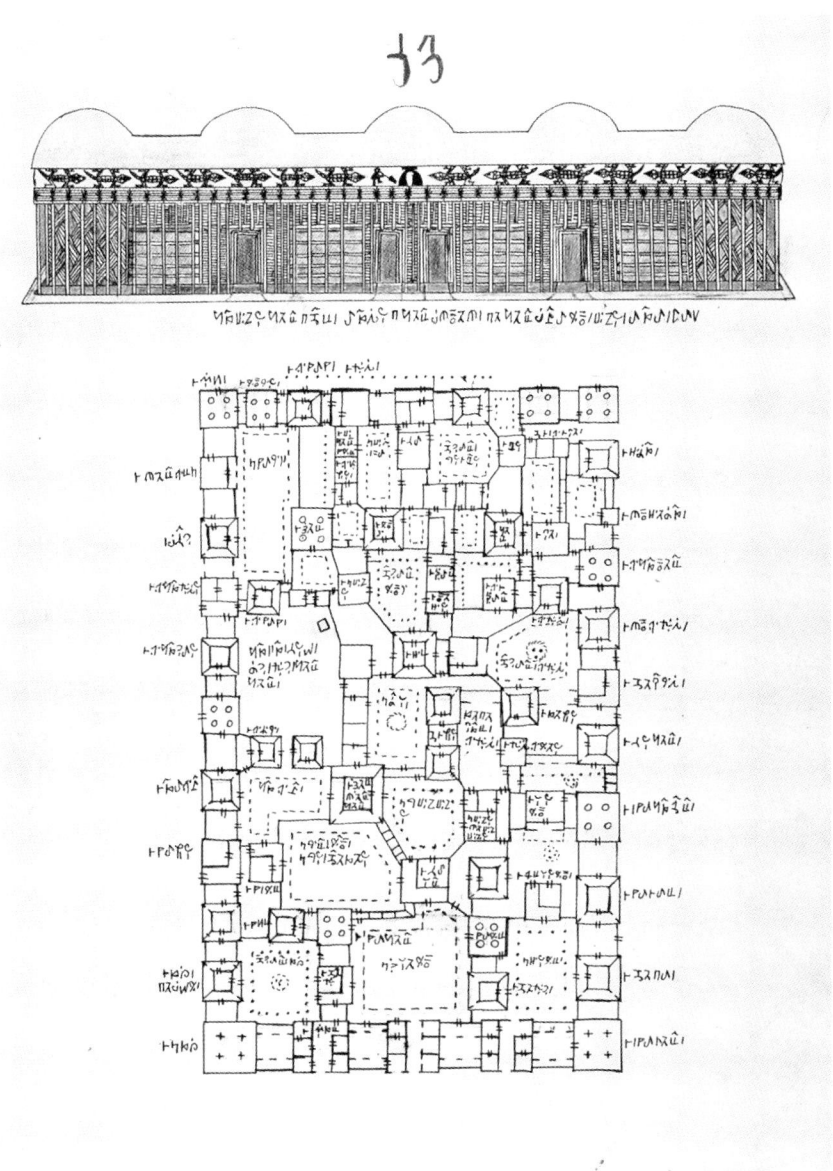

Figure 4.16. Ibrahim Njoya, 'The palace of the Bamum Kings',
ink and graphite on paper, 35×29 cm. 1927-1930.

of abstraction. As such, the drawing is at odds with earlier Bamum representations of the palace [Fig. 4.17]. In this tapestry example, the various precincts of
the palace are represented by symbols and presented so as to indicate hierarchies
and interrelations, not just of precincts but of their users. Such hierarchies cannot be represented directly in a version of the plan conformed to a scale; accordingly, in the sheet with the plan and elevation the draughtsman has had to have
recourse to a Bamum script to designate the uses of the different areas. Thus the
scheme for representing co-ordinate space is a rejection of a cosmological and
hierarchical conception of space. The co-ordinate space of the plan is part of
a system which denies "ontological uniqueness and hierarchy" and is intended
"to undercut traditional centres together with the ways of life that have formed
around them".[102] In this version of the plan the authority of the palace — its
centrality — is at once represented and displaced.

The displacement and the transition of power are marked in the suite of the
portraits by the presence of Njoya's rivals. Yet the transition is also articulated
in the drawing of Yeyap's museum [Fig. 4.18]. This image should be understood
as the converse of the earlier drawings in the suite representing the secret societies. The societies belonged in restricted sites, with reserved objects, and were
emphatically not open to view; they belonged
within the series of defined places and precincts
which made up the palace. By overturning these
prohibitions on access and viewing, the "public"
museum becomes the opposite of the societies'
meeting places.

The public status of Yeyap's museum is al-
luded to in the drawing in the positioning of the
mounted, ranked figures, which seem to form
a guard or escort. To the extent that they have
an honorific function they are an acknowledgement and articulation of authority, and as such
they are related to the deferentially posed figures
carved on the pillars of the palace. However,
the carved figures were posed in deference to
the King — and as such were markers of royal authority — and this is not the case for the
mounted figures in the drawing. The palace was
for the king; it was for him to occupy the threshold; by contrast, in the image of the museum the

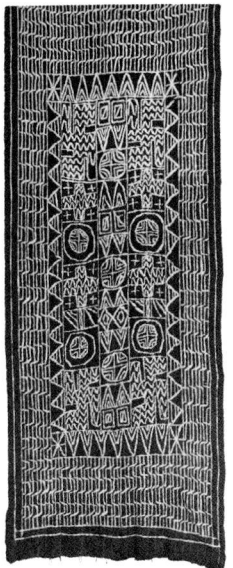

Figure 4.17. Fumban, Bamum,
Royal Tapestry, 549×183 cm, cotton,
indigo dyes.

threshold is unoccupied. The king does not preside and the viewer — the arriving visitor — cannot be specified in advance, precisely because anyone may approach and enter a public building. Whilst various people might approach the palace as the seat of royal authority, entry and access could by no means be taken for granted. The drawing, then, is *of* the museum in representing its building but it also stands in analogy *to* the museum in presenting a properly modern public space. As such it is wholly of a piece with Huguenin's portrait of the proprietorial Yeyap [Fig. 4.7]. Here the logic of the museum is not merely secured, but is asserted over that of the palace.

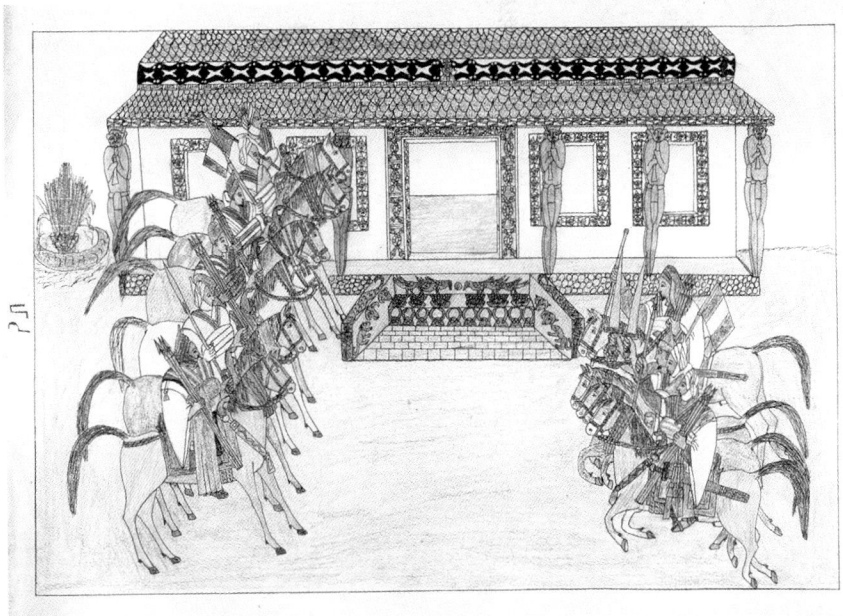

Figure 4.18. Ibrahim Njoya, 'Riders in front of the museum', ink and graphite on paper, 29×35 cm. 1927-1930.

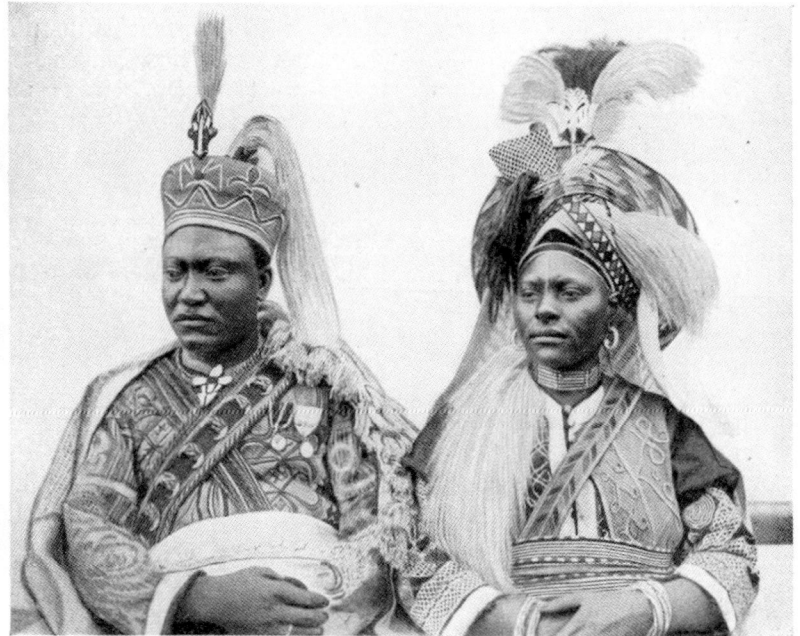

König Njchoja mit einer Lieblingsfrau.

Figure 4.19. King Njoya, 'King Njoya with favoured wife', 1912, illustration, p. 155 in Anna Rein-Wuhrmann, *Mein Bamumvolk im Grasland von Kamerun*, Basel: Basler Missionsbuchhandlung, 1925.

The final pair of portraits in the suite, those of Njoya, submit to this logic of representation. Yet the portraits also reposition Njoya, and suggest something of his response to the new conditions. These portraits emerge from a complex working of sources and precedents, from a mining of Njoya's own history.

The drawn portraits are both derived from photographs and in one case, at least, the photographic source can be stated with some certainty. The adorned portrait, with a literally decorated Njoya [Fig. 4.11], is traced from a photograph of around 1912, which Rein-Wuhrmann had published in her book of 1925, *Mein Bamumvolk im Grasland von Kamerun* [Fig. 4.19]. In her book the photograph is described as a self-portrait of the King. The tracing of this photograph does not seem a matter of serendipity or convenience.[103] Before becoming a precedent, Njoya's photograph had itself been derived from precedents. His self-portrait followed a template offered by the image of Kaiser Wilhelm II and his consort,

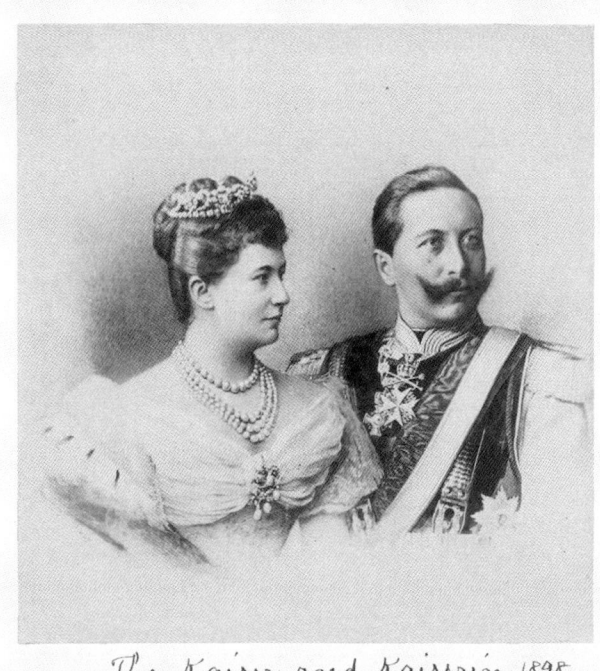

The Kaiser and Kaiserin, 1898.

Figure 4.20. Eric Bieber, 'The Emperor and Empress', postcard, 1898.

an image which was endlessly recycled during the Kaiser's reign [Fig. 4.20]. Once again, Njoya took up something from afar. He and the Kaiser have arranged for their likenesses to be taken and in his self-portrait Njoya adopts something of the pose of the Kaiser, distanced both from his consort and the viewer. Yet unlike the Kaiser, Njoya assumes two roles in his photograph, for the self-portrait is a double performance — a presentation of appearance and of skill. As in the self-portait with which I began this chapter, here the maker is doubly present. There is no need to ask whether Njoya models in order to display his skills with photographic technology or uses the technology to render the modelling permanent and transmissible. What is important is to recognise that Njoya controls both processes. In Fumban he is at once object and subject. In Berlin, of course, there was a different division of labour; it was for the Kaiser to delegate. As a result of this kind of delegation it has become quite common to draw a distinction between state portraits and self-portraits, yet it was in Njoya's interest to collapse such a distinction.[104] In Fumban, Njoya's authority was confirmed in his double performance.

However, Njoya's authority and status changed dramatically between his taking the photograph in 1912 and Rein-Wuhrmann's decision to reproduce it in 1925. The missionary's attitude had also changed, in large part as a result of Njoya's increased engagement with Islam. After the German withdrawal in 1915 Njoya first elaborated his own syncretic religion, *Nuet Kuete*, then, in 1916, a mosque was built in Fumban. In 1918, Njoya asked Bobo Amadou of Yola to send a marabout to Fumban to prepare his conversion.[105] If the missionaries in Fumban were exercised by paganism and neopaganism, they were even more anxious about what they saw as the threat posed by a competing religion of the book. So Rein-Wuhrmann felt betrayed. Her use of Njoya's image is an expression of her frustration. She positions the self-portrait of 1912 at the end of an increasingly embittered narrative, offering this summation of what she found on her return to Fumban after the war:

> Islam left the king with everything he had possessed as a heathen. Yes, it gave him even more sorcery in the form of amulets to keep animals and people from evil. Now he is a Mohammedan and most of his wives have given themselves to Islam too. Not only has Njoya been lost to Christianity, now he belongs to the supporters of Islam, who hold fast to every fanatical commandment of the Koran: 'Above all else, the Holy War against unbelievers.' Those for him are the Christians. He hates them, he persecutes them, he does them harm whenever he can, and lives therefore in madness and in this he serves Allah.[106]

Rein-Wuhrmann then offers a futher reflection, which serves to introduce her reproduction of Njoya's image:

> When one has observed the inner and outer development of Njoya, one has to say to oneself: It could not have been otherwise! And one cannot even be angry with the King, rather one turns, with a kind of quiet self-reproach, to the words of the poet:
> wretches pile up guilt from birth,
> And then you yield them up to pain.[107]

In Rein-Wuhrmann's view, Njoya's madness and fanaticism mean he is now bound for perdition; he is truly lost. In this context the reproduction of the self-portrait is to show a man enmired in his own pride and pretension, in a "royal wretchedness" of his own making. This coding of the portrait is established not just through the emphatic text but also by the inclusion of another image of Njoya, reproduced a few pages earlier. In this image, most unusually, Njoya is photographed from a distance [Fig. 4.21].[108] Here he is an isolated — almost lost — figure. The juxtaposition of this image with Njoya's double performance of authority underlines the changes which have taken place between 1912 and 1925. For Rein-Wuhrmann, the King's isolation is a result of his estrangement from Christianity and from the colonial authorities; this is considered inevitable: "It could not have been otherwise."

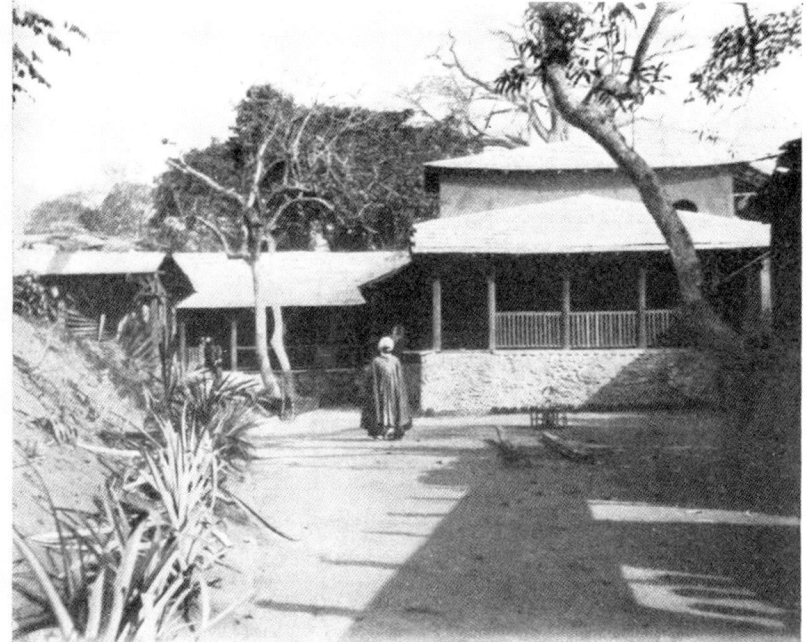

König Nschoja in Mantum.

Figure 4.21. King Njoya, 'King Njoya in Mantum, c. 1924 [?], illustration, p. 151 in Anna Rein-Wuhrmann, *Mein Bamumvolk im Grasland von Kamerun*, Basel: Basler Missionsbuchhandlung, 1925.

The final pair of portraits in the suite of illustrations offers a conclusion which is more ambiguous than Rein-Wuhrmann's.[109] The first portrait is a survey of achievements [Fig. 4.11]. A further iteration of Njoya's self-portrait, it shows more than a reworking of the double performance; it also alludes to Njoya's celebrated innovations in weaving, dying and writing. The internal frame of the portrait contains motifs found on Bamum textiles and includes some designs in indigo, a prized colour and one formerly used in prestige goods.[110] And below this frame is a developed form of the Bamum alphabet. Yet while the portrait is a survey, it is perhaps not a very orderly one. It offers a view of a rather disparate and disorganised set of materials. Various signs are piled up here. What relation is to be construed between the star of Islam above Njoya's head and the Bamum motifs connected to quite different religious practices? What relation between the European medals pinned to Njoya's chest and the Bamum sword hanging awkwardly over the lower part of the frame? Can these signs be properly marshalled or is the piling up to be understood as a form of listing, a collation, and thus a visual counterpart to the list of Bamum arts to be advertised in the *Journal officiel*? Is this an image, then, of the King as curator? Is this, ultimately, an image of the King dispossessed? The answer is not clear, and this is in part because the artist seems to have worked quite hard to create ambiguity in the portrait. He first drew the internal frame of motifs with a curved lower edge corresponding to the framing above Njoya's head; this would have given the King a more secure placing as a figure standing at a window. Yet in the final version this lower edge has been erased, although traces of it remain just visible. The result increases the viewer's uncertainty as to the King's relation to the frame, prompting futher questions. Why create such an effect? What purposes might ambiguity serve here?

Perhaps the portrait is neither a celebration of the King's authority nor a concession of its loss. Authority and its loss are opposed terms — a stark choice — and the portrait should perhaps be understood differently, outside this polarity, as representing another kind of relation between the King and his people. The caption to the portrait suggests as much; it is drawn from the text of Njoya's history, from his account of the end of his reign:

> Here is the speech that Njoya addressed to the Bamum when he governed them. He said to the Bamum: 'I was named king when I was still young, aged 19. It was the Bamum who brought me up. The Bamum are like my fathers; I cannot be afraid of them and they must not be afraid of me. The help I want to give my fathers is without limits, it will only end when God calls me.'[111]

There are in fact no less than three versions of this speech in Njoya's history; it is something of a signature.[112] The words cited in the caption are closest to those in the speech which is appended to a list of laws Njoya had decided to abrogate.[113]

The abrogation was presented as an act of service to the Bamum people, and the speech is also an acknowledgement of service. However, in turn, the speech dedicates Njoya and the Bamum to Allah, closing with a prayer:

> We pray to God, that God will grant us the Holy Spirit, that he will put his blessing on the things that everyone accepts because of Mohammed, the prophet of God. *Amen!*[114]

The pairing of portraits in the suite should, I think, be interpreted in this context. Yet it is important to consider that a context need not serve to resolve ambiguity into a single meaning. It may be that the pairing of images generates equivocation. On the one hand, a missionary could persist in deploring Njoya's conversion to Islam and could view the second portrait, of Njoya in Muslim dress, in this light [Fig. 4.12]. Such, clearly, would be Rein-Wurhmann's view. And Yeyap would probably have shared this view. On the other hand, the second portrait may be understood as signalling precisely the renunciation of what is shown in the first portrait. This renunciation would be of a piece with the abrogation of laws, and would give a different inflection to the images.

The portrait of Njoya in Muslim dress is shorn of framing and here the King has shrugged off his elaborate costume and his decorations. Such renunciation of the worldly was anticipated in his early engagement with Islam. A prayer in Njoya's *Nuet Kuete* contains the following injunctions:

> All listen: God will pardon your sins and not punish them. You see the world? It will pass and all things with it. I am speaking to you: you see the world? It will pass and all things with it. I am speaking to you: you see the world? It deceives, as do all things in it.[115]

So renunciation here is something other than a reflex. It is not merely part of Njoya's rejection of Christianity and nor does it need to be understood, narrowly, as a response to his dispossession. This, finally, seems too prescriptive.

The portrait of Njoya in Muslim dress has its place in the longer history of his reign. Recall that in 1894 Njoya had requested the help of the Fula to secure a victory in the civil war with Gbentkom. Following his victory, Njoya asked what sorcery the Fula had used to achieve it. In reply the Lamido Oumarou sent Njoya "a rosary, a white tunic, a turban and loose trousers" and "he told him to pray to God and that the war medicine came from this prayer".[116] In the end, this did not help Oumarou, who was to be killed by Sandrock. Yet in the final portrait Njoya wears a white tunic and turban. The Muslim dress may be part of a renunciation and it may also represent a form of independence and even resistance. This is what remained.

I have described Njoya's photographic self-portrait of 1912 as a double performance, and the final pairing of portraits also casts the King in roles, although with a different script to that of 1912. However, the pair of images do not establish the kind of proscenium familiar from European portraiture. Njoya's portraits are thus quite different from Élie Allégret's photographs of the Pastors Kuo, Ekollo and Modi Din, which were decisively shaped by European conventions [Figs 0.1 and 0.2]. Allégret's photographs were designed to contribute to a network of relations extending from Paris to Fumban; they were to affirm a quite particular community of belief and so the use of European conventions was appropriate in this particular African context. After all, Allégret would wish to show his friends in a manner which would be intelligible to all members of the Société des Missions Évangéliques de Paris. The photographed performance of each pastor in Fumban was directed to "an essentially *like* subjectivity" in Paris.[117] These portraits were oriented to a European horizon. Njoya's pair of portraits may also have been directed to a community of belief, yet they were oriented to a different horizon. What is imagined here is not what was imagined by Allégret and Rein-Wuhrmann. Njoya's portraits have different frames of reference.

Yeyap's arts in France

In 1931 the campaign against Njoya came to its conclusion when he was sent into exile. Governor Marchand left an exceptionally bitter and hostile account of Njoya's reign, a reign he ended with an order of exile dated 5 April 1931.[118] Just over a month later Lyautey inaugurated the *Exposition coloniale*. This exhibition of course included pavilions dedicated to Togo and Cameroon, the territories for which Marchand was responsible. Thus, a little over a year after Yeyap's exhibition in Fumban, Governor Marchand came to preside over another exhibition of the arts of the Bamum. Needless to say, his portrait appeared in the souvenir brochure dedicated to this section of *Exposition coloniale*. Yeyap also made his contribution by supplying the organisers with artefacts for display.[119]

By the time the *Exposition* opened, Njoya's palace in Fumban was already falling into disrepair. However, in the Parc de Vincennes buildings inspired by the "traditional" palace architecture of the Bamum had been erected. The role of the palace in Fumban had been eroded and finally removed and the buildings in

Vincennes preserved this shell, retaining something of the palace's architectural style but without its functions. There was another inversion here. Njoya had sought to preserve the social and religious functions of his palace whilst adopting a European style; conversely, in Vincennes the removal of "traditional" functions and practices was one sign of the success of the civilising project. In the souvenir brochure, the visitor was welcomed to a series of pavilions which "give an impression of cleanliness most appealing to all those who prefer an Africa humanised and improved through colonisation to that barbarous, savage Africa which has almost everywhere ceased to be a reality".[120] Here appropriation of an architectural style served to measure a distance travelled towards civilisation. This, at least, was one part of the fantasy constituting the display.

The exhibition site for Togo and Cameroon had five important buildings and some lesser huts. "Le Grand Pavillon" was the point of orientation where it was explained that exports from Cameroon had increased from 27,000 tonnes in 1921 to 175,000 in 1930.[121] Such was the French success in exploiting Cameroon's resources. Thus, the economic policy of Carde was celebrated as new mechanisms of exchange wrought their effects. And the products of the Bamum artisans were subject to these mechanisms. The authors of the souvenir brochure commented of one arrangement of these products: "In the centre, a cluster of native spears and lances mounted on a Bamum table makes a display which is at once decorative and informative."[122] As in Yeyap's museum, objects could be presented to convey different kinds of pleasure and information, without the hierarchies and monopolies which had obtained in the royal palace. In Fumban, it had served Yeyap's immediate ends to produce "the arts of the Bamum", to convert the objects of the secret societies into representations. This conversion had been an effective part of Yeyap's campaign against Njoya. Yet, ultimately, Yeyap was not to control representation.

On 30 May 1933, Njoya died. Then, in early July, it was the turn of another missionary to write to his superiors at the Société des Missions Évangéliques. Now it was Henri Martin's duty to inform the directors that following Njoya's death, Yeyap, their protégé, had been obliged to take a period of leave.[123] He had been suspended as official interpreter. And at the end of his period of leave Yeyap was compelled to retire. He would no longer be permitted to perform his role.

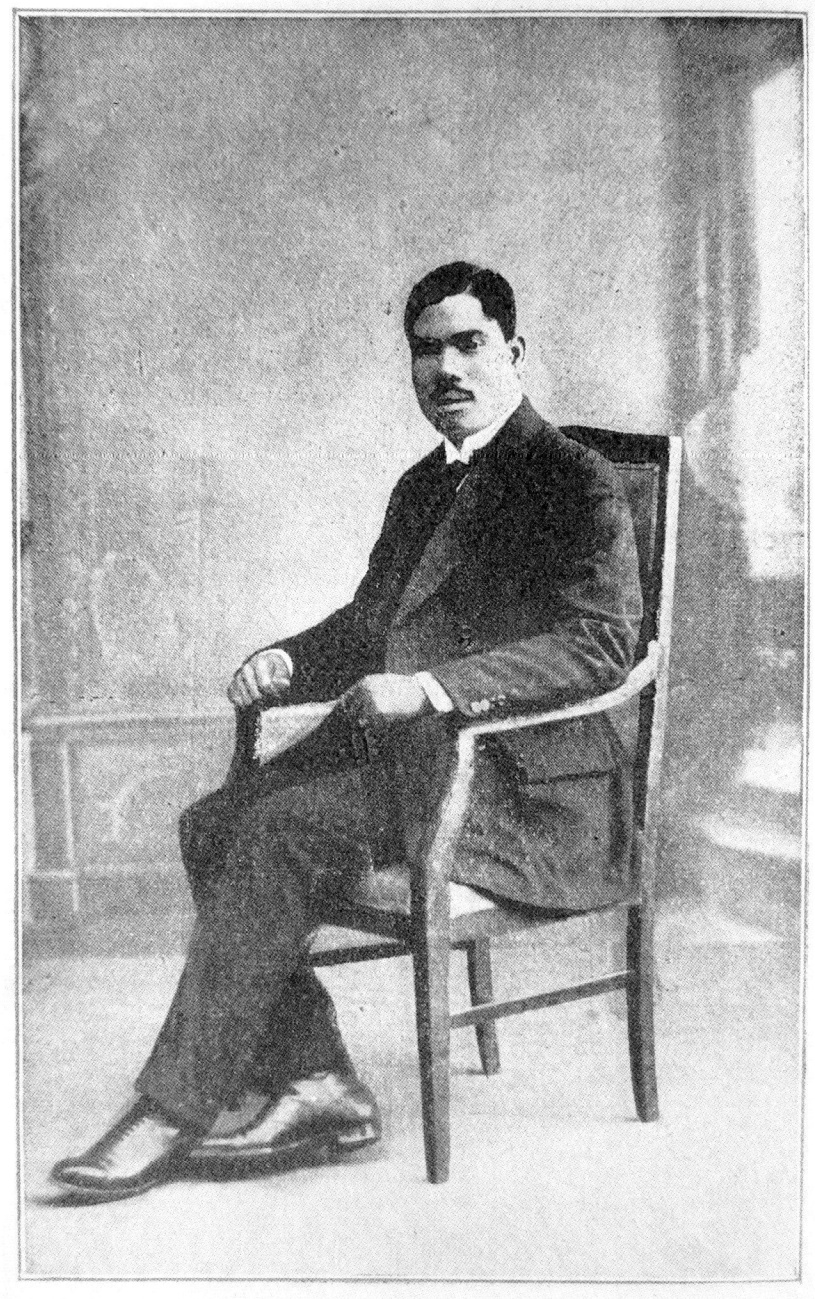

Figure 5.1. Anon. 'Charles Atangana', frontispiece, in Charles Atangana, *Paix Humanité Justice*, Madrid: Privately circulated, 1920.

Epilogue

Charles Atangana between Africa and France

In Madrid, towards the end of 1919, Charles Atangana arranged to have his portrait made [Fig. 5.1]. As chief of the Jaundes and Banes, Atangana had assisted the Germans in Cameroon at the beginning of the war and so was forced to flee the country when they withdrew. Atangana was first interned on the island of Fernando Poo (as it was then known), and from there made his way to Spain once the war ended. He then had to petition the French repeatedly for his repatriation. In 1919 Atangana decided to publish privately a text entitled *Paix Humanité Justice* in order to garner support for his case; he judged that this appeal required his portrait as a frontispiece.[1]

Atangana's text makes deft use of the terms of the colonial imaginary. A paean to "the law of progress" and humanity's "successive transformations", it is also a celebration of the formula of *liberté, égalité, fraternité*.[2] In Atangana's account, history is nothing other than a progress towards these ideals. Implicitly, if the French remain in the vanguard of this history — as surely their role in the war had attested — then they would also see the justice in allowing Atangana to return to his homeland. Thus Atangana's petition is insinuated into the larger claims made for a Greater France. These were the only tactics available to him. Accordingly, Atangana prefaces his account with a declaration of loyalty; he, too, is dedicated to pursuing the great French formula. His portrait is placed opposite his declaration, with his signature positioned prominently below the image. Signature and portrait are proxies, offered to confirm Atangana's declaration. Sworn declarations require a physical presence before witnesses yet this is precisely what Atangana could not perform, stranded in Spain. He could only hope that his portrait would do something of the work by showing him to be an exemplary product of the colonial encounter.

Atangana's hope was rewarded. His potential was recognised by the first French governor of Cameroon, Lucien Fourneau, who had the delicate task of establishing a new colonial administration and was therefore properly sensible to the value of figures such as Atangana. Already in August 1919, in a report recommending Atangana's return, Fourneau concludes: "In sum, if Atangana returned we would have in our hands a powerful instrument, which would be of the greatest use to us."[3] On his return to Cameroon Atangana was indeed energetic. He was determined to remain exemplary and thus it is not surprising that, when Njoya was exiled, he was placed in Atangana's care.[4] The latter would work with his ambiguous status as an instrument of the French in Africa.

The portrait of Atangana shows a calm, collected individual. His displacement to Madrid is perhaps discreetly acknowledged in the anonymity of the setting, which is probably a photographer's studio. Atangana was experienced in many ways and knew what was required from his portrait. He knew what was involved in making a representation. So at one level this photograph shows the colonial imaginary functioning well enough; once again its terms are used with some care. Yet at another level the fantasy of the civilising mission could barely sustain itself. After all, the inescapable context of *Paix Humanité Justice* was a global, imperial conflict, and the portrait is of a refugee, a stateless person. Ambiguities persist.

This book has been concerned with the ambiguities generated by colonial encounters, and with the functions of the portrait within these encounters. In Atangana's case, the portrait works to frame someone who has been made a civilised man. It is to provide the proscenium for an exemplary performance. The portraits of the Pastors Modi Din, Kuo and Ekollo had similar functions. In colonial contexts, the portrait is a means of organising different frames of reference. Yet I have tried to show that portraits may perform this function in many different ways, taking different positions within temporal, spatial, and racial coordinates. To the extent that portraits combine frames of reference, they are, like metaphors, unstable. I want to conclude with a few reflections on this instability, by briefly considering a last pairing of photographs, one of which features Atangana [Figs 5.2 and 5.3].

In the early 1930s Atangana would petition the colonial authorities for permission to visit France; his wish was granted in 1935. The organisers of the Conférence Économique Impériale required "appropriate indigenous representation" and Atangana was duly nominated.[5] In January 1935 the minister for the colonies, Louis Rollin, endorsed the proposal to send the chief to the conference.[6] As it happened, Atangana's visit coincided with an exhibition of the arts of Cameroon at the Musée du Trocadéro. Here one of Njoya's thrones was on display.

The exhibition was organised by Henri Labouret and it was he who had brought the throne to France in the previous year. Labouret had succeeded Maurice Delafosse as professor of African ethnography at both the École coloniale and the Institut d'ethnologie; he had also succeeded Delafosse as co-director of the Institut International des Langues et Civilisations Africaines. In these roles,

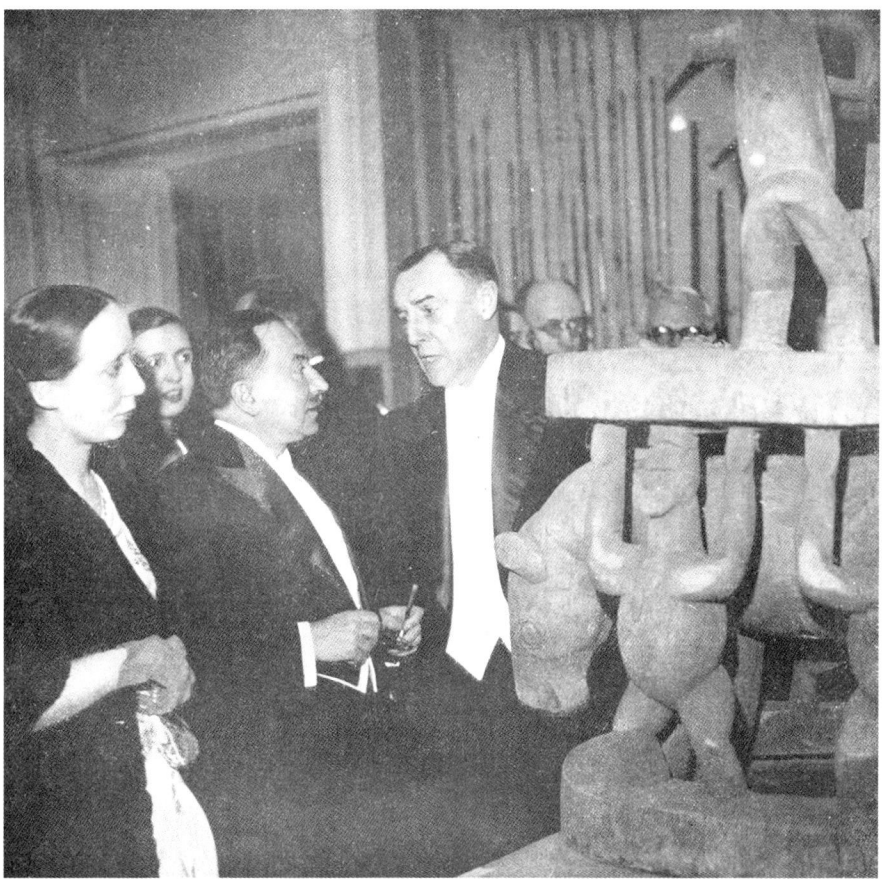

Figure 5.2. Anon. 'The Trocadéro Museum', illustration, p. 166 in *Togo-Cameroun*, April-July 1935.

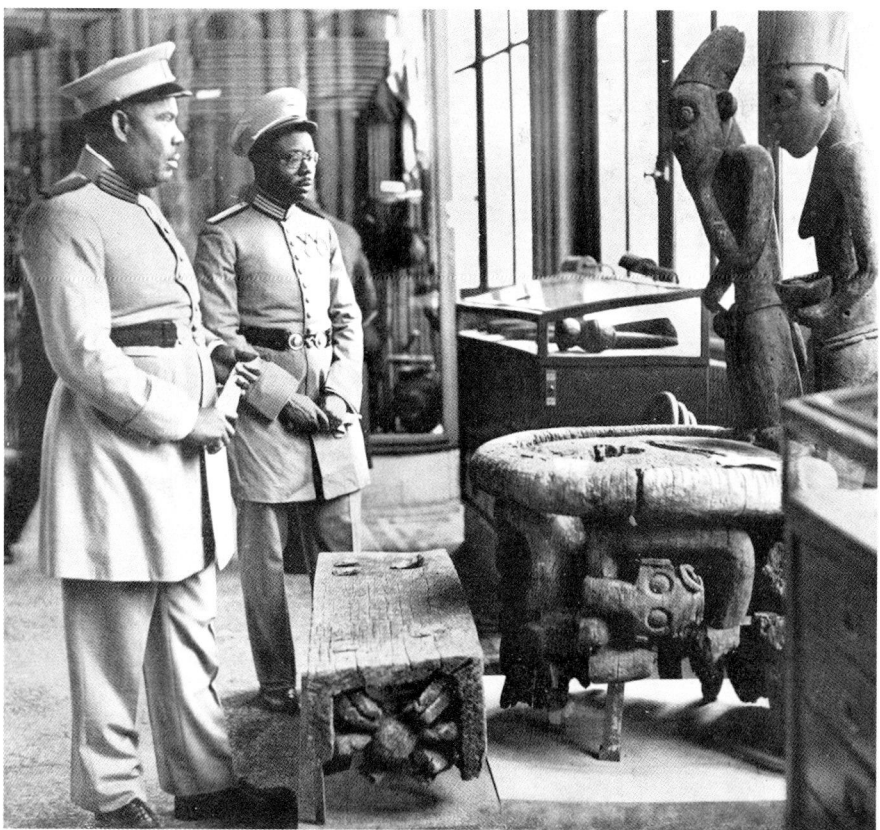

Figure 5.3. Anon. 'Before his return to Cameroon, Atangana, high chief of the Yaoundé-Bané, delegate at the Conférence Économique Impériale (left) and his secretary Essomba visit the Trocadéro exhibition of Labouret's mission', illustration, p. 167 in *Togo-Cameroun*, April-July 1935.

Labouret insisted on the importance of studying the transformations resulting from colonisation and he was quite candid in presenting himself in the service of the colonial project; in his view ethnographic knowledge made an important contribution to good governance.[7] Like Schwab, Labouret had visited Fumban, and like Schwab he was able to acquire formerly reserved objects. These acquisitions were to be an important part of the Parisian exhibition dedicated to his fieldwork.[8] The organisers of this exhibition took pains to give it appropriate publicity. *Togo-Cameroun*, the organ of the Agence Économique des Territoires Africains Sous Mandat, dedicated a special issue to Labouret's work, precisely to showcase ethnographic knowledge in the service of the state. One article by Labouret, on art in Cameroon, was introduced by a photograph of the professor with Rollin [Fig. 5.2]. The composition gives Labouret his proper role; he is presented using his expertise to mediate the minister's experience of Cameroonian artefacts, in this case an empty throne. Knowledge and power are pictured in their reciprocity; this, after all, was one of the principal tasks of *Togo-Cameroun*.

In this publication, the image of the professor and the minister has as its pendant a photograph showing Njoya's throne on display in the Trocadéro; the caption explains the situation: "Before his return to Cameroon, Atangana, high chief of the Yaoundé-Bané, delegate at the *Conférence Économique Impériale* (left) and his secretary Essomba visit the Trocadéro exhibition of Labouret's mission" [Fig. 5.3]. The photograph of Atangana has an organisation akin to that with the professor, with a throne as an object of contemplation in both. Of course, Labouret is not present, for it is to be understood that Atangana does not on this occasion require a lecture on ethnography. The pendant photographs juxtapose minister and chief, colonial and indigenous authorities; this would have been clear enough to the reader of *Togo-Cameroun*, at least at first glance. However, the juxtaposition creates instability in the photograph of Atangana. For where does his authority lie? From the comparative perspective established at the *Exposition coloniale*, it might lie in Atangana's destination, in the distance he has travelled from the culture represented by the throne, toward that represented by Labouret and Rollin. Yet authority might also lie in Atangana's proximity to the throne; as the caption states, he is a chief, and one about to return to Cameroon. The instability in the photograph is created by these different destinations. Standing still, Atangana is pulled in quite different directions. This difficult status is underlined through his contemplation of the empty throne. In both photographs, the throne may be taken to stand for the monarch. Empty thrones are reminders of absent performers. In the photograph of Labouret and Rollin, colonial performers have clearly supplanted indigenous ones. In the photograph of Atangana this supplanting is less obvious. Atangana does, after all, have a role to play. He remains a powerful instrument.

The photographer has captured a fall of light which illuminates both Atangana's neatly pressed uniform and quite roughly hewn wood; this could be an invitation to make a sharp distinction between European and African materials and workmanship, just as in the photograph of Labouret and Rollin. Thus the photographs could be and were drawn together, and, in the process, Atangana was portrayed as an example of the civilising mission at its most successful. Care was certainly taken to secure this impression; Atangana and Essomba received a designated allowance for clothing.[9] Yet the civilising mission has to sustain and prolong itself rather than be completed; its object must be preserved. And so Atangana cannot remain in Paris; he must be sent back to that other place, as the caption to his photograph insists. Proximity and distance cannot be reconciled here. In some respects Atangana remained estranged. His status had certainly changed since 1919, but looking at Njoya's throne, he perhaps understood both what it means to make men and what it means to find oneself so created.

This pair of portraits creates equivocation. This must be attended to. The history of the photograph of the minister and the professor cannot be written without that of the chief and his secretary. Imagine a parallel case, where the history of colonialism was written so as to be confined to activity in the "whited sepulchres" of Paris, London, Brussels and Berlin![10] How could this be considered adequate? And yet histories of portraiture have often been similarly confined, framed too exclusively, and therefore separated from the larger global histories to which they belong.

Portraits may thematise the business of looking, and they may also serve within the colonial imaginary. They may contribute to the process in which the colonised are to be remade in the image of the European, to fall under the sway of the colonising power. Yet the business of looking need not always be about securing the mastery of the viewer and the objectification of the viewed; in certain encounters this mastery may be called into question. 'The strangeness of the Other, his irreducibility to the I, to my thoughts and my possessions, is precisely accomplished as a calling into question (...) as ethics.'[11] Such moments of encounter are rare enough in the history of colonialism but that is no reason to disregard them. This book — and its movement through different perspectives — has been an attempt to grasp these moments and rethink them. The book arose by questioning at least some of the procedures of art history, where these are used to maintain borders and restrict enquiry. It has been an attempt to imagine an ethics of art history.

Notes

Introduction

1. Élie Allégret, 'Rapport confidentiel présenté au Comité de la Société des Missions Évangéliques de Paris sur la Mission au Cameroun, mai 1919', typescript in *Njoya et le royaume bamoum: Les archives de la Société des Missions Évangéliques de Paris, 1917-1937*, ed. Alexandra Loumpet-Galitzine, Paris: Karthala, 2006, 221-23, 221. Translations are my own unless otherwise stated.
2. Ibid.
3. Ibid.
4. For the domestic arrangements of the Société's missionaries see Dagmar Konrad, 'The Mission Station', in *Mission Possible? The Basel Mission Collection - Reflecting Cultural Encounters*, ed. Anna Schmid, Kathrin Fischer, Basel: Christoph Merian Verlag and Museum der Kulturen Basel, 2015, 69-75.
5. Élie Allégret, 'Á Foumban et au Grassfield', *Journal de la Société des Missions Évangéliques de Paris*, 1 (1918), extracts in Loumpet-Galitzine, *Njoya*, 213-16, 215.
6. See amongst other sources, Abraham Njoya and Paulo Pepuere, 'Histoire de l'Église bamoun depuis 1905 par les missionaires de Balle', manuscript in Loumpet-Galitzine, *Njoya*, 138-152, 146.
7. Élie Allégret, 'The Missionary Question in the French Colonies', *International Review of Mission*, 12: 2, April 1923, 161-81, 170.
8. Ibid. 167.
9. Albert Sarraut, *Projet de loi portant fixation d'un programme général de mise en valeur des colonies françaises*, No. 2449, Paris: Imprimerie de la Chambre des Députés, 1921, 33. An almost identical phrase is used in a later work for a popular readership: see Albert Sarraut, *Grandeur et servitude coloniales*, Paris: Éditions du sagittaire, Anciennes Éditions Kra, 1931, 115.
10. Frantz Fanon, *Black Skin, White Masks*, trans. by Charles Lam Markmann, London: Pluto Press, 1986, 98. The citation is from Aimé Césaire, *Cahier d'un retour au pays natal*, Paris: Présence Africaine, 1956.
11. The shifting of perspectives in these chapters is intended to have at least something of the movement between colony and metropole to be found in Césaire, *Cahier d'un retour* and Cheikh Hamidou Kane, *L'Aventure ambiguë*, Paris: René Juillard, 1962.
12. Okwui Enwezor and Octavio Zaya, 'Colonial Imaginary, Tropes of Disruption: History, Culture, and Representation in the Works of African Photographers', in *In/sight: African Photographers, 1940 to the Present*, Solomon R. Guggenheim Museum, New York: Abrams, 1996, 17-47, 20.
13. See Horacio Fernández, *Fotografía pública: Photography in Print*, Madrid: Museo Nacional Centro d'Arte Reina Sofía, 2000.
14. For an overview of these issues see John Tagg, *The Disciplinary Frame: Photographic Truths and the Capture of Meaning*, Minneapolis: The University of Minnesota Press, 2009.
15. See for example David Summers, *Real Spaces: World Art History and the Rise of Western Modernism*, London: Phaidon Press, 2003; David Carrier, *A World Art History and Its Objects*, University Park: The Pennsylvania State University Press, 2008; Whitney Davis, *A General Theory of Visual Culture*, Princeton and Oxford: Princeton University Press, 2011.
16. The groundbreaking work of 1986 was Melissa Banta and Curtis M. Hinsley with Joan Kathryn O'Donnell, *From Site to Sight: Anthropology, Photography, and the Power of Imagery*, 30th Anniversary edition, Cambridge, Mass: Peabody Museum Press, Harvard University,

2017: see the new introduction to this edition. See also Elizabeth Edwards, ed. *Anthropology and Photography, 1860-1920*, New Haven and London: Yale University Press in association with the Royal Anthropological Institute, 1992, the fruit of a research project begun in 1984. For an early critical account see David Green, 'Photography and Anthropology: The Technology of Power', *Ten: 8*, 14, 1984, 30–37.

17.   Anne Maxwell, *Colonial Photography and Exhibitions: Representations of the 'Native' and the Making of European Identities*, London and New York: Leicester University Press, 1999; Eleanor M. Hight and Gary D. Sampson ed. *Colonialist Photography: Imag(in)ing race and place*, London and New York: Routledge, 2002; Paul S. Landau and Deborah D. Kaspin, ed. *Images and Empires: Visuality in Colonial and Postcolonial Africa*, Berkeley, Los Angeles and London: University of California Press, 2002.

18.   See for example Erin Haney, *Photography and Africa*, London: Reaktion, 2010, and for a discussion of these developments, 7–12.

19.   Here the *Black Photo Album* developed by Santu Mofokeng from the late 1980s has been a significant precedent. The most important early surveys of African photography are New York, Solomon R. Guggenheim Museum, *In/sight: African Photographers, 1940 to the Present*, New York: Abrams, 1996 and Pascal Martin Saint Léon and N'Goné Fall, ed. *Anthology of African and Indian Ocean Photography*, Paris: Revue noire, 1999. See also Okwui Enwezor, ed. *Contemporary African Photography from the Walther Collection: Events of the Self, Portraiture and Social Identity*, Göttingen: Steidl, 2010 and John Peffer and Elisabeth L. Cameron, ed. *Portraiture and Photography in Africa*, Bloomington: Indiana University Press, 2013. In this context it is significant that the monumental study of the image of the black in Western art has recently concluded with a shift of focus to different agencies: see David Bindman, Susan Preston Blier and Henry Louis Gates Jr., ed. *The Image of the Black in African and Asian Art*, Cambridge, Mass: The Belknap Press of Harvard University Press, 2017.

20.   These are now large fields. For a sense of how they have developed, compare the collections which specifically draw together contributions from art historians, historians and anthropologists: Lucien Taylor, ed. *Visualizing Theory: Selected Essays from V.A.R., 1990-1994*, New York and London: Routledge, 1994, and Martin Jay and Sumathi Ramaswamy, ed. *Empires of Vision: A Reader*, Durham and London: Duke University Press. 2014.

21.   This observation is not as tautological as it sounds; the debate over France's colonial legacy has been complicated by the relations between republicanism and colonialism. The (delayed) opening of the French debate may be dated to the publication of Pascal Blanchard, Nicolas Bancel and Sandrine Lemaire, ed. *La Fracture coloniale: La Société française au prisme de l'héritage colonial*, Paris: La Découverte, 2005. For one account of this debate see Robert J. C. Young, 'Bayart's Broken Kettle', *Public Culture*, 23:1, 2011, 167–175. In turn, *La Fracture coloniale* took its place within the historical project of the Association Connaissance de l'histoire de l'Afrique contemporaine, beginning with Nicolas Bancel, Pascal Blanchard and Laurent Gervereau, ed, *Images et colonies: Iconographie et propagande colonial sur l'Afrique française de 1880 à 1962*, Nanterre and Paris: Bibliothèque de documentation internationale contemporaine and Association Connaissance de l'histoire de l'Afrique contemporaine, 1993. This work continues and is of continued relevance: see more recently Pascal Blanchard, Nicolas Bancel and Dominic Thomas, ed. *Vers la guerre des identités? De la fracture coloniale à la révolution ultranationale*, Paris: La Découverte, 2016.

22.   Frederick Cooper and Laura Stoler, ed. *Tensions of Empire: Colonial Culture in a Bourgeois World*, Berkeley, Los Angeles and London: University of California Press, 1997, 4. On the importance of this for colonial France in the interwar period see Jennifer Anne Boittin, *Colonial Metropolis: The Urban Grounds of Anti-Imperialism and Feminism in Interwar Paris*, Lincoln and London: University of Nebraska Press, 2010, xxiii. For an alternative method of moving between France and Africa see Steven Nelson, *From Cameroon to Paris: Mousgoum Architecture in and out of Africa*, Chicago and London: University of Chicago Press, 2007.

Of course, metropole and colony are not static entities: Europe produced "the rest of the world" as part of the work of constituting itself: see Mary Louise Pratt, *Imperial Eyes: Travel Writing and Transculturation*, London and New York: Routledge, 1992.

23. Emmanuel Levinas, *Totality and Infinity: An Essay on Exteriority*, trans. by Alphonso Lingis, Pittsburgh: Duquesne University Press, 1969, 38, emphasis retained.

24. Ibid. 39.

25. Ibid. emphasis retained.

26. Ibid. emphasis retained.

27. Ibid. 43.

28. My reading of Levinas is certainly an unsophisticated one. For an account of the issue Levinas raises in relation to the discipline of anthropology see Bernhard Leistle, 'Introduction', in *Anthropology and Alterity: Responding to the Other*, ed. Bernhard Leistle, New York and London: Routledge, 2017, 1–24. And for an assessment of the place of representation in the philosophy of Levinas see Jacques Derrida, 'Violence and Metaphysics: An Essay on the Thought of Emmanuel Levinas', in *Writing and Difference*, trans. by Alan Bass, London: Routledge, 1977, 79–153.

1. Making men: Citizens and subjects

1. Here cited from David Bindman and Henry Louis Gates Jr., ed. *The Image of the Black in Western Art: From the American Revolution to World War I, Slaves and Liberators*, Cambridge, Mass. and London: The Belknap Press of Harvard University Press, 2012, 81–2.

2. The more recent literature on the painting has tended to equivocal or antithetical descriptions. See for example Thomas Crow, *Emulation: Making Artists for Revolutionary France*, New Haven and London: Yale University Press, 1995, 225ff and Michèle Bocquillon, 'Le "Portrait parlant" de Jean-Baptiste Belley', *Nineteenth-Century French Studies*, 33: 1/2, Fall-Winter 2004–2005, 35–56.

3. Belley [Jean-Baptiste], *Le Bout d'oreille des colons, ou le système de l'hôtel de Massiac, mis au jour par Gouli*, Paris: De l'Imprimerie de Pain, 1794, 5.

4. Cited ibid. emphasis retained.

5. Ibid. 5 and 4.

6. Ibid. 5.

7. For this role for thresholds and boundary markers see the classic account in Arnold van Gennep, *The Rites of Passage*, trans. by Monika B. Vizedom and Gabrielle L. Caffre, London: Routledge and Kegan Paul, 1960, 15ff.

8. For Girodet's views on the universal language of painting see 'Le Peintre, poème', in *Œuvres posthumes de Girodet-Trioson, peintre d'histoire; suivi de sa correspondence; précédés d'une notice historique*, I, ed. P. A. Coupin, Paris: Librairie Jules Renouard, 1829, 1–199, 192.

9. David Bindman, 'Subjectivity and Slavery in Portraiture: From Courtly to Commercial Societies', in *Slave Portraiture in the Atlantic World*, ed. Angela Rosenthal and Agnes Lugo-Ortiz, New York: Cambridge University Press, 2013, 71–87, 75.

10. Fanon, *Black Skin*, 110. Being caught between the frames of reference could be characterised as an ambiguous position: see for example Kane, *L'Aventure ambiguë*. Fanon also recognised this but regarded ambiguity as lived psychopathologically: *Black Skin*, 192.

11. Fanon, *Black Skin*, 228, 226, translation modified.

12. André Gide and Élie Allégret, *L'Enfance de l'Art: Correspondance avec Élie Allégret (1886–1896), Lettres d'André Gide, Juliette Gide, Madeleine Rondeaux et Élie Allégret*, ed. Daniel Durosay, Paris: NRF, Gallimard, 1998, 106, emphasis retained.

13. Ibid. 127.

14.   Ibid. The allusion is to Luke, 10: 2.

15.   For Ferry's role in the early Republic see François Furet, ed. *Jules Ferry: Fondateur de la République: Actes du colloque*, Paris: Éditions due l'École des Hautes Études en Sciences Sociales, 1985.

16.   These different campaigns have complicated histories. For one clear narrative and an explication of Ferry's roles see Thomas F. Jr. Power, *Jules Ferry and the Renaissance of French Imperialism*, New York: Octagon Books, 1966. Apologists of empire made a refrain of Ferry's greatness during the first decades of the twentieth century. For a typical example see the introduction to Maurice Allain, *Notre belle France d'outre-mer, I*, Paris: A. Quillet, 1934.

17.   Jules Ferry, *Discours et opinions de Jules Ferry, V*, Paris: Colin, 1897, 199. Sources as diverse as Paul Deschamps et al. *Les Colonies et la vie française pendant huit siècles*, Paris: Firmin-Didot, 1933, 194 and Raoul Girardet, *L'Idée coloniale en France de 1871–1962*, Paris: La Table ronde, 1972, 46 give Ferry's speech and his preface to *Le Tonkin et la Mère-Patrie* as the *loci classici* of colonial policy in the early Third Republic. Ferry's accusers were from both the radical extreme left and the nationalist extreme right. For Sarraut's view of the importance of this debate, see Sarraut, *Grandeur et servitude coloniales*, 70.

18.   Ferry, *Discours*, 199–200.

19.   Ibid. 200ff.

20.   Ibid. 210.

21.   Ibid. 210.

22.   Ibid. 211.

23.   Here cited from David Bindman and Henry Louis Gates Jr., ed. *The Image of the Black in Western Art: From the "Age of Discovery" to the Age of Abolition, The Eighteenth Century*, Cambridge, Mass. and London: The Belknap Press of Harvard University Press, 2011, 298.

24.   Ferry, *Discours*, 220.

25.   Ibid. 220.

26.   Jean-Antoine-Nicolas de Caritat, marquis de Condorcet, *Sketch for a Historical Picture of the Progress of the Human Mind*, trans. by June Barraclough, Westport: Greenwood Press, 1955, 128ff and 177ff. For an astute commentary on the differences between Condorcet's views and those of later colonialists, see Tzvetan Todorov, *On Human Diversity: Nationalism, Racism, and Exoticism in French Thought*, trans. by Catherine Porter, Cambridge, Mass. and London: Harvard University Press, 1993, esp. 252ff.

27.   My account draws on that of Marx in 'The Class Struggles in France: 1848-1850', 'The Eighteenth Brumaire of Louis Bonaparte' and 'The Civil War in France'. See, respectively, Karl Marx, *Surveys from Exile: Political Writings, II*, trans. by Paul Jackson, Harmondsworth: Penguin Books, 1992, 35–142 and 143–249 and *The First International and After: Political Writings, III*, Harmondsworth: Penguin Books, 1992, 143–249. I have also relied on the analysis of Republicanism in Antonio Gramsci, *Prison Notebooks, I and II*, trans. by Joseph A. Buttigieg and Antonio Callari, New York: Columbia University Press, 1992 and 1996.

28.   Marx, 'The Class Struggles in France', 43.

29.   Ibid. 71.

30.   Karl Marx, *Capital: A Critique of Political Economy*, trans. by Ben Fowkes, Harmondsworth: Penguin Books, 1990, 280.

31.   See Jacques Juillard, 'Le Peuple', in *Les Lieux de mémoire, III*, ed. Pierre Nora, Paris: Gallimard, 1992, 184–229.

32.   The argument developed here builds on earlier discussions of Republicanism and colonialism: see, amongst others, Girardet, *L'Idée coloniale*, esp. 43ff and Jean-Paul Sartre, *Critique of Dialectical Reason, I*, trans. by Alan Sheridan-Smith, London: New Left Books, 1976, 714ff. Work in this field has been recently advanced by Pascal Blanchard, Nicolas Bancel and Sandrine Lemaire and their collaborators: see Pascal Blanchard and Sandrine Lemaire,

ed. *Culture coloniale: La France conquise par son Empire, 1871-1931*, Paris: Éditions Autrement – collection Mémoires, 2003; Pascal Blanchard, Sandrine Lemaire and Nicolas Bancel, ed. *Culture coloniale en France: De la Révolution française à nos jours*, Paris: Éditions Autrement and Association Connaissance de l'histoire de l'Afrique contemporaine, 2003. Whilst it is difficult to overestimate the importance of this recent work for understanding the history of French colonialism, I feel it is necessary to augment it with the analysis of Republicanism given here.

33. Gramsci, *Prison Notebooks*, II, 178.

34. Marx, 'The Eighteenth Brumaire of Louis Bonaparte', 176. This is a comment on the programme of the Second Republic but it holds up well as an analysis of the Third.

35. See Simon Dell, *The Image of the Popular Front: The Masses and the Media in Interwar France*, Basingstoke and New York: Palgrave Macmillan, 2007, 11-27.

36. Louis Althusser, 'Ideology and Ideological State Apparatuses (Notes towards an Investigation), in *Lenin and Philosophy and Other Essays*, trans. by Ben Brewster, Delhi: Aakar Books, 2006, 85-126, 122.

37. Ibid. emphases retained.

38. Ibid. 123.

39. Marx, 'The Class Struggles in France', 43. On the exercise of power and exchanges between 'leaders and led' see Gramsci, *Prison Notebooks*, II, 173-174.

40. Althusser, 'Ideology', 89.

41. The term "colonial imaginary" has had a certain currency yet the concept has remained largely undeveloped. See for example Dominique Taffin, 'Le Musée des colonies et l'imaginaire colonial', in *Images et colonies: Iconographie et propagande colonial sur l'Afrique française de 1880 à 1962*, ed. Nicolas Bancel, Pascal Blanchard and Laurent Gervereau, Nanterre and Paris: Bibliothèque de documentation internationale contemporaine and Association Connaissance de l'histoire de l'Afrique contemporaine, 1993, 140-144 and Okwui Enwezor and Octavio Zaya, 'Colonial Imaginary'.

42. Frédéric Gaëtan de la Rochefoucauld-Liancourt had articulated his vision for the liberation of Algeria in these terms in 1835, as did Republicans of different stripes such as Louis Blanc in 1839 and Eugène Bodichon in 1847: see Charles-Robert Ageron, *France coloniale ou parti colonial?*, Paris: Presses Universitaires de France, 1978, 62-64.

43. Althusser, 'Ideology', 99ff. For a good account of how colonial policies played out in practice see William B. Cohen, *Rulers of Empire: The French Colonial Service in Africa*, Stanford: Hoover Institution Press, Stanford University, 1971.

44. Allégret, 'Rapport confidentiel', 221.

45. For an account of the postwar context for the civilising mission see Ageron, *France coloniale*. The scope of this narrative permits Ageron to position specific developments within the longer trajectory of French colonialism yet his work is usefully complemented by more focused studies; for an assessment of responses to the War in the context of French West Africa see the later chapters of Alice L. Conklin, *A Mission to Civilize: The Republican Idea of Empire in France and West Africa, 1895-1939*, Stanford: Stanford University Press, 1997.

46. For Sarraut's view of his context see the 'Avant-Propos' and 'Introduction': Albert Sarraut, *La Mise en valeur des colonies françaises*, Paris: Payot, 1923, 15-33 and esp. 26ff. (This work is the *Projet de loi* published as a book.)

47. Ibid. 83.

48. Ibid. 88, emphasis retained. For a discussion of this view of indigenous peoples as a resource see Nicolas Bancel and Pascal Blanchard, 'Civiliser: L'invention de l'indigène' in *Culture coloniale: La France conquise par son Empire, 1871-1931*, ed. Pascal Blanchard and Sandrine Lemaire, Paris: Éditions Autrement – collection Mémoires 2003, 149-61.

49. Sarraut, *La Mise en valeur*, 88, emphasis retained.

50. For the debate over the virtues of association see Raymond, F. Betts, *Assimilation and Association in French Colonial Theory, 1890-1914*, New York: Columbia University Press, 1961. See also Todorov, *On Human Diversity*.

51. Sarraut, *La Mise en valeur*, 88, emphasis retained.

52. Ibid. 89. In a similar fashion it should be made clear that Sarraut's project for the *mise en valeur* drew on a range of sources. The immediate one was the programme of his predecessor Henri Simon: see ibid. 26. The postwar project of development should thus be seen as one further stage in the longer process of colonisation: see the trajectory sketched in Conklin, *A Mission*, esp. 23-72.

53. Sarraut, *La Mise en valeur*, 99ff. In theory the three *départements* of Algeria were under the same laws as metropolitan France but in practice only European settlers enjoyed full citizenship. Inhabitants of the four *Communes* of Senegal could vote and were under French jurisdiction but the majority remained Muslim and used Muslim courts.

54. Sarraut, *Grandeur et servitude coloniales*, 121.

55. For a discussion of the contradictions between the discourse of equality and the profoundly unequal relations of colonialism see Bancel and Blanchard, 'Civiliser'.

56. Both works are included in Olympe de Gouges, *Œuvres*, Paris: Mercure de France, 1986.

57. For possessive individualism see C. B. MacPherson, *The Political Theory of Possessive Individualism: Hobbes to Locke*, Oxford: Clarendon Press, 1962, and for the possessive market society 47ff.

58. Allégret, 'The Missionary Question', 164.

59. Ibid. 168. The formulation is again derived from Sarraut: see Ageron, *France coloniale*, 228.

60. Allégret, 1919, 221, emphasis added.

61. This is the characterisation in Shearer West, *Portraiture*, Oxford and New York: Oxford University Press, 2004, 21. Similar definitions are starting points in other synoptic works: see for example Richard Brilliant, *Portraiture*, London: Reaktion, 1991, 23-44 and Joanna Woodall, ed. *Portraiture: Facing the Subject*, Manchester and New York: Manchester University Press, 1997, 1-23.

62. Summers, *Real Spaces*, 257, for a broad definition of the term "sightlike". My account here is intended only as a statement of the issues; for an elaboration see ibid, 431-547.

63. Ibid. 29.

64. Ibid. 30.

65. Ibid. 323, with reference to Aristotle's *De memoria*.

66. Ibid. 29, 30.

67. Ibid. 575.

68. Ibid.

69. Ibid.

70. Ulrich Thieme and Curtis Becker, ed. *Allgemeines Lexikon der Bildenden Künstler*, *33*, Leipzig: Veb E. A. Seemann, no date, 182.

71. Gide-Allégret, *L'Enfance de l'Art*, 124-125. The anxiety is noted in the same letter where Gide responds to Allégret's moralising.

72. Philippe Peltier, 'From Oceania', in *"Primitivism" in 20th Century Art: Affinity of the Tribal and Modern*, ed. William Rubin, New York: Museum of Modern Art, 1984, 99-123, 105.

73. Paul Gauguin, *Lettres de Paul Gauguin à Émile Bernard*, Geneva: Pierre Cailler, 1954, 73.

74. For the role of such imagery in relation to histories of modernism see Christian F. Feest, 'From North America' and Jean-Louis Paudrat, 'From Africa', in *"Primitivism" in 20th Century Art: Affinity of the Tribal and Modern*, ed. William Rubin, New York: Museum of Modern Art, 1984, 85-97 and 125-175, as well as Peltier, 'From Oceania'. For an overview of the role of these villages in constructions of the "primitive" see Pascal Blanchard, Gilles Boëtsch and Nanette Jacomijn Snoep, ed, *Human Zoos: The Invention of the Savage*, Paris and Arles: Musée du quai Branly and Actes Sud, 2011.

75. Summers, *Real Spaces*, 28–36 and 624–627. This account of formalism is engaged with Kant's *Critique of Judgement* and as Summers notes, "the issues Kant treated have been foundational, and still have broad intellectual and even popular currency", 624.

76. On the early modern development of the distinction between arts and sciences, with the latter elucidated as 'epistemologically superior' see Michel de Certeau, *The Practice of Everyday Life*, trans. by Steven Rendall, Berkeley, Los Angeles and London: University of California Press, 1984, 64–68, 67.

77. Summers, *Real Spaces*, 624, 625.

78. Ibid. 625.

79. Ibid. emphasis retained.

80. Ibid.

81. Whilst the formalist position derived from this has the potential to embrace "the productions of all cultures" it has also "demanded that all art be addressed and understood in the ways European philosophy and criticism had come to think art should be addressed and understood". Ibid. 34.

82. This is a necessarily brief summary of the most sustained attempt to review European art history without reproducing its governing principles. Yet the arguments presented in *Real Spaces* should be seen as part of a larger arc tracing the relationship between naturalism and aesthetics: see David Summers, *The Judgement of Sense: Renaissance Naturalism and the Rise of Aesthetics*, Cambridge: Cambridge University Press, 1987 and *Vision, Reflection, and Desire in Western Painting*, Chapel Hill: The University of North Carolina Press, 2007.

83. Sarraut, *La Mise en valeur*, 88.

84. See for example the commentary on the village in the issue of *Le Monde illustré* which carried Tinayre's image: G. Lenôtre, 'Courrier de l'exposition', *Le Monde illustré*, 1687, 27 July 1889, 51.

85. For the conformity of the photographic image to earlier pictorial precedents see Joel Snyder, 'Picturing Vision', *Critical Inquiry*, 6: 3, 1980, 499–526.

86. For the first debates over the status of photography in France see André Rouillé, ed. *La Photographie en France: Textes et controversies, une anthologie 1816–1871*, Paris: Macula, 1989. For important discussions of photography and art see Steve Edwards, *The Making of English Photography: Allegories*, University Park, Pennsylvania: The Pennsylvania University Press, 2006.

87. For a view of competing photographic processes see Ian Jeffrey, *ReVisions: An Alternative History of Photography*, Bradford: National Museum of Photography, Film and Television, 1999. For the transition to large-scale industry see Marx, *Capital*, 461–491.

88. See Mark Haworth-Booth, Anne McCauley and Heidi Humphrey, *The Museum and the Photograph: Collecting Photography at the Victoria & Albert Museum, 1853–1900*, Williamstown, Mass. Sterling and Francine Clark Art Institute, 1998.

89. This view of photography is that given in the report for the Exposition universelle. See Alfred Picard, *Exposition universelle internationale de 1889 à Paris: Rapport général: Tome IV: Les beaux-arts, l'éducation, l'enseignement, les arts libéraux*, Paris: Imprimerie nationale, 1891, 473. For a commentary on such views see Allan Sekula, 'The Traffic in Photographs', *Art Journal*, 41: 1, Spring 1981, 15–25, 17.

90. For discussions of the difficulties in classifying photography see Edwards, *The Making of English Photography*, esp.165–203.

91. Picard, *Exposition universelle*, 473–492.

92. Lenôtre, 'Courrier de l'exposition', 51.

93. Idid.

94. Ibid.

95. This will be clear from even a cursory glance at the images assembled in Blanchard, Boëtsch and Snoep, *Human Zoos*.

96. Georg Wilhelm Friedrich Hegel, *Aesthetics: Lectures on Fine Art, I*, trans. by T. M. Knox, Oxford: Clarendon Press, 2010, 505–506.

97. Ibid. 435. See also Charles Taylor, *Hegel*, Cambridge: Cambridge University Press, 1975, 478–479 on the relationship of art and Incarnation.

98. Hegel, *Aesthetics*, 531, emphasis retained.

99. Ibid. 532.

100. Ibid. 519. Here Hegel refers back to the passage at 435. Deleuze and Guattari make different arguments to arrive at the conclusion: "The face is not universal. It is not even the white man; it is the White Man himself, with his broad white cheeks and the black holes of his eyes. The face is Christ. The face is the typical European". Gilles Deleuze and Félix Guattari, *A Thousand Plateaus: Capitalism and Schizophrenia*, trans. by Brian Massumi, London and New York: Continuum, 1987, 196.

101. For this process see Philippe Descola, *Beyond Nature and Culture*, trans. by Janet Lloyd, Chicago and London: University of Chicago Press, 2013. For one overview of the implications of the Incarnation for European modes of representation see Michael Houseman, 'La chair est image: Europe occidentale', in *Qu'est-ce qu'un corps?*, ed. Stéphane Breton, Paris: Flammarion, 2006, 59–80.

102. Georg Wilhelm Friedrich Hegel, *Lectures on the Philosophy of World History: Introduction: Reason in History*, trans. by H. B. Nisbet, Cambridge: Cambridge University Press, 1975, 197.

103. Ibid. 130.

104. Georg Wilhelm Friedrich Hegel, *Phenomenology of Spirit*, trans. by A. V. Miller, Oxford: Clarendon Press, 1977, 458, emphases retained.

105. Ibid. emphases retained.

106. This is precisely the force of the passage from the *Aesthetics* cited above, on God as man, with an actuality which is contrasted with the imagined gods of the classical era: Hegel, *Aesthetics*, 505.

107. Althusser, 'Ideology', 122

108. Ibid. 123.

109. Ibid. emphasis retained.

110. Ibid.

111. Ibid.

112. Hegel, *Lectures*, 197.

113. Ibid.

114. Ibid. 190.

115. Many involved in colonial encounters subscribed to views similar to those set down by Hegel, yet there is no necessary connection between Christian beliefs and developmental schemata. Prompted by the conquest of the Americas, Bartolomé de Las Casas developed the contrary argument, that "barbarians" are created in God's image and so are not forsaken. See Bartolomé de las Casas, *In Defense of the Indians*, trans. by Stafford Poole, DeKalb: Northern Illinois University Press, 1992, 39.

116. Summers, *Real Spaces*, 625.

117. This is implicit in the account of portrayal in Michael Podro, *Depiction*, New Haven and London: Yale University Press, 1998, 87–106.

2. Perception, apperception and disavowal: André Gide and Marc Allégret in the Congo

1. André Gide, *Souvenirs et voyages*, ed. Pierre Masson, with Daniel Durosay and Martine Sagaert, Paris: NRF, Bibliothèque de la Pléiade, Gallimard, 2001, 331. My quotations are from this critical edition rather than from the illustrated volume.

2. Ibid. 1218.

3. Léon Blum, 'Aux colonies: *Voyage au Congo*', *Le Populaire*, 5 July 1927, in 'Le Problème du colonialisme', *L'Œuvre de Léon Blum, 1914–1928, III: i*, Paris: Éditions Albin Michel, 1972, 480–490, 486. It is important to maintain some equivocation here. Too much commentary on Gide's text has begun by ascribing a role to the author as either an attacker or defender of colonialism and this has had the effect of flattening his account of his perceptions. For example, this is a limitation of Albert Sonnenfeld, 'André Gide's Congo Journals: A Reappraisal', *L'Esprit créateur*, 1: 1, Spring 1961, 21–28, and remains so for Phyllis Clark, 'Gide's Africa', *South Central Review*, 14: 1, Spring 1997, 56–73.

4. Roland Barthes, 'Notes sur André Gide et son «Journal»', in *Œuvres complètes, 1, 1942–1965*, ed. Éric Marty, Paris: Éditions du Seuil, 1993, 23–33, 23. This essay is amongst Barthes' first published works; he remained deeply attached to the themes sketched here and returned to them in his last writings. See Roland Barthes, *Roland Barthes*, trans. by Richard Howard, New York: Hill and Wang, 1977, 95 and Roland Barthes, *The Preparation of the Novel: Lecture Courses and Seminars at the Collège de France (1978–79 and 1979–80)*, ed. Nathalie Léger, trans. by Kate Briggs, New York: Columbia University Press, 2011, 209. Taken together these texts form one of the most subtle accounts of Gide's work.

5. The scale of the œuvre may be judged from the fact that the bibliography of Gide's writings extends to 544 pages: see Jacques Cotnam, *Bibliographie chronologique de l'Œuvre d'André Gide (1889–1973)*, Boston, Mass.: G. K. Hall & Co., 1974. This work must be supplemented by Arnold Naville, *Bibliographie des écrits de André Gide*, Paris: Guy Le Prat, 1952, which supplies greater detail on individual publications, including print runs.

6. André Gide, *Journal: I: 1887–1925*, ed. Éric Marty, Paris: NRF, Bibliothèque de la Pléiade, Gallimard, 1996 and *Journal: II: 1926–1950*, ed. Martine Sagaert, Paris: NRF, Bibliothèque de la Pléiade, Gallimard, 2001. Henceforth *Journal* will designate this critical edition. The scrupulous work of Pierre Masson, Éric Marty, Daniel Durosay and Martine Sagaert in establishing the edition makes it the point of departure for any account of Gide's work. For the genesis of the *Journal* see Marty's 'Notice' in Gide, *Journal: I*, 1297–1317.

7. See Jean Delay, *La Jeunesse d'André Gide: I, André Gide avant André Walter, 1869–1890*, Paris: Gallimard, 1956, 543.

8. Naville, *Bibliographie*, 37.

9. Delay, *Jeunesse*, 572.

10. Alan Sheridan, *André Gide: A Life in the Present*, London: Hamish Hamilton, 1998, 143–47.

11. On *Les Faux-Monnayeurs* as Gide's "true" novel and for a broader discussion of Gide's genres, see C. D. E. Tolton, *André Gide and the Art of Autobiography: A Study of Si le Grain ne meurt*, Toronto: The Macmillan Company of Canada Ltd., 1975, 4–22.

12. Barthes, *Preparation of the Novel*, 209.

13. Barthes, 'Notes', 23–4.

14. Barthes, 'Notes', 25. See also Delay, *Jeunesse*, 56.

15. Barthes, 'Notes', 25.

16. Ibid.

17. Gide, *Journal: I*, 490.

18. Barthes, 'Notes', 24.

19. Ibid. 27.

20.   Gide, *Souvenirs*, 333.
21.   Ibid.
22.   Gide-Allégret, *Enfance*, 77. The influence of Élie Allégret on Gide is explored in Daniel Durosay's introduction to Marc Allégret, *Carnets du Congo: Voyage avec André Gide*, ed. Daniel Durosay, text established by Claudia Rabel-Jullien, Paris: CNRS Éditions, 1993.
23.   Gide, *Souvenirs*, 333.
24.   Ibid.
25.   Ibid.
26.   Joseph Conrad, 'Geography and Some Explorers', in *Tales of Hearsay and Last Essays*, London: J. M. Dent & Sons Ltd., 1926, 10–17, 2
27.   Ibid. 15.
28.   Ibid. 3
29.   Ibid. 6 and 3.
30.   Gide, *Journal: I*, 1259.
31.   Ibid. 149. For discussions of this passage see Delay, *Jeunesse*, 12 and 290.
32.   André Gide, *Les Cahiers et les Poésies d'André Walter*, ed. Claude Martin, Paris: NRF, Gallimard, 1986 and Gide, *Journal: I*, 51 and 59: an editorial note draws out the similarity, ibid. 243.
33.   See Barthes, 'Notes', 30, where he offers numerous citations in suport of this. See also Jacques Lacan, 'The Youth of Gide, or the Letter and Desire', in *Écrits*, trans. Bruce Fink, New York and London: W.W. Norton & Company, 2006, 623–644.
34.   Barthes, *Preparation of the Novel*, 209.
35.   Barthes, 'Notes', 26.
36.   Barthes, *Preparation of the Novel*, 44.
37.   Gide, *Journal: I*, 1269.
38.   Ibid. 1296. Something of this is adumbrated in Gide, *Les Cahiers*, 44.
39.   Gide, *Journal: I*, 1271.
40.   Ibid. 1271, emphasis retained. For the role of such reflections in Gide's project see Pierre Masson's 'Introduction' in Gide, *Souvenirs*, xi–xxxv.
41.   Gide, *Journal: I*, 1271.
42.   Ibid. The relationship between the entries is underlined by repeated reference to Keats' *Letters*, as Marty notes ibid. 1736.
43.   André Gide, *Les Faux-Monnayeurs*, Paris: Gallimard, 1963, 93 and 127.
44.   André Gide, *Journal des Faux-Monnayeurs*, Paris: Gallimard, 1967, 68. Steven Nelson also discusses this passage in relation to *Voyage au Congo*, although he reaches different conclusions to mine: see Nelson, *From Cameroon to Paris*, 84.
45.   Gide, *Journal des Faux-Monnayeurs*, 86–87.
46.   Ibid. 107.
47.   Barthes, 'Notes', 24.
48.   Gide, *Journal des Faux-Monnayeurs*, 107.
49.   André Gide, *Les Nourritures terrestres*, Paris: Gallimard, 1935, 21–22.
50.   Ibid. 185.
51.   Ibid. 41.
52.   Ibid 125. See also Delay, *Jeunesse*, 245–7.
53.   Gide, *Souvenirs*, 268. As with many of Gide's works, *Si le grain ne meurt* has a complex publication history. Gide was working on an edition in October 1924, at the moment he made his journal entry about being an adventurer: see Gide, *Journal: I*, 1258–1259. For the publication history see Gide, *Souvenirs*, 1093–1116.
54.   Gide, *Souvenirs*, 269.
55.   Ibid.

56. Ibid. 309–310. This passage has generated considerable discussion. For insightful analyses see Michael Lucey, *Gide's Bent: Sexuality, Politics, Writing*, New York and Oxford: Oxford University Press, 1995, 32–37 and Naomi Segal, *André Gide: Pedarasty and Pedagogy*, Oxford: Clarendon 1998, 43–46 and 82–86.

57. Gide, *Souvenirs*, 309–310.

58. Ibid. 309.

59. Ibid. 310.

60. Ibid. 311, ellipsis added.

61. Ibid. 312.

62. See Delay, *Jeunesse*, 425–6.

63. See ibid. 394–6 and 424–6. For Gide's attempts at absolution in the late *Carnets d'Égypte*, see Joseph Allen Boone, *The Homoerotics of Orientalism*, Columbia University Press: New York and Chichester, 2014, 224–9.

64. Gide, *Journal: I*, 1217.

65. Barthes, *Roland Barthes*, 69.

66. Ibid.

67. Barthes further reflects: "Am I not justified in considering everything I have written as a clandestine and stubborn effort to bring to light again, someday, quite freely, the theme of the Gidean 'journal'?" Ibid, 95.

68. Robert Aldrich, *Colonialism and Homosexuality*, London and New York: Routledge 2003, 342. For properly cautious comments on the relation of Gide's sexuality and his writing see Segal, *André Gide*, 45–6.

69. The photographic archive is held at the Mediathèque de l'Architecture et du Patrimoine. Some of the material has been digitised and is available at: http://www.mediatheque-patrimoine.culture.gouv.fr/pages/bases/memoire_cible.html (last accessed 14 September 2019). The size of the holdings was confirmed by the archivist, Matthieu Rivallin (personal communication, June 2013).

70. This is the version held by the British Film Institute, London (BFI 8.067 405 A A).

71. These writings are dispersed. Some notebooks are held at the Bienecke Rare Books and Manuscript Library of Yale University: Marc Allégret Papers: GEN MSS 651. The personal journal has been published with the 'Note' as an appendix: Allégret, *Carnets*.

72. Allégret indeed speculated that a thesis could be written as a partial fulfilment of his course at the École Libre des Sciences Politiques: André Gide and Marc Allégret, *Correspondance avec Marc Allégret 1917–1949: Cahiers André Gide 19*, ed. Claude Martin and Pierre Masson, Paris: NRF, Gallimard, 2005, 601.

73. See for example Marc Allégret, 'Sous le soleil des tropiques: En Afrique Équatoriale Française chez les enfants Massas', *Le Monde Colonial Illustré*, 45, May 1927, 107.

74. Allégret was in contact with the editors of various publications, not just in France but also in Germany, Austria, the United Kingdom and the United States. See Marc Allégret Papers: Bienecke, GEN MSS 651: Box 9: Folder 95: Voyage au Congo: Correspondence.

75. Gide, *Souvenirs*, 335.

76. For Allégret's contacts at this point and his appointments with Man Ray, see his diary for 1925: Marc Allégret Papers: Bienecke, GEN MSS 651: Box 10: Folder 114: Voyage au Congo: Notes and Notebooks 8 of 8.

77. See the holdings in the archives of the Service protestant de mission Défap. Some of the images are available online: http://digitallibrary.usc.edu/cdm/search/searchterm/Allegret (last accessed 7 July 2019).

78. Gide, *Souvenirs*, 333.

79. Gide, *Journal: I*, 1283–84.

80. Joseph Conrad, *Heart of Darkness and Other Tales*, Oxford: Oxford World's Classics, 1998, 151.

81. Ibid, 151.

82.   Gide, *Souvenirs*, 334.

83.   Ibid. 334–335.

84.   Ibid. 339.

85.   Ibid. 339.

86.   For one example involving Élie Allégret, see anon. 'Cameroun, dernières nouvelles', *Journal de la Société des Missions Évangéliques de Paris*, 1918, reprinted in Loumpet-Galitzine, *Njoya*, 219–221. For an example from the New Testament, see the narrative of Paul's sea journey (Acts 27: 9–44).

87.   Gide, *Souvenirs*, 342.

88.   Ibid. 342.

89.   See Alfred Chaumel, 'Une Mission de propagande par le film en Afrique Équatoriale Française', *Bulletin de la Société des recherches congoliases*, 5, 1924, 11–15.

90.   Gide, *Souvenirs*, 342.

91.   Ibid, 342–343. Durosay notes that the ms. has Chaumel named as the interlocutor: ibid, 1222.

92.   Ibid, 343.

93.   Ibid.

94.   Ibid. Here I am following the conventions of the 1929 translation by Dorothy Bussy, in rendering "le blanc" as "the white man". Gide's use of the terms "white" and "black" is typical of the period and problematic but cannot be expunged.

95.   Gide, *Souvenirs*, 344.

96.   Ibid.

97.   Ibid.

98.   Ibid.

99.   Ibid.

100.   Ibid. 345.

101.   Ibid. Footnotes are used sparingly in the journal but with sufficient frequency to underline the complex processes of editing involved in its production.

102.   Ibid. 345–346.

103.   For Gide as lepidopterist, see ibid. 335, 341.

104.   One might compare Gide's disposition here with the view of Édouard in *Les Faux-Monnayeurs*: "By localising and specifying one restricts." Gide, *Les Faux-Monnayeurs*, 238.

105.   Gide, *Souvenirs*, 353, emphasis retained.

106.   Ibid. 368.

107.   On this formula as an initial response see Marja Warehime, 'Exploring Connections and Rediscovering Difference: Gide *au Congo*', *The French Review*, 68: 3, February 1995, 457–465, 462.

108.   See Banta and Hinsley, *From Site to Sight*, and for the matching of photography to the traits of a culture, 108–110.

109.   Gide, *Souvenirs*, 389.

110.   Ibid.

111.   Ibid.

112.   Ibid. 371.

113.   Ibid. 393.

114.   Ibid. 394.

115.   Ibid. 396–397.

116.   Ibid. 398–399.

117.   Ibid. The most detailed account of the context for these events is to be found in Daniel Maleyasse, 'En marge du "Voyage au Congo" d'André Gide: l'affaire Pacha, 1925–1932',

Mémoire de maîtrise, Université de Bangui, 1987-1988. This draws on the relevant holdings of the Archives nationales d'Outre-Mer (AF ANOM, AEF, Série 5D60).

118. Gide, *Souvenirs*, 400. Gide repeated this formulation in a letter to the interim governor, Mateo Alfassa: this is reprinted ibid. 657-661.

119. Ibid. 401.

120. Ibid.

121. Ibid.

122. Ibid. 402.

123. Gide and Allégret, *Correspondance*, 106.

124. Gide, *Souvenirs*, 402.

125. Ibid. 398.

126. Two minor exceptions would be encounters with "the 'young Mélèze'" and with the sultan of Rafaï: ibid. 359 and 377-378. In these accounts, however, no direct speech is reported.

127. Ibid. 368.

128. See for example the entries for 31 October and 1 November: ibid. 403, 405, 406.

129. Ibid. 406.

130. Ibid. 407.

131. Levinas, *Totality and Infinity*, 39, emphasis retained.

132. Ibid. 40.

133. Ibid. 43.

134. Ibid. 66.

135. Ibid. 40, emphasis retained.

136. Ibid. 43.

137. That this photograph is a representation of an encounter rather than the encounter itself is of course significant. An image of a face is not a face and one does not sustain the same ethical relations with images as with faces: for an account of this see ibid. 294-298.

138. Gide, *Souvenirs*, 407, emphasis retained.

139. Ibid. 408.

140. Ibid.

141. Ibid. 412.

142. Ibid. 414 and 417-419.

143. Ibid. 420.

144. Ibid. 421.

145. Ibid. 343.

146. Ibid. 421.

147. Ibid. 419.

148. Ibid. 423. There are echoes of *Heart of Darkness* here, of the journey through the forest as "travelling in the night of first ages": Conrad, *Heart of Darkness*, 186.

149. Gide, *Souvenirs*, 423-424.

150. Ibid. 424.

151. Ibid. 425.

152. Ibid. 425-426.

153. Ibid. 447, ellipsis retained.

154. Ibid. 448.

155. Ibid. 449.

156. Ibid. 310.

157. Ibid. 449.

158. Ibid. 453.

159. That this is a climax of the first volume is registered by a number of commentators. See for example Warehime, 'Exploring', 463; Clark, 'Gide's Africa', 71.

160. Homi Bhabha, 'Of Mimicry and Man: The Ambivalence of Colonial Discourse', *October*, 28, Spring 1984, 125–33, 126.

161. Gide, *Souvenirs*, 454–455.

162. Levinas, *Totality and Infinity*, 38, 39.

163. Gide, *Souvenirs*, 454.

164. Ibid. 455.

165. Ibid.

166. Gide, *Les Faux-Monnayeurs*, 12–16. The absence of the conventional devices of the novel is commented on in Barthes, 'Notes', 32.

167. Gide, *Souvenirs*, 363.

168. It should be conceded that Gide was often vague in describing the physical appearance of individuals: see Delay, *Jeunesse*, 30. However, there is precision in his psychological portraits and these are also absent from *Voyage au Congo*.

169. There is perhaps one small exception. Gide gives a tip to the pilot of the *Léon-Blot* and as it is unexpected "his face, which had been sullen, lit up. I joked with him about his gloomy looks and he began to laugh". Gide, *Souvenirs*, 487.

170. André Gide, 'Voyage au Congo', *La Nouvelle Revue Française*, 28: 162, January-June 1927, 320–361.

171. Ibid. 332.

172. Ibid.

173. Again, there is an exception. Gide makes a cruel report of a moment in the Sambry trial when witnesses are invited to take the oath and "they repeat stupidly: 'Say: I swear', much to the amusement of the audience". Gide, *Souvenirs*, 344.

174. One set of proofs has the appendix at the end of chapter 5 and another at the end of chapter 7, that is, as an appendix to the entire volume. This latter set anticipates a printing in April 1927 whereas the first edition was in fact printed on 11 June 1927, the delay presumably the result of the deletions and a subsequent resetting. See André Gide: *Voyage au Congo*, proofs, corrected, 1927, Marc Allégret Papers: Bienecke, GEN MSS 651, Box 13: Folders 138 and 139. The only remnant of the appendix is the rueful conclusion, which is incorporated into a note accompanying the account of Pacha's activities: see Gide, *Souvenirs*, 400.

175. The campaign may be followed through Gide's subsequent journals: see Gide, *Journals: II*. For a concise account of the campaign see Durosay's 'Notice' in Gide, *Souvenirs*, 1194–211.

176. This is to register a continuity in Gide's writing. Much has been made of the change wrought in Gide by the African journey, and his transition from personal concerns to "commitment". See for example Jacqueline M. Chadourne, *André Gide et l'Afrique: Le role de l'Afrique dans la vie et l'oeuvre de l'écrivain*, Paris: A. G. Nizet, 1968. For some reflections on this see Lucey, *Gide's Bent*, 145. For a nuanced account of the place of *Voyage au Congo* see Masson's introduction in Gide, *Souvenirs*, xi-xxxv.

177. Gide, *Souvenirs*, 661. The appendices to *Le Retour du Tchad* contain this letter and other relevant correspondence: ibid, 1287–96.

178. Blum, 'Aux colonies', 485.

179. Ibid. 485–486.

180. Ibid. 486.

181. Ibid. 489.

182. Ibid. 489.

183. Ibid. 489.

184. Ibid. 484.

185. Ibid. 484.

186. Ibid. 485.

187. Léon Blum, 'L'Idéal socialiste', *Revue de Paris*, 1 May 1924, in *L'Œuvre de Léon Blum, 1914-1928, III: i*, Paris: Éditions Albin Michel, 1972, 347–362, 354.

188. Ibid. 355.
189. Léon Blum, 'Bolchevisme et socialisme', *Le Populaire*, 17, 19, 20, 21, 22 and 25 March 1927, in *L'Œuvre de Léon Blum, 1914–1928, III: i*, Paris: Éditions Albin Michel 1972, 451–460.
190. Ibid. 459.
191. Blum, 'Aux colonies', 483.
192. Gide and Allégret, *Correspondance*, 658.
193. Anon. 'Nouelle interpelle sur le recrutement de la main-d'œuvre indigène en Afrique Occidentale', *Le Populaire*, 8 July 1927, 2.
194. Gide, *Souvenirs*, 675–685. The article originally appeared in *La Revue de Paris*, 15 October 1927.
195. C.L. 'À la Chambre: Le Budget des colonies', *Le Populaire*, 24 November 1927, 2.
196. Ibid.
197. Ibid. Blum also believed in stages of development, which accorded with his own sense of socialist progress: Blum, 'L'Idéal socialiste'.
198. Marie-Louise Sicard, 'Écrivains coloniaux... et d'ailleurs', *Les Annales Coloniales*, 2 May 1928, 1.
199. Ibid.
200. Ibid. ellipsis added.
201. Ibid.
202. Louis Perrier, *Enquête sur les Indigènes*, Montauban: Société des amis des Missions et des indigènes 1909, 3. This volume may be found amongst the papers relating to Allégret's journey. Marc Allégret Papers: Beinecke, GEN MSS 651: Box 9: Folder 98. Voyage au Congo: Notes and Notebooks.
203. Perrier, *Enquête*, 5–10.
204. Allégret, *Carnets*, 267–289.
205. See Gide and Allégret, *Correspondance*, 628–631.
206. Chaumel, 'Mission', 1924, 12.
207. Ibid. 13.
208. For an analysis of the Allégret's film see Durosay's account in Allégret, *Carnets*, 297–306 and for the genesis of the film see Daniel Durosay, 'Images et imaginaire dans le *Voyage au Congo*', *Bulletin des Amis d'André Gide*, 16: 60, October 1988, 9–30. Durosay had access to two versions of the film, the longer of which is 94 minutes; the version held at the BFI is considerably longer, at 114 minutes, and accordingly it is this version which I discuss here.
209. Marc Allégret, dir. *Voyage au Congo: Scènes de la Vie indigène en Afrique Équatoriale*, Les Éditions P. Braunberger, 114 mins., British Film Institute, London (BFI 8.067 405 A A), intertitle, 17.11 mins.
210. Ibid. intertitle, 17.33 mins.
211. This is not to say that the arc was easy to construct. The editing of the film seems to have been difficult. On 21 March 1927 Maria van Rysselberghe attended a private projection of a cut which lasted one hour; she did not find it entirely successful and her opinion was shared by Léon Poirier, the director of the 1926 film about the Citroën African expedition, *La Croisière noire*. See Maria van Rysselberghe, *Les Cahiers de la Petite Dame: Notes pour l'historique authentique d'André Gide, 1918–1929: Cahiers André Gide 4*, Paris: NRF, Gallimard, 1973, 306–307.
212. Allégret, *Voyage*, intertitle, 43.14 mins.
213. Gide and Allégret, *Correspondance*, 625.
214. Allégret, *Voyage*, intertitle, 96.06 mins.
215. Ibid. intertitles, 105 mins., ellipsis retained.
216. Ibid. intertitle, 107.09 mins.
217. Durosay notes the various elisions which help to constitute this arc, without registering their purpose: see his introduction in Allégret, *Carnets*, 51.
218. Conrad, *Heart of Darkness*, 252.

219.   Ibid. 252 and 138.

220.   See Durosay, 'Image', 19–20.

221.   Daniel Couve, letter to Marc Allégret, 23 June 1927, Marc Allégret Papers: Bienecke, GEN MSS 651, Box 9: Folder 96: Voyage au Congo: Correspondence 2 of 2.

222.   Marc Allégret, letter to Daniel Muller, 22 June 1927, Marc Allégret Papers: Bienecke, GEN MSS 651, Box 9: Folder 96: Voyage au Congo: Correspondence 2 of 2.

223.   Ibid.

224.   Ibid.

225.   Daniel Couve, letter to Marc Allégret, 23 June 1927.

226.   Ibid.

227.   Ibid.

228.   Marc Allégret, letter to Daniel Couve, 26 June 1927, Marc Allégret Papers: Bienecke, GEN MSS 651, Box 9: Folder 96: Voyage au Congo: Correspondence 2 of 2.

229.   Gide and Allégret, *Correspondance*, 602.

230.   Daniel Couve, letter to Marc Allégret, 28 June 1927, Marc Allégret Papers: Bienecke, GEN MSS 651, Box 9: Folder 96: Voyage au Congo: Correspondence 2 of 2.

231.   André Muller, letter to Marc Allégret, 1 July 1927, Marc Allégret Papers: Bienecke, GEN MSS 651, Box 9: Folder 96: Voyage au Congo: Correspondence 2 of 2.

232.   Ibid.

233.   Ibid.

234.   The charges of immorality were not only levelled at the film. The display of Allégret's photographs in a bookshop window provoked a response from the Ligue pour la relèvement de la moralité publique. See the unsigned letters to the press of July 1927 in Marc Allégret papers Box 9: Folder 96: Voyage au Congo: Correspondence 2 of 2.

235.   André Gide, 'Conférence de Bruxelles', *Bulletin des Amis d'André Gide*, 16: 60, October 1988, 31–36, 32.

236.   Ibid.

237.   Ibid.

238.   Ibid. 33.

239.   Gide, *Souvenirs*, 345.

240.   Gide, 'Conférence', 34.

241.   Ibid. 34–35.

242.   Ibid. 35.

243.   The Brussels screening was held on 22 May. Gide had finished correcting the proofs of the illustrated edition on 10 May, at least according to a letter of that date to Martin du Gard. See André Gide and Roger Martin du Gard, *Correspondance: I*, Paris: NRF, Gallimard, 1968, 342–343. However, an entry in his journal for 9 June 1928 show he was still working on the proofs: Gide, *Journal: II*, 82. Gide's positive reception of the illustrated edition as the result of collaboration with Allégret is noted in Van Rysselberghe, *Cahiers*, 17.

244.   For this definition see Cynthia Freeland, *Portraits and Persons: A Philosophical Inquiry*, Oxford: Oxford University Press, 2010, 17.

245.   Summers, *Real Spaces*, 625, emphasis retained.

246.   Anon. 'Strange "Beauty Culture": Face Scars; Distended Lips and Ears', *The Illustrated London News*, 951, 26 November 1927, np.

247.   Compare this image with those of Christian converts in the archives of the Service protestant de mission Défap, and in particular with those included in the "album gris" compiled by Élie Allégret and his wife Suzanne in Gabon. See https://defap-bibliotheque.fr/ressources/images/galerie-photos-par-pays/ (last accessed 14 September 2019).

248.   The photograph is cropped and the original reveals that the background is the wall of a brick building over which torn sheeting has been hung to make the poorly improvised

backdrop. See No. 69L00254 in the Marc Allégret holdings of the Médiathèque de l'Architecture et du Patrimoine.

249. Marc Allégret, untitled inventory, undated: Marc Allégret Papers: Bienecke, GEN MSS 651, Box 9: Folder 97: Voyage au Congo: Notes and Notebooks 1 of 10.
250. Allégret, letter to Muller, 22 June 1927.
251. Allégret, letter to Couve, 26 June 1927.
252. The Allégret family was Calvinist but the missionaries of the Société came from a range of Protestant denominations and were quite prepared to collaborate. See Michael Bangert, 'Phenomenon of a Threshold Period' and 'The BM and its International Network', in *Mission Possible? The Basel Mission Collection: Reflecting Cultural Encounters*, ed. Anna Schmid and Kathrin Fischer, Basel: Christoph Merian Verlag and Museum der Kulturen Basel 2015, 19–33 and 34–38.
253. Allégret, untitled inventory.
254. Allégret, *Carnets*, 173–175.
255. Ibid. 175.

3. Staging, actors and audiences: *The Exposition coloniale internationale* in Paris

1. Lenôtre, 'Courrier', 51.
2. G.A. [Georges Altman], 'Images d'exposition et chronique coloniale', *Monde*, 164, 25 July 1931, 12.
3. Sarraut, *La Mise en valeur*, 88.
4. Max Deauville, 'Un peu d'Humour... Exposition des blancs chez les noirs', *Le Journal de l'Exposition coloniale*, June 1931, 3.
5. See Boittin, *Colonial Metropolis*, 9–10 for the comparisons, and Elizabeth Ezra, *The Colonial Unconscious: Race and Culture in Interwar France*, Cornell University Press, Ithaca and London, 2000, 19 for Baker as Queen.
6. Robert Artus, 'Ce que nous dit le Maréchal Lyautey', *Le Journal de l'Exposition coloniale*, June 1931, 1.
7. Ibid.
8. There is now a very extensive literature dedicated to the colonial exhibitions. The first scholar to make effective use of the principal archive for the *Exposition coloniale* was Hermann Lebovics: see *True France: The Wars over Cultural Identity, 1900-1945*, Ithaca and London: Cornell University Press, 1992. There are two monographs dedicated to the exhibition: Patricia A. Morton, *Hybrid Modernities: Architecture and Representation at the 1931 Colonial Exhibition, Paris*, Cambridge, Mass. and London: MIT Press, 2000 and Catherine Hodeir and Michel Pierre, *L'Exposition coloniale de 1931*, Brussels: André Versaille, 2011. For an extremely important view of the exhibition in its broader context see Benoît de L'Estoile, *Le Gout des Autres: De l'Exposition coloniale aux Arts premiers*, Paris: Flammarion, 2007. For the alternative perspective of those exhibited see the authoritative collection: Pascal Blanchard, Nicolas Bancel, Gilles Boëtsch, Éric Deroo and Sandrine Lemaire, ed. *Zoo humains et exhibitions coloniales: 150 ans d'invention de l'Autre*, Paris: La Découverte, 2011. For the broader context see Laure Blévis, Hélène Lafont-Couturier, Nanette Jacomijn Snoep and Claire Zalc, ed. *1931: Les étrangers au temps de l'Exposition coloniale*, Paris: Gallimard and Cité nationale de l'histoire de l'immigration, 2008.
9. Hubert Lyautey, 'Discours prononcé le 5 novembre 1928', AF ANOM, Fonds ministériels: Exposition coloniale: ECI/1 Divers, ellipsis added.

10.   The speech of 5 November was cited at various points during the planning of the exhi-
        bition: see for example anon. 'L'Exposition internationale de 1931 et l'oeuvre coloniale
        française: Schémas de Conférence: Plan développé No. 2', AF ANOM, Fonds ministériels,
        Exposition coloniale: ECI/1 Divers. Lyautey was happy to rehearse his own rhetoric: his
        speech opening the exhibition in 1931 preserved much of that of 1928: see Hubert Lyautey
        'Discours de l'ouverture' in Marcel Olivier, *Exposition coloniale internationale et de pays
        d'outre-mer: Rapport général présenté par le gouverneur général Olivier, délégué général: Tome IV: Vie
        d'exposition*, Paris: Imprimerie nationale, 1934, 374–377.

11.   Lyautey, 'Discours prononcé le 5 novembre 1928', emphasis retained.

12.   Ibid, emphasis retained.

13.   Sarraut, *La Mise en valeur*, 88. For the immediate political context supporting these views
        in 1931 see Pascal Blanchard, 'L'union nationale: la «rencontre» des droits et des gauches à
        travers la presse et autour de l'Exposition de Vincennes', in *Culture coloniale: La France con-
        quise par son Empire, 1871–1931*, ed. Pascal Blanchard and Sandrine Lemaire, Paris: Éditions
        Autrement – collection Mémoires, 2003, 213–231.

14.   For important observations on the *Rapport général* as *a posteriori* rationalisation see De l'Es-
        toile, *Le Goût des Autres*, 40–41.

15.   As the exhibition was an international one – as opposed to the national colonial exhibition
        held in Marseille in 1922 – there were pavilions organised by a number of colonial powers.
        However, here I shall only address the French contributions.

16.   See Alfred Picard, *Exposition universelle internationale de 1889 à Paris: Rapport général: II: Travaux
        de l'Exposition universelle de 1889*, Paris: Imprimerie nationale, 1891.

17.   The idea of an exhibition of the industry of all nations as a test of development is conven-
        tionally attributed to Prince Albert, Prince Consort of Queen Victoria: see anon. 'History
        of the Great Exhibition' in 'The Crystal Palace Exhibition: Illustrated Catalogue', *The Art
        Journal*, Special Issue, 1851, xi-xxvi.

18.   André Bonamy, letter to Hubert Lyautey, Maréchal de France, Commissaire général de
        l'Exposition coloniale internationale, 20 November 1930, AF ANOM, Fonds ministériels,
        Exposition coloniale: ECI/II Togo et Cameroun.

19.   Marx, *Surveys from Exile*, 43.

20.   Marcel Olivier, *Exposition coloniale internationale et de pays d'outre-mer: Rapport général présenté
        par le gouverneur général Olivier, délégué général: Tome V: Les sections coloniales*, Paris: Imprimerie
        nationale, 1933, 1069.

21.   Olivier also refers to Sarraut's work in his introduction to the *Rapport*: see Marcel Olivier,
        *Exposition coloniale internationale et de pays d'outre-mer: Rapport général présenté par le gouverneur
        général Olivier, délégué général: Tome I: Conception and organisation*, Paris: Imprimerie nationale,
        1933, xiii and xvi. The early histories of French colonialism confirm this position: see for
        example Stephen Henry Roberts, *The History of French Colonial Policy: 1870–1925*, London:
        Cass, 1963 (first edition 1928).

22.   Paul Reynaud, 'Discours de l'ouverture', in Olivier, *Rapport général: IV*, 380–385, 383.

23.   Marcel Olivier, 'Avant-propos', in *Le Livre d'or de l'exposition coloniale internationale de 1931*,
        Fédération Française des Anciens Coloniaux, Paris: Librairie ancienne Honoré Campion,
        1931, 11.

24.   Marcel Peyrouton, 'L'Algérie métropole second', in *Le Livre d'or*, 36–38, 37.

25.   Ibid. and Georges Fontagnol, 'L'Algérie à Vincennes', in *Le Livre d'or*, 39–40.

26.   P. Marc-Vincent, 'Cinquante ans d'efforts français en Tunisie', in *Le Livre d'or*, 44–45, 44.

27.   Fanon, *Black Skin*, 110.

28.   Françoise Denoyelle, *La Lumière de Paris: Les Usages de la photographie, 1919–1939*, Paris:
        L'Harmattan, 1997, 73ff.

29.   Ibid. and Françoise Denoyelle, *La Lumière de Paris: La Marché de la photographie, 1919–1939*,
        Paris: L'Harmattan, 1997, 146–156.

30. On this role for newspapers see Benedict Anderson, *Reflections on the Origins and Spread of Nationalism*, London and New York: Verso, 2006, 61ff and 138ff.

31. Paul Reynaud, 'Introduction', in *Le Livre d'or*, 9.

32. Olivier, 'Avant-Propos', 11.

33. Ibid.

34. Ibid.

35. André Demaison, *Exposition coloniale internationale à Paris en 1931: Guide officiel*, Paris: Éditions Mayeux, 1931, 18.

36. Ibid.

37. Ibid. 20.

38. Sarraut, *Grandeur et servitude*, 102.

39. See Durosay, 'Images', 20.

40. Félicien Challaye, 'Discours de M. Challaye', in *Le Congrès national de 1931: Compte-rendu sténographique (23–25 mai 1931)*, Ligue des Droits de l'Homme, Paris: Ligue des Droits de l'Homme, 1931, 288–309, 307.

41. Ibid. 291.

42. Ibid. 296, ellipses retained.

43. Ibid. ellipses retained.

44. Ibid. 308–309, emphasis retained.

45. Maurice Violette, 'Discours de M. Violette', in *Le Congrès national*, 309–324, 313. See Sarraut, *Grandeur et servitude*, 121.

46. Violette, 'Discours', 317.

47. Ibid. 318–319.

48. Anon. 'L'attitude du Parti Communiste et de la C.G.T.U. à propos de l'Exposition Coloniale', 1931, AF ANOM, Fonds ministériels: 3 SLOTFOM, Carton 5, 1. For the colonial policy of the PCF in this period see Jacob Moneta, *La Politique du Parti communiste français dans la question coloniale, 1920–1963*, Paris: François Maspero, 1971, 38–104.

49. Anon. 'L'attitude', 2.

50. The progress of the anti-exhibition may be tracked through the surveillance reports filed in 3 SLOTFOM, Carton 5: see also the separate folder: 'Ligue contre l'Impérialisme'. This small exhibition has generated an extensive literature. A first-hand account is given in André Thirion, *Revolutionaries Without Revolution*, trans. by Joachim Neugroschel, London: Cassell, 1975, 283–290. 3 SLOTFOM, Carton 5 was first used effectively in Lebovics, *True France*, yet see Adam Jolles, *The Curatorial Avant-Garde: Surrealism and Exhibition Practice in France, 1925–1941*, University Park: The Pennsylvania State University Press, 2013, 93–137, for further archival materials and analyses. An extended account is given in Morton, *Hybrid Modernities*, 99–110.

51. Joé, 'Rapport', 20 June 1931, AF ANOM, Fonds ministériels: 3 SLOTFOM, Carton 5. Ligue contre l'Impérialisme. Boittin has plausibly identified 'Joé' as Edmond Thomas Ramananjato: see Boittin, *Colonial Metropolis*, xxvi.

52. This echoed the title of a tract the PCF had circulated: *Le véritable guide de l'Exposition coloniale.*

53. A similar point is made in Morton, *Hybrid Modernities*, 317.

54. G. Faralicq, letter to Directeur général de la Police Municipale, 15 July 1931, AF ANOM, Fonds ministériels: 3 SLOTFOM, Carton 5.

55. Anon. [Nguyên Van Nhi], untitled tract appended to Ministre des Colonies, letter to Résident Supérieur, Commissaire général de l'Exposition coloniale, 20 July 1931, AF ANOM, Fonds Ministériels: 3 SLOTFOM, Carton 5.

56. Ibid.

57. Ibid.

58.   G. A. [Georges Altman] 'A travers les carcasses de l'exposition coloniale', *Monde*, 154, 16 May 1931, 11, ellipses retained.

59.   Ibid. ellipsis retained.

60.   Ibid.

61.   Ibid. ellipsis retained.

62.   G. A. [Georges Altman] 'Images d'exposition', 12.

63.   Ibid.

64.   Jean-Paul Sartre, *Being and Nothingness: An essay on phenomenological ontology*, trans. by Hazel E. Barnes, London and New York: Routledge, 2003, 245, emphases retained.

65.   Ibid. 246, emphases retained.

66.   Ibid. 284.

67.   Challaye, 'Discours', 291.

68.   Léon Werth, 'Croquis d'exposition: Un vieux noir dansait', *Monde*, 169, 29 August 1931, Special number, 3.

69.   Werth, 'Croquis', 3, ellipsis added. This takes up a theme Werth had developed in an article on the displays in the Jardin d'acclimatation published in *La Grande Revue* in 1912.

70.   Gide, *Souvenirs*, 402.

71.   An extract of Werth's book *Cochinchine* was reprinted in *Monde*. See 'Sur la terre d'Annam', *Monde*, 169, 29 August 1931, Special number, 14.

72.   For biographical details see Mouna Mekouar et al. *Roger Parry: Photographies, dessins, mises en pages*, Paris: Gallimard, 2007.

73.   Léon-Paul Fargue, *Banalité: illustré de réogrammes et recherches d'objets de Loris et Parry*, Paris: NRF, Gallimard, 1930.

74.   André Breton, 'Manifeste du surréalisme', in *Manifestes du surréalisme*, Paris: Gallimard, 1979, 13–60, 31.

75.   See Dell, *The Image of the Popular Front*, 32–43.

76.   There is also some diversity in Parry's later work in Tahiti, although here he was certainly prepared to recycle tropes of the exotic. See Tahiti, Musée de Tahiti et des îles, *Roger Parry, 1931: Au-delà du mythe tahitien*, Pirae: Au vent des îles 2006.

77.   For one attack see Diane Richmond, 'Le quartier réservé de Casablanca', *Nos Regards*, 1, May 1928, n.p.

78.   For some discussion see Simon Dell, 'The Difficult Conjunction of 'Worker' and 'Photographer' in France,' in *The Worker Photography Movement (1926–1939): Essays and Documents*, ed. Jorge Ribalta, Madrid: Museo Nacional Centro de Arte Reina Sofia, 2011, 354–362.

79.   Anon. 'Objectif du Congrès', *Congrès International et Intercolonial de la Société Indigène: II*, Paris: École coloniale, 1931, 5. Part of the tone may be attributed to the rather late decision to hold this event. It was not included in the series anticipated in the spring of 1930: see anon. 'Note sur les congrès', 15 May 1930, AF ANOM, Fonds ministériels: Exposition coloniale: ECI/18.

80.   Hubert Lyautey, 'Discours', in *Congrès Internationale: II*, 15–18, 16.

81.   Élie Allégret, 'Rapport général sur l'amélioration des conditions familiales et sociales', in *Congrès Internationale: II*, 143–148.

82.   Paul Hazoumé, 'Amélioration des conditions familiales et sociales en Afrique-Occidentale Française', in *Congrès International et Intercolonial de la Société Indigène: I*, Paris: École coloniale, 1931, 305–314, 314.

83.   Maurice Leenhardt, 'Rapport général sur l'action coloniale et les mentalités indigènes', in *Congrès internationale: II*, 205–209, 208.

4. Performance, appropriation and dispossession: King Ibrahim Njoya and Mosé Yeyap in the Cameroon Grassfields

1. Anon. 'König Nschoya von Bamum mit einer seiner Frauen', *Der evangelischer Heidenbote*, 86: 1, January 1913, 4.

2. For the status of the person of the king see Claude Tardits, *Le Royaume Bamoum*, Paris: Librairie Armand Colin, 1980, 700–760. This monumental work is central to any study of the history of the Bamum.

3. See Christraud M. Geary, *Images from Bamum: German Colonial Photography at the Court of King Njoya: Cameroon, West Africa, 1902-1915*, Washington D.C. and London: National Museum of African Art, Smithsonian Institution Press, 1988, 40.

4. Jean-François Bayart, *The Illusion of Cultural Identity*, trans. by Steven Rendall, Janet Roitman and Jonathan Derrick, London and Paris: Hurst and Company, in association with the Centre d'Etudes et de Recherches Internationales, 2005, 33.

5. Ibid. 107. The reference is to Terence Ranger, 'The Invention of Tradition in Colonial Africa', in *The Invention of Tradition*, ed. Eric Hobsbawm and Terence Ranger, Cambridge: Cambridge University Press, 1992, 211–262.

6. Bayart, *Illusion*, 71.

7. Ibid. 72.

8. See an editor's comment in Loumpet-Galitzine, *Njoya*, 113-14. This collection of documents is indispensable for the study of Njoya's relationship with colonisers and missionaries.

9. For Sandrock's actions in Banyo and Fumban see Jean Hurault, 'Une Phase de la conquête allemande du Cameroun: l'occupation de Banyo (1902)', *Revue française d'histoire d'Outre-Mer*, 61: 225, Winter 1974, 579-593.

10. See Tardits, *Le Royaume*, 204ff.

11. Ibrahim Njoya, *Histoire et coutumes des Bamoum*, trans. by Henri Martin, Paris: Mémoires de l'Institut Français d'Afrique Noire, Centre du Cameroun, 1952, 42–43. Yeyap's alternative history has Njoya following the advice of the Sultan of Tibati in not fighting: see Mosé Yeyap, 'Histoire des Bamouns', in Loumpet-Galitzine, *Njoya*, 101-128, 117.

12. Njoya, *Histoire*, 43.

13. Ibid.

14. There is a debate concerning the role of Europeans, and especially missionaries, in stimulating these innovations. Tardits does give a role to Eugen Schwartz: see Claude Tardits, *L'Histoire singulière de l'art Bamoum, Cameroun*, Paris: Maisonneuve & Larose, 2004, 51.

15. Dating the text is difficult and the history clearly went through a number of drafts but Bernhard Ankermann saw one version during his visit of 1908: see 'Bericht über eine ethnographische Forschungsreise ins Grasland von Kamerun', *Zeitschrift für Ethnologie*, 42, 1910, 288-310, 291. It has been suggested that the missionary Martin Göhring had a role in encouraging Njoya to compose the history: see I. Dugast and M.D.W. Jeffreys, *L'Écriture des Bamum: Sa naissance, son evolution, sa valeur phonétique, son utilisation*, Paris: Mémoires de l'Institut Français d'Afrique Noire, Centre du Cameroun, Série: Populations. No. 4, 1950, 63–64. This is also suggested in Paul Dubié, 'Christianisme, Islam et Animisme chez les Bamoun (Cameroun)', *Bulletin de l'Institut Français d'Afrique Noire*, 19: 3-4, Series B, 1957, 337-381, 348. Tardits dates the history to around 1912: *Le Royaume*, 229.

16. Njoya, *Histoire*, 22.

17. Ibid. 26. For the importance of Mbuembue see Tardits, *Le Royaume*, 127-69.

18. For the significance of these appropriations see Christraud Geary, *Things of the Palace: a Catalogue of the Bamum Palace Museum in Foumban (Cameroon)*, Wiesbaden: Franz Steiner Verlag, GMBH, 1983, 91, and 117ff.

19.   For *Ngüri* see Tardits, *Le Royaume*, 112 and for *Mbansié*, 104, and for *Mtungu*, Geary, *Things*, 145. For comments on the manner in which vanquished populations were obliged to surrender sacred objects to the Bamum see J. Binet, 'Le commandement chez les Bamoun', *Le Monde Non-Chrétien*, 24, 1952, 399–415, 406.

20.   Anticipating Bayart, Binet could view Bamum practices as taking place almost entirely within the sphere of appropriation: Binet, 'Le commandement', 415.

21.   For the school see Tardits, *Le Royaume*, 229–230.

22.   Ernst Vollbehr, *Mit Pinsel und Palette durch Kamerun: Tagebuchaufzeichnungen und Bilder*, Leipzig: List und von Bressendorf 1912, cited in Walter Hirschberg, *Die Künstlerstrasse: Auf Studienreise durch Kamerun*, Vienna: Wollzeilen Verlag, 1962, 40.

23.   The three identifications are drawn from an archival source: see Geary *Images*, 42.

24.   For uses of the apotropaic see Pierre Harter, *Arts anciens du Cameroun*, Arnouville: Arts d'Afrique Noire, 1986, 61.

25.   The date of 1903 is given in Geary, *Images*, 39.

26.   See ibid. 53ff.

27.   Roland Barthes, *A Lover's Discourse: Fragments*, trans. by Richard Howard, New York: Hill and Wang, 1978, 3.

28.   Tardits, *Le Royaume*, 572. See ibid. 572–601 for the organisation of the palace but also 308, 401, 483, 512–515, *inter alia* for the importance of the palace.

29.   Ibid. 572.

30.   For one discussion of such photographs see Geary, *Images*, esp. 85–117.

31.   The first photographers were members of the German forces, including Captain von Ramsay. They were soon followed by missionaries such as Rein-Wuhrmann and then ethnographers such as Ankermann. See Geary, *Images*, and also Christraud M. Geary and Adamou Ndam Njoya, *Mandou Yénou: Photographie du pays Bamoum*, Munich: Trickster Verlag, 1985.

32.   See the account of *Nja* by Ankermann cited and discussed in Geary, *Images*, 106.

33.   Njoya, *Histoire*, 43.

34.   Sartous, [?], 'Étude sur le Bamoum', report to the Ministre des colonies, 25 April 1917, AF ANOM, Fonds ministériels: Série géographique TGO, Carton 34, Dossier 318, 35.

35.   After the killing of the Lamido Oumarou left Banyo without effective leadership, the Germans swiftly came to realise the advantages of maintaining local structures of power in the region. See Hurault, 'Une Phase', esp. 586–588.

36.   Further support for this would come from the friendly relations Njoya maintained with the Germans. Gift exchanges between these parties continued on the model Njoya had established with the Fula of Banyo: see Christraud Geary, 'Political Dress: German-Style Military Attire and Colonial Politics in Bamum', in *African Crossroads: Intersections between History and Anthropology in Cameroon*, ed. Ian Fowler and David Zeitlyn, Providence and Oxford: Berghahn, 1996, 165–92.

37.   On the religious practices of the Bamum and the role of the palace see Tardits, *Le Royaume*, 850ff.

38.   For an account of Yeyap's life see Jean Njimonya, 'Moïse Yeyap', manuscript in Loumpet-Galitzine, *Njoya*, 161–164.

39.   Ibid. 162 and Anna Rein-Wuhrmann, *Fumban, die Stadt auf dem Schutte: Arbeit und Ernte im Missionsdienst in Kamerun*, Basel: Basler Missionsbuchhandlung, 1948, 63.

40.   Njoya and Pepuere, 'Histoire', 140.

41.   For the vicissitudes of the mission from the point of view of the missionaries, see Élie Allégret, *La Mission du Cameroun*, Paris: Société des Missions Évangéliques, 1924, and for this period 25ff. The Bamum Christians detail a confrontation with Njoya at this point: see Njoya and Pepuere, 'Histoire', 149. For Njoya's account of the arrival of the French see his *Histoire*, 216ff.

42. Allégret had the rank of captain and so was the superior of the lieutenant post-
ed in Fumban. For the relations between colonial and missionary projects see
Alexandra Loumpet-Galitzine, 'Dieu et le roi: les Bamoun et le protestantisme',
in Loumpet-Galitzine, *Njoya*, 16–33.

43. Élie Allégret, 'Chez le Sultan de Foumban', *Journal de la Société des Missions Évangéliques de
Paris*, 1918, in Loumpet-Galitzine, *Njoya*, 216–219.

44. According to Njimonya, Yeyap was appointed by Lieutenant Auguste-Ernest Clapot: see
his 'Moïse Yeyap', 164. Clapot was stationed at Fumban between December 1917 and
December 1919.

45. Allégret, 'Rapport', 221.

46. The postcard is probably derived from a photograph by Rein-Wuhrmann:
Loumpet-Galitzine, *Njoya*, 503.

47. Tardits, *Le Royaume*, 679–680.

48. The need for a gradual transition is a refrain in administrative reports of the period. See
for example Jules Carde, 'Lettre du Commissaire de la République au Cdt. Martin, 14
novembre 1919', typescript in Tardits, *Le Royaume*, 982–984. A series of difficulties were
encountered with Lt. Prestat in 1919, which to the French underlined the need for caution:
see Njoya, *Histoire*, 242ff, and Tardits, *Le Royaume*, 991.

49. France, Ministère des affaires étrangères, *Rapport annuel du gouvernement français sur l'administration sur mandat des territoires du Caméroun pour l'année 1922*, Paris: Imprimerie Générale
Lahure, 1923, 61-2 and 164.

50. De Certeau, *Practice*, xix. For De Certeau a "strategy assumes a place that can be circumscribed as *proper* and thus serve as a basis for generating relations" while "because it does
not have a place, a tactic depends on time". Ibid.

51. On the foundation of the museum see Eva Maclean, 'Kunst in Kamerun', *Deutsche
Kolonialzeitung*, 52/11, 1940: 209–212 and also Geary, *Things*, 14ff.

52. For an account of this palace and the context of earlier Bamum architecture see Tardits,
L'Histoire.

53. For the team of artisans see Adamou Ndam Njoya, *Le Palais de Foumban: Chef d'oeuvre d'art
et d'architecture*, Yaoundé: Éditions Ndam et Raynier, 1975, 11. For Njoya's workshops more
generally see Geary, *Things*, 60–74 and 147–153.

54. This event is documented in a chronology established by Jean-René Brutsch: see
Loumpet-Galitzine, *Njoya*, 460.

55. For details of this monopoly see Geary, *Things*, 41, 79 and 85. The tradition had already
been curtailed by Njoya insofar as at some point in the second decade of the twentieth century he had abrogated a number of relevant laws, including a range addressed to reserved
goods: see Njoya, *Histoire*, 125ff.

56. The description is that of Eugène Pittard, who corresponded with Yeyap in 1930. See Floriane
Morin, 'Mosé Yeyap (1895–1941), cet «eminent révolutionnaire»...', *Totem*, 63, 2013, 6–9.

57. This account is drawn from Gaston Ripert, 'Lettre de l'Administrateur des Colonies Ripert
de la Circonscription de Dschang à Monsieur le Commissaire de la République, 3 juin
1924', typescript in Tardits, *Le Royaume*, 1004-16.

58. On the role of the tribute in the Bamum economy see Tardits, *Le Royaume*, 310ff; for the
Nguon see 773-96.

59. For the new system and Yeyap's role see: Yeyap, 'Histoire' and Loumpet-Galtzine's comments. A system of regional chiefs had been created in 1922 within the Bamum political
structure: see Gaston Ripert, 'Une appréciation sur le sultan Njoya', typescript in Tardits,
Le Royaume, 997-1003.

60. The phrasing is borrowed from Gaston Ripert, 'Lettre de l'Administrateur Ripert au Sultan
Njoya, Foumban, 26 mai 1924', published in Loumpet-Galitzine, *Njoya*, 461–464. This

document gives the terms for the suppression of the tribute. Here it should be recognised that the Bamum economy under Njoya was sustained by a large slave population.

61.   See Roberts, *French Colonial Policy*, 372. For a commentary on Carde's policy see Camille Guy, 'La France au Cameroun', *Bulletin de la Comité de l'Afrique Française*, 23: 6, June 1923, 325–330.

62.   Jules Carde, 'Chronique: Afrique Occidentale Française: Un discours-programme de M. le Gouverneur général Carde', *Journal officiel des territories occupies de l'ancien Caméroun*, 1–2, January-February 1924, 96–106, 100.

63.   On the reorganisation of 1924 Tardits cites a report of Veauver, *Le Royaume*, 373. Different sources give different dates for the construction of the new museum. In a document datable to 1927–29, Yeyap gives the date of 1926 for the new building: Yeyap, 'Histoire', 122. The reorganisation of the artisans is mentioned in Njoya's history but here it precedes the political reorganisation: Njoya, *Historie*, 250–251.

64.   See Théodore Paul Marchand, 'Arrèté créant une école d'artisanat à Foumban', *Journal officiel des territoires occupés de l'ancien Cameroun*, 163: 1, 1 March 1927, 133.

65.   Henri Nicod, *Sur les sentiers de l'Afrique Équatoriale*, Paris: Société des Missions Évangéliques, 1931, 287.

66.   Jürgen Habermas, *The Structural Transformation of the Public Sphere: An Enquiry into a Category of Bourgeois Society*, trans. by Thomas Burger, Cambridge: Polity, 1989, 11.

67.   For this condition of representation see ibid. 7ff.

68.   Letter of 2 May 1930 in the archive of the Musée d'ethnographie de Genève (CH AVG, 350.A.1.1.1.4/9) as cited in Morin, 'Yeyap', 6.

69.   Charles Frey, 'Coutumes africaines. Un peu d'histoire. Les panjou! Initiation. Clans et associations. Le Mountngou messagers de mort. Libération', *Journal de la Société des Missions Évangéliques de Paris*, April 1930, in Loumpet-Galitzine, *Njoya*, 373–378, 374.

70.   Ibid. 373

71.   E. Huguenin, 'Cameroun: fin d'année à Foumban', *L'Ami des Missions*, March 1930, in Loumpet-Galitzine, *Njoya*, 328–330, 329.

72.   Ibid.

73.   Ibid.

74.   See Tardits, *Le Royaume*, for the role of *Mbansié*, 680–690; for *Ngüri*, 634–45; for an account of the relations between the societies, 690–693.

75.   On the prohibition see Njoya, *Histoire*, 126 and 130 and Tardits, *Le Royaume*, 690. Jean Texier underlines the prohibition on sight in his account of fetishism: *Les Bamoum*, 52, 1933–34, AF ANOM, 3ECOL20 Mémoires ENFOM. See also Michael Rowlands, 'Of substances, palaces, and museums: The visible and the invisible in the constitution of Cameroon', *Journal of the Royal Anthropological Institute*, 17, s1 May 2011, 23–38.

76.   Binet, 'Le commandement', 406.

77.   For Schwab's account of the visit see his letter to W. Reginald Wheeler, 1 February 1930, Archives of the Presbyterian Historical Society in Philadelphia: RG 142: United Presbyterian Church in the U.S.A. Commission on Ecumenical Mission and Relations. Secretaries' files: West Africa Mission, 1911–1965, Box 4, Folder 22.

78.   The photographic record of this visit is held at the Peabody Museum: see cat. nos. 2004.24.8416–2004.24.8494. This record was undated but Schwab's letter to Wheeler confirms the timing of his visit: see Simon Dell, 'Yeyap's Resources: The Arts of the Bamum in Cameroon and France, c. 1902–1935', in *World Art and the Legacies of Colonial Violence*, ed. Daniel J. Rycroft, Farnham: Ashgate, 2013, 4–31.

79.   None of this is to argue that the objects were somehow without representational status before the intervention of Yeyap and Schwab but it is to assert that this status was transformed. For some of the difficulties here see Thomas McEvilley, 'Doctor, Lawyer, Indian Chief', *Artforum*, 23, November 1984, 54–60. The very idea that all objects

should be collected as "representative" of their culture is evidence of a quite specific set of assumptions: see Philip L. Ravenhill, 'The Passive Object and the Tribal Paradigm: Colonial Museography in French West Africa', in *African Material Culture*, es. Mary Jo Arnoldi, Christraud M. Geary and Kris L. Hardin, Bloomington and Indianapolis: Indiana University Press, 1996, 265–282.

80.   Hugeunin, 'Cameroun', 329.

81.   Anna Rein-Wuhrmann, *Mein Bamumvolk im Grasland von Kamerun*, Basel: Basler Missionsbuchhandlung, 1925, 65.

82.   See Tardits, *Le Royaume*, 784.

83.   Huguenin, 'Cameroun', 329.

84.   Tardits is emphatic on this point: *Le Royaume*, 774.

85.   Frey, 'Coutumes africaines', 378.

86.   Ibid.

87.   Ibid. From a different perspective, Texier notes a similar transition: see his account of 'Les biens collectifs', *Les Bamoums*, np.

88.   The term "néopaganisme" is used in Edouard Oeschner de Coninck, 'Lettre addressée au Directeur des Missions de Paris, 5 septembre 1934', manuscript in Loumpet-Galitzine, *Njoya*, 346. Oeschner de Coninck was one of the first three missionaries to arrive in Cameroun in January 1917. Loumpet-Galitzine has established that the dangers of civilisation became a recurrent theme in missionaries' writings of this period.

89.   See for example Allégret, *La Mission*, 56.

90.   Allégret, 'The Missionary Question', 164.

91.   Loumpet-Galitzine, *Njoya*, 32. The exact date of the museum's foundation has not been established. Paul Gebauer makes reference to a visit in 1931 in 'Art of Cameroon', *African Arts*, 4: 2, Winter 1971, 24–35, 31.

92.   Njoya's heir, Njimoluh Seidou, who acceded to the throne on 24 June 1933, was officially described by Marchand simply as 'heir of the sultans of Fumban, keeper of the museum of the Bamum race': see Théodore Paul Marchand, 'Arrète portant attribution d'allocation à des chefs indigènes', *Journal officiel des territoires occupés de l'ancien Cameroun*, 332, 15 March 1934, 168–169, 169.

93.   For beads as reserved objects see Geary, *Things*, 86ff. Advertisements in subsequent issues indicate the way in which production diversified to include objects that conjured the "savagery" of Africa. In 1935 fetishes and masks were included alongside objects fulfilling more mundane functions.

94.   See the advertisement in *Journal officiel des territoires occupés de l'ancien Cameroun*, 369, 15 September 1935, 744. For the spider as reserved see Njoya, *Histoire*, 133.

95.   This at least inflects the familiar responses to the perceived decay of "traditional" arts. For examples in the Bamum case see Clement Egerton, *African Majesty: A Record of Refuge at the Court of the King of Bangangté in the French Cameroons*, London: George Routledge and Sons, 1938. The works produced on the artists' avenue are described as having "not the life of the old things", ibid. 273.

96.   For the history of the alphabet see Dugast and Jeffreys, *L'Écriture des Bamum*.

97.   Njoya, *Histoire*, 22–34.

98.   For the dating see Claude Tardits, 'Un grand dessinateur: Ibrahim Njoya', Marseille, Musée d'Arts Africains, Océaniens, Amérindiens, *Les dessins bamum*, Marseille and Milan: Skira, 1997, 55–57. Tardits interviewed the artist in 1960–61.

99.   For the appointments see anon. 'Tribunaux des races', *Journal officiel des territoires occupies de l'ancien Caméroun*, 138, 1 February 1926, 73.

100.   For the enmity of Njoya and Njinchara see Ripert, 'Une appréciation', 1000–1001.

101.   Summers, *Real Spaces*, 21.

102.   Ibid. 250.

103.   The dimensions of the figure in Njoya's drawing match those of the figure in photograph as published by Rein-Wuhrmann. That the version in the book is the source is confirmed by the fact that this photograph by Njoya is only known through its published version; it does not form part of Rein-Wührmann's archive, as has been confirmed by Anke Shürer-Ries of the Basel Mission Archive (personal communication, February 2014). That Ibrahim Njoya frequently made use of tracing paper is confirmed in Tardits, 'Un grand dessinateur', 55.

104.   On the distinction see Podro, *Depiction*, 106.

105.   This is the sequence of events given in Dubié, 'Christianisme', 348–350.

106.   Rein-Wuhrmann, *Mein Bamumvolk*, 154.

107.   Ibid. 155. The citation is from Goethe, *Wilhelm Meister's Years of Apprenticeship*.

108.   For this change in the picturing of Njoya see Geary, *Images*, 128.

109.   I have suspended discussion of the commission of the suite of illustrations. The presence of Yeyap and the regional chiefs suggests he may have had a role in commissioning the work, yet arguments could also be made for Njoya initiating it. However, what concerns me here are the ambiguous effects the suite generates and not the kind of circular argument where an agent's given position or ideology is seen to be represented in an artefact and this is then confirmed by analysis of the artefact.

110.   Geary, *Things*, 101. For an example of the motifs see Ankermann's photograph [Fig. 4.4].

111.   Marseille, *Les dessins*, cited 141.

112.   Njoya, *Histoire*, 42, 133 and 136.

113.   Ibid. 133.

114.   Ibid. 136.

115.   Cited in annex in Tardits, *Le Royaume*, 972–973.

116.   From a history of the introduction of Islam to the Bamum: Ismaïla Mouchili, 'Introduction de la religion musulmane dans la région bamoum', extracts in Tardits, *Le Royaume*, 976. See also the account given in Dubié, 'Le commandement', 343.

117.   Summers, *Real Spaces*, 625.

118.   Théodore Paul Marchand, letter to the Ministre des colonies, 16 April 1931, AF ANOM, Fonds ministériels: Série géographique TGO, Carton 30, Dossier 264.

119.   Morin, 'Yeyap', 8.

120.   Commissariat des territoires africains sous mandat à l'exposition coloniale internationale, *Territoires africains sous mandat de la France: Cameroun et Togo: exposition coloniale internationale de Paris*, Mulhouse-Dornach: Commissariat des territoires africains sous mandat 1931, np.

121.   Ibid.

122.   Ibid.

123.   Henri Martin, letter to the Directeur de la Société des Missions Évangéliques de Paris, 3 July 1933, extracts in Loumpet-Galitzine, *Njoya*, 340–341.

Epilogue: Charles Atangana between Africa and France

1.   Charles Atangana, *Paix Humanité Justice*, Madrid: Privately circulated, 1920. Atangana's appeal is to Georges Clemenceau, yet as the latter resigned in January 1920 Atangana must have completed his text and commissioned his portrait in the last months of 1919. For biographical details of Atangana see Paul Auguste Françoise Bonnecarrère, letter to the Ministre des colonies, 27 December 1933, AF ANOM, Fonds ministériels: Série géographique TGO, Carton 33, Dossier 270. See also Philippe Laburthe-Tolra, 'Charles Atangana (c. 1881-1943): Un chef camerounais entre deux colonisations', in *Les Africains: V*, ed. Charles-André Julien, Magali Morsy, Catherine Coquery-Vidrovitch and Yves Person, Paris: Éditions J. A., 1977, 107-141.

2.   Atangana, *Paix*, 8.

3.   Lucien Fourneau, 'Rapport', 11 August 1919, AF ANOM, Fonds ministériels: Série géo-
     graphique TGO Carton 31, Dossier 279.

4.   For this period see Eugène Désiré Eloundou and Arouna Ngapna, *Un Souverain bamoun en
     exil: Le roi Njoya Ibrahima à Yaoundé (1931–1933)*, Paris: L'Harmattan, 2011, esp.33–54.

5.   This phrasing is to be found in Louis Rollin, telegram to the Commissaire de la République
     du Cameroun, 8 November 1934, AF ANOM, Fonds ministériels: Série géographique
     TGO, Carton 33, Dossier 310.

6.   Louis Rollin, letter to the Commissaire de la République du Cameroun, 30 January 1935,
     AF ANOM, Fonds ministériels: Série géographique TGO, Carton 33, Dossier 310.

7.   For a statement to this effect relevant to the Cameroonian case see Henri Labouret, 'Avant
     Propos', *Togo-Cameroun*, April-July 1935, 87. More generally see De L'Estoile, *Le Goût des
     autres*, 151–156.

8.   For the range of material displayed see Paris, Musée du Trocadéro, *Catalogue de l'exposition
     de la mission au Cameroun de M. H. Labouret*, Paris: Musée du Trocadéro, 1935.

9.   Commissaire de la République du Cameroun, 'Arrêté 2036', 13 November 1934, AF
     ANOM, Fonds ministériels: Série géographique TGO, Carton 33, Dossier 310.

10. Conrad, *Heart of Darkness*, 145.

11. Levinas, *Totality and Infinity*, 43.

Sources

Abbreviations

AF ANOM: Archives françaises: Archives nationales d'Outre-Mer, Aix-en-Provence.
Bienecke: Bienecke Rare Books and Manuscript Library, Yale University, New Haven, Connecticut.

Unpublished Sources

Archives françaises: Archives nationales d'Outre-Mer, Aix-en-Provence

Anon. 'L'attitude du Parti Communiste et de la C.G.T.U. à propos de l'Exposition Coloniale', 1931, Fonds ministériels: 3 SLOTFOM, Carton 5, 1.

—— 'L'Exposition internationale de 1931 et l'œuvre coloniale française: Schémas de Conférence: Plan développé No. 2', Fonds ministériels: Exposition colonial, ECI/1 Divers.

—— 'Note sur les congrès', 15 May 1930, Fonds ministériels: Exposition colonial, ECI/18.

Anon. [Nguyên Van Nhi], untitled tract appended to Ministre des Colonies, letter to Résident Supérieur, Commissaire général de l'Exposition coloniale, 20 July 1931, Fonds Ministériels: 3 SLOTFOM, Carton 5.

Bonamy, André, letter to Hubert Lyautey, Maréchal de France, Commissaire général de l'Exposition coloniale internationale, 20 November 1930, Fonds ministériels: Exposition colonial, ECI/11 Togo et Cameroun.

Bonnecarrère, Paul Auguste Françoise, letter to the Ministre des colonies, 27 December 1933, Fonds ministériels: Série géographique TGO, Carton 33, Dossier 270.

Commissaire de la République du Cameroun, 'Arrêté 2036', 13 November 1934, Fonds ministériels: Série géographique TGO, Carton 33, Dossier 310.

Faralicq, G., letter to Directeur général de la Police Municipale, 15 July 1931, Fonds ministériels: 3 SLOTFOM, Carton 5.

Fourneau, Lucien, 'Rapport', 11 August 1919, Fonds ministériels: Série géographique TGO, Carton 31, Dossier 279.

Joé, 'Rapport', 20 June 1931, Fonds ministériels: 3 SLOTFOM, Carton 5, Ligue contre l'Impérialisme.

Lyautey, Hubert, 'Discours prononcé le 5 novembre 1928', Fonds ministériels: Exposition coloniale, ECI/1 Divers.

Marchand, Théodore Paul, letter to the Ministre des colonies, 16 April 1931, Fonds ministériels: Série géographique TGO, Carton 30, Dossier 264.

Rollin, Louis, letter to the Commissaire de la République du Cameroun, 30 January 1935, Fonds ministériels: Série géographique TGO, Carton 33, Dossier 310.

—— telegram to the Commissaire de la République du Cameroun, 8 November 1934, Fonds ministériels: Série géographique TGO, Carton 33, Dossier 310.

Sartous, [?], 'Étude sur le Bamoum', report to the Ministre des colonies, 25 April 1917, Fonds ministériels: Série géographique TGO, Carton 34, Dossier 318.

Texier, Jean, *Les Bamoum*, 52, 1933–34, 3ECOL20 Mémoires ENFOM.

Archives of the Presbyterian Historical Society, Philadelphia.

Schwab, George, letter to W. Reginald Wheeler, 1 February 1930, RG 142: United Presbyterian
Church in the U.S.A. Commission on Ecumenical Mission and Relations. Secretaries' files:
West Africa Mission, 1911-1965, Box 4, Folder 22.

Bienecke Rare Books and Manuscript Library, Yale University, New Haven, Conn.
Marc Allégret Papers: GEN MSS 651

Allégret, Marc, diary, Box 10: Folder 114: Voyage au Congo: Notes and Notebooks 8 of 8.
—— letter to Daniel Couve, 26 June 1927, Box 9: Folder 96: Voyage au Congo: Correspondence
2 of 2.
—— letter to Daniel Muller, 22 June 1927, Box 9: Folder 96: Voyage au Congo: Correspondence
2 of 2.
—— untitled inventory, undated, Box 9: Folder 97: Voyage au Congo: Notes and Notebooks 1 of 10.
Couve, Daniel, letter to Marc Allégret, 23 June 1927, Box 9: Folder 96: Voyage au Congo:
Correspondence 2 of 2.
—— letter to Marc Allégret, 28 June 1927, Box 9: Folder 96: Voyage au Congo: Correspondence
2 of 2.
Gide, André, *Voyage au Congo*, proofs, corrected, 1927, Box 13: Folders 138 and 139.
Muller, André, letter to Marc Allégret, 1 July 1927, Box 9: Folder 96: Voyage au Congo:
Correspondence 2 of 2.

Université de Bangui

Maleyasse, Daniel, 'En marge du "Voyage au Congo" d'André Gide: l'affaire Pacha, 1925-1932',
Mémoire de maîtrise, 1987-1988. [A copy of this work is available in the library of AF
ANOM.]

Filmography

Allégret, Marc, dir. *Voyage au Congo: Scènes de la Vie indigène en Afrique Équatoriale*, Les Éditions
P. Braunberger, 114 mins., British Film Institute, London (BFI 8.067 405 A A).

Bibliography

Ageron, Charles-Robert, *France coloniale ou parti colonial?*, Paris: Presses Universitaires de France,
1978.
Allain, Maurice, *Notre belle France d'outre-mer, I*, Paris: A. Quillet, 1934.

Allégret, Élie, 'Á Foumban et au Grassfield', *Journal de la Société des Missions Évangéliques de Paris*, 1 (1918), extracts in *Njoya et le royaume bamoum: Les archives de la Société des Missions Évangéliques de Paris, 1917-1937*, ed. Alexandra Loumpet-Galitzine, Paris: Karthala, 2006, 213-16.

—— 'Chez le Sultan de Foumban', *Journal de la Société des Missions Évangéliques de Paris* (1918), in *Njoya et le royaume bamoum: Les archives de la Société des Missions Évangéliques de Paris, 1917-1937*, ed. Alexandra Loumpet-Galitzine, Paris: Karthala, 2006, 216-219.

—— *La Mission du Cameroun*, Paris: Société des Missions Évangéliques, 1924.

—— 'The Missionary Question in the French Colonies', *International Review of Mission*, 12: 2, April 1923, 161-81.

—— 'Rapport confidentiel présenté au Comité de la Société des Missions Évangéliques de Paris sur la Mission au Cameroun, mai 1919', typescript in *Njoya et le royaume bamoum: Les archives de la Société des Missions Évangéliques de Paris, 1917-1937*, ed. Alexandra Loumpet-Galitzine, Paris: Karthala, 2006, 221-23.

—— 'Rapport général sur l'amélioration des conditions familiales et sociales', in *Congrès International et Intercolonial de la Société Indigène: II*, Paris: École coloniale, 1931, 143-148.

Allégret, Marc, *Carnets du Congo: Voyage avec André Gide*, ed. Daniel Durosay, text established by Claudia Rabel-Jullien, Paris: CNRS Éditions, 1993.

—— 'Sous le soleil des tropiques: En Afrique Équatoriale Française chez les enfants Massas', *Le Monde Colonial Illustré*, 45, May 1927, 107.

Althusser, Louis, 'Ideology and Ideological State Apparatuses (Notes towards an Investigation), in *Lenin and Philosophy and Other Essays*, trans. by Ben Brewster, Delhi: Aakar Books, 2006, 85-126.

Altman, Georges [G.A.], 'A travers les carcasses de l'exposition coloniale', *Monde*, 154, 16 May 1931, 11.

—— 'Images d'exposition et chronique coloniale', *Monde*, 164, 25 July 1931, 12.

Anderson, Benedict, *Reflections on the Origins and Spread of Nationalism*, London and New York: Verso, 1991.

Ankermann, Bernhard, 'Bericht über eine ethnographische Forschungsreise ins Grasland von Kamerun', *Zeitschrift für Ethnologie*, 42, 1910, 288-310.

Anon. 'Cameroun, dernières nouvelles', *Journal de la Société des Missions Évangéliques de Paris*, 1918, in *Njoya et le royaume bamoum: Les archives de la Société des Missions Évangéliques de Paris, 1917-1937*, ed. Alexandra Loumpet-Galitzine, Paris: Karthala, 2006, 219-221.

—— 'History of the Great Exhibition' in 'The Crystal Palace Exhibition: Illustrated Catalogue', *The Art Journal*, Special Issue, 1851, xi-xxvi.

—— 'König Nschoya von Bamum mit einer seiner Frauen', *Der evangelischer Heidenbote*, 86: 1, January 1913, 4.

—— 'Nouelle interpelle sur le recrutement de la main-d'œuvre indigène en Afrique Occidentale', *Le Populaire*, 8 July 1927, 2.

—— 'Objectif du Congrès', in *Congrès International et Intercolonial de la Société Indigène: II*, Paris: École coloniale, 1931, 5.

—— 'Strange "Beauty Culture": Face Scars; Distended Lips and Ears', *The Illustrated London News*, 951, 26 November 1927, np.

—— 'Tribunaux des races', *Journal officiel des territoires occupies de l'ancien Caméroun*, 138, 1 February 1926, 73.

Artus, Robert, 'Ce que nous dit le Maréchal Lyautey', *Le Journal de l'Exposition coloniale*, June 1931, 1.

Atangana, Charles, *Paix Humanité Justice*, Madrid: Privately circulated, 1920.

Bancel, Nicolas and Pascal Blanchard, 'Civiliser: L'invention de l'indigène' in *Culture coloniale: La France conquise par son Empire, 1871-1931*, ed. Pascal Blanchard and Sandrine Lemaire, Paris: Éditions Autrement — collection Mémoires 2003, 149-61.

Bancel, Nicolas, Pascal Blanchard and Laurent Gervereau, ed, *Images et colonies: Iconographie et propaganda colonial sur l'Afrique française de 1880 à 1962*, Nanterre and Paris: Bibliothèque de documentation internationale contemporaine and Association Connaissance de l'histoire de l'Afrique contemporaine, 1993.

Bangert, Michael, 'The BM and its International Network', in *Mission Possible? The Basel Mission Collection: Reflecting Cultural Encounters*, ed. Anna Schmid and Kathrin Fischer, Basel: Christoph Merian Verlag and Museum der Kulturen Basel, 2015, 34-38.

—— 'Phenomenon of a Threshold Period', in *Mission Possible? The Basel Mission Collection: Reflecting Cultural Encounters*, ed. Anna Schmid and Kathrin Fischer, Basel: Christoph Merian Verlag and Museum der Kulturen Basel, 2015, 19-33.

Banta, Melissa, and Curtis M. Hinsley with Joan Kathryn O'Donnell, *From Site to Sight: Anthropology, Photography, and the Power of Imagery*, 30th Anniversary edition, Cambridge, Mass: Peabody Museum Press, Harvard University, 2017.

Barthes, Roland, *A Lover's Discourse: Fragments*, trans. by Richard Howard, New York: Hill and Wang, 1978.

—— 'Notes sur André Gide et son «Journal»', in *Œuvres complètes, I, 1942-1965*, ed. Éric Marty, Paris: Éditions du Seuil, 1993, 23-33.

—— *Roland Barthes*, trans. by Richard Howard, New York: Hill and Wang, 1977.

—— *The Preparation of the Novel: Lecture Courses and Seminars at the Collège de France (1978-79 and 1979-80)*, ed. Nathalie Léger, trans. by Kate Briggs, New York: Columbia University Press, 2011.

Bayart, Jean-François, *The Illusion of Cultural Identity*, trans. Steven Rendall, Janet Roitman and Jonathan Derrick, London and Paris: Hurst and Company, in association with the Centre d'Etudes et de Recherches Internationales, 2005.

Belley [Jean-Baptiste], *Le Bout d'oreille des colons, ou le système de l'hôtel de Massiac, mis au jour par Gouli*, Paris: De l'Imprimerie de Pain, 1794.

Betts, Raymond, F. *Assimilation and Association in French Colonial Theory, 1890-1914*, New York: Columbia University Press, 1961.

Bhabha, Homi, 'Of Mimicry and Man: The Ambivalence of Colonial Discourse', *October*, 28, Spring 1984, 125-33.

Bindman, David, 'Subjectivity and Slavery in Portraiture: From Courtly to Commercial Societies' in *Slave Portraiture in the Atlantic World*, ed. Angela Rosenthal and Agnes Lugo-Ortiz, New York: Cambridge University Press, 2013, 71-87.

Bindman, David, Susan Preston Blier and Henry Louis Gates Jr., ed. *The Image of the Black in African and Asian Art*, Cambridge, Mass: The Belknap Press of Harvard University Press, 2017.

Bindman, David, and Henry Louis Gates Jr., ed. *The Image of the Black in Western Art: From the "Age of Discovery" to the Age of Abolition, The Eighteenth Century*, Cambridge, Mass. and London: The Belknap Press of Harvard University Press, 2011.

—— *The Image of the Black in Western Art: From the American Revolution to World War I, Slaves and Liberators*, Cambridge, Mass. and London: The Belknap Press of Harvard University Press, 2012.

Binet, J., 'Le commandement chez les Bamoun', *Le Monde Non-Chrétien*, 24, 1952, 399-415.

Blanchard, Pascal, 'L'union nationale: la «rencontre» des droits et des gauches à travers la presse et autour de l'Exposition de Vincennes', in *Culture coloniale: La France conquise par son Empire,*

1871-1931, ed. Pascal Blanchard and Sandrine Lemaire, Paris: Éditions Autrement — collection Mémoires, 2003, 213-231.

Blanchard, Pascal, Nicolas Bancel, Gilles Boëtsch, Éric Deroo and Sandrine Lemaire, ed. *Zoo humains et exhibitions coloniales: 150 ans d'invention de l'Autre*, Paris: La Découverte, 2011.

Blanchard, Pascal, Nicolas Bancel and Sandrine Lemaire, ed. *La Fracture coloniale: La Société française au prisme de l'héritage colonial*, Paris: La Découverte, 2005.

Blanchard, Pascal, Nicolas Bancel and Dominic Thomas, ed. *Vers la guerre des identités? De la fracture coloniale à la révolution ultranationale*, Paris: La Découverte, 2016.

Blanchard, Pascal, Gilles Boëtsch and Nanette Jacomijn Snoep, ed, *Human Zoos: The Invention of the Savage*, Paris and Arles: Musée du quai Branly and Actes Sud, 2011.

Blanchard, Pascal, and Sandrine Lemaire, ed. *Culture coloniale: La France conquise par son Empire, 1871-1931*, Paris: Éditions Autrement — collection Mémoires, 2003.

Blanchard, Pascal, Sandrine Lemaire and Nicolas Bancel, ed. *Culture coloniale en France: De la Révolution française à nos jours*, Paris: Éditions Autrement and Association Connaissance de l'histoire de l'Afrique contemporaine, 2003.

Blévis, Laure, Hélène Lafont-Couturier, Nanette Jacomijn Snoep and Claire Zalc, ed. *1931: Les étrangers au temps de l'Exposition coloniale*, Paris: Gallimard and Cité nationale de l'histoire de l'immigration, 2008.

Blum, Léon, 'Aux colonies: *Voyage au Congo*', *Le Populaire*, 5 July 1927, in 'Le Problème du colonialisme', *L'Œuvre de Léon Blum, 1914-1928, III: i*, Paris: Éditions Albin Michel, 1972, 480-490.

—— 'Bolchevisme et socialisme', *Le Populaire*, 17, 19, 20, 21, 22 and 25 March 1927, in *L'Œuvre de Léon Blum, 1914-1928, III: i*, Paris: Éditions Albin Michel 1972, 451-460.

—— 'L'Idéal socialiste', *Revue de Paris*, 1 May 1924, in *L'Œuvre de Léon Blum, 1914-1928, III: i*, Paris: Éditions Albin Michel, 1972, 347-362.

Bocquillon, Michèle, 'Le "Portrait parlant" de Jean-Baptiste Belley', *Nineteenth-Century French Studies*, 33: 1/2, Fall-Winter 2004-2005, 35-56.

Boittin, Jennifer Anne, *Colonial Metropolis: The Urban Grounds of Anti-Imperialism and Feminism in Interwar Paris*, Lincoln and London: University of Nebraska Press, 2010.

Boone, Joseph Allen, *The Homoerotics of Orientalism*, Columbia University Press: New York and Chichester, 2014.

Breton, André, 'Manifeste du surréalisme', in *Manifestes du surréalisme*, Paris: Gallimard, 1979, 13-60.

Brilliant, Richard, *Portraiture*, London: Reaktion, 1991.

C.L. 'À la Chambre: Le Budget des colonies', *Le Populaire*, 24 November 1927, 2.

Carde, Jules, 'Chronique: Afrique Occidentale Française: Un discours-programme de M. le Gouverneur général Carde', *Journal officiel des territories occupies de l'ancien Caméroun*, 1-2, January-February 1924, 96-106.

—— 'Lettre du Commissaire de la République au Cdt. Martin, 14 novembre 1919', typescript in *Le Royaume Bamoum*, Claude Tardits, Paris: Librairie Armand Colin, 1980, 982-984.

Carrier, David, *A World Art History and Its Objects*, University Park: The Pennsylvania State University Press, 2008.

Certeau, Michel de, *The Practice of Everyday Life*, trans. by Steven Rendall, Berkeley, Los Angeles and London: University of California Press, 1984.

Césaire, Aimé, *Cahier d'un retour au pays natal*, Paris: Présence Africaine, 1956.

Chadourne, Jacqueline M. *André Gide et l'Afrique: Le role de l'Afrique dans la vie et l'oeuvre de l'écrivain*, Paris: A. G. Nizet, 1968.

Challaye, Félicien, 'Discours de M. Challaye', in *Le Congrès national de 1931: Compte-rendu sténographique (23-25 mai 1931)*, Ligue des Droits de l'Homme, Paris: Ligue des Droits de l'Homme, 1931, 288-309.

Chaumel, Alfred, 'Une Mission de propagande par le film en Afrique Équatoriale Française', *Bulletin de la Société des recherches congoliases*, 5, 1924, 11-15.

Clark, Phyllis, 'Gide's Africa', *South Central Review*, 14: 1, Spring 1997, 56-73.

Cohen, William B. *Rulers of Empire: The French Colonial Service in Africa*, Stanford: Hoover Institution Press, Stanford University, 1971.

Commissariat des territoires africains sous mandat à l'exposition coloniale internationale, *Territoires africains sous mandat de la France: Cameroun et Togo: exposition coloniale internationale de Paris*, Mulhouse-Dornach: Commissariat des territoires africains sous mandat 1931.

Condorcet, Jean-Antoine-Nicolas de Caritat, marquis de, *Sketch for a Historical Picture of the Progress of the Human Mind*, trans. by June Barraclough, Westport: Greenwood Press, 1955.

Conklin, Alice L. *A Mission to Civilize: The Republican Idea of Empire in France and West Africa, 1895-1939*, Stanford: Stanford University Press, 1997.

Conrad, Joseph, 'Geography and Some Explorers', in *Tales of Hearsay and Last Essays*, London: J. M. Dent & Sons Ltd., 1926, 10-17.

—— *Heart of Darkness and Other Tales*, Oxford: Oxford World's Classics, 1998.

Cooper, Frederick, and Laura Stoler, ed. *Tensions of Empire: Colonial Culture in a Bourgeois World*, Berkeley, Los Angeles and London: University of California Press, 1997.

Cotnam, Jacques, *Bibliographie chronologique de l'Œuvre d'André Gide (1889-1973)*, Boston, Mass.: G. K. Hall & Co., 1974.

Crow, Thomas, *Emulation: Making Artists for Revolutionary France*, New Haven and London: Yale University Press, 1995.

Davis, Whitney, *A General Theory of Visual Culture*, Princeton and Oxford: Princeton University Press, 2011.

Deauville, Max, 'Un peu d'Humour... Exposition des blancs chez les noirs', *Le Journal de l'Exposition coloniale*, June 1931, 3.

Delay, Jean, *La Jeunesse d'André Gide: I, André Gide avant André Walter, 1869-1890*, Paris: Gallimard, 1956.

Deleuze, Gilles and Félix Guattari, *A Thousand Plateaus: Capitalism and Schizophrenia*, trans. by Brian Massumi, London and New York: Continuum, 1987

Dell, Simon, 'The Difficult Conjunction of 'Worker' and 'Photographer' in France,' in *The Worker Photography Movement (1926-1939): Essays and Documents*, ed. Jorge Ribalta, Madrid: Museo Nacional Centro de Arte Reina Sofia, 2011, 354-362.

—— *The Image of the Popular Front: The Masses and the Media in Interwar France*, Basingstoke and New York: Palgrave Macmillan, 2007.

—— 'Yeyap's Resources: The Arts of the Bamum in Cameroon and France, c. 1902-1935', in *World Art and the Legacies of Colonial Violence*, ed. Daniel J. Rycroft, Farnham: Ashgate, 2013, 4-31.

Demaison, André, *Exposition coloniale internationale à Paris en 1931: Guide officiel*, Paris: Éditions Mayeux, 1931.

Denoyelle, Françoise, *La Lumière de Paris: La Marché de la photographie, 1919-1939*, Paris: L'Harmattan, 1997.

—— *La Lumière de Paris: Les Usages de la photographie, 1919-1939*, Paris: L'Harmattan, 1997.

Derrida, Jacques, 'Violence and Metaphysics: An Essay on the Thought of Emmanuel Levinas', in *Writing and Difference*, trans. by Alan Bass, London: Routledge, 1977, 79-153.

Deschamps, Paul, et al. *Les Colonies et la vie française pendant huit siècles*, Paris: Firmin-Didot, 1933.

Descola, Philippe, *Beyond Nature and Culture*, trans. by Janet Lloyd, Chicago and London: University of Chicago Press, 2013.

Dubié, Paul, 'Christianisme, Islam et Animisme chez les Bamoun (Cameroun)', *Bulletin de l'Institut Français d'Afrique Noire*, 19: 3-4, Series B, 1957, 337-381.

Dugast, I., and M.D.W. Jeffreys, *L'Écriture des Bamum: Sa naissance, son evolution, sa valeur phonétique, son utilisation*, Paris: Mémoires de l'Institut Français d'Afrique Noire, Centre du Cameroun, Série: Populations. No. 4, 1950.

Durosay, Daniel, 'Images et imaginaire dans le *Voyage au Congo*', *Bulletin des Amis d'André Gide*, 16: 60, October 1988, 9-30.

Edwards, Elizabeth, ed. *Anthropology and Photography, 1860-1920*, New Haven and London: Yale University Press in association with the Royal Anthropological Institute, 1992.

Edwards, Steve, *The Making of English Photography: Allegories*, University Park, Pennsylvania: The Pennsylvania University Press, 2006.

Egerton, Clement, *African Majesty: A Record of Refuge at the Court of the King of Bangangté in the French Cameroons*, London: George Routledge and Sons, 1938.

Eloundou, Eugène Désiré, and Arouna Ngapna, *Un Souverain bamoun en exil: Le roi Njoya Ibrahima à Yaoundé (1931-1933)*, Paris: L'Harmattan, 2011.

Enwezor, Okwui, ed. *Contemporary African Photography from the Walther Collection: Events of the Self, Portraiture and Social Identity*, Göttingen: Steidl, 2010.

Enwezor, Okwui, and Octavio Zaya, 'Colonial Imaginary, Tropes of Disruption: History, Culture, and Representation in the Works of African Photographers', in *In/sight: African Photographers, 1940 to the Present*, New York, Solomon R. Guggenheim Museum, New York: Abrams, 1996, 17-47.

Ezra, Elizabeth, *The Colonial Unconscious: Race and Culture in Interwar France*, Cornell University Press, Ithaca and London, 2000.

Fanon, Frantz, *Black Skin, White Masks*, trans. by Charles Lam Markmann, London: Pluto Press, 1986.

Fargue, Léon-Paul, *Banalité: illustré de réogrammes et recherches d'objets de Loris et Parry*, Paris: NRF, Gallimard, 1930.

Fédération Française des Anciens Coloniaux, *Le Livre d'or de l'exposition coloniale internationale de 1931*, Paris: Librairie ancienne Honoré Campion, 1931.

Feest, Christian F. 'From North America', in *"Primitivism" in 20th Century Art: Affinity of the Tribal and Modern*, ed. William Rubin, New York: Museum of Modern Art 1984, 85-97.

Fernández, Horacio, *Fotografía pública: Photography in Print*, Madrid: Museo Nacional Centro d'Arte Reina Sofía, 2000.

Ferry, Jules, *Discours et opinions de Jules Ferry, V*, Paris: Colin, 1897.

Fontagnol, Georges, 'L'Algérie à Vincennes', in *Le Livre d'or de l'exposition coloniale internationale de 1931*, Fédération Française des Anciens Coloniaux, Paris: Librairie ancienne Honoré Campion, 1931, 39-40.

France, Ministère des affaires étrangères, *Rapport annuel du gouvernement français sur l'administration sur mandat des territoires du Caméroun pour l'année 1922*, Paris: Imprimerie Générale Lahure, 1923.

Freeland, Cynthia, *Portraits and Persons: A Philosophical Inquiry*, Oxford: Oxford University Press, 2010.

Frey, Charles, 'Coutumes africaines. Un peu d'histoire. Les panjou! Initiation. Clans et associations. Le Mountngou messagers de mort. Libération', *Journal de la Société des Missions Évangéliques de Paris*, April 1930, in *Njoya et le royaume bamoum: Les archives de la Société des Missions Évangéliques de Paris, 1917-1937*, ed. Alexandra Loumpet-Galitzine, Paris: Karthala, 2006, 373-378.

Furet, François, ed. *Jules Ferry: Fondateur de la République: Actes du colloque*, Paris: Éditions due l'École des Hautes Études en Sciences Sociales, 1985.

Gauguin, Paul, *Lettres de Paul Gauguin à Émile Bernard*, Geneva: Pierre Cailler, 1954.

Geary, Christraud M., *Images from Bamum: German Colonial Photography at the Court of King Njoya: Cameroon, West Africa, 1902-1915*, Washington D.C. and London: National Museum of African Art, Smithsonian Institution Press, 1988.

—— 'Political Dress: German-Style Military Attire and Colonial Politics in Bamum', in *African Crossroads: Intersections between History and Anthropology in Cameroon*, ed. Ian Fowler and David Zeitlyn, Providence and Oxford: Berghahn, 1996, 165-92.

—— *Things of the Palace: a Catalogue of the Bamum Palace Museum in Foumban (Cameroon)*, Wiesbaden: Franz Steiner Verlag, GMBH, 1983.

Geary, Christraud M., and Adamou Ndam Njoya, *Mandou Yénou: Photographie du pays Bamoum*, Munich: Trickster Verlag, 1985.

Gebauer, Paul, 'Art of Cameroon', *African Arts*, 4: 2, Winter 1971, 24-35.

Gennep, Arnold van, *The Rites of Passage*, trans. by Monika B. Vizedom and Gabrielle L. Caffre, London: Routledge and Kegan Paul, 1960.

Gide, André, *Les Cahiers et les Poésies d'André Walter*, ed. Claude Martin, Paris: NRF, Gallimard, 1986.

—— 'Conférence de Bruxelles', *Bulletin des Amis d'André Gide*, 16: 60, October 1988, 31-36.

—— *Les Faux-Monnayeurs*, Paris: Gallimard, 1963.

—— *Journal: I: 1887-1925*, ed. Éric Marty, Paris: NRF, Bibliothèque de la Pléiade, Gallimard, 1996.

—— *Journal: II: 1926-1950*, ed. Martine Sagaert, Paris: NRF, Bibliothèque de la Pléiade, Gallimard, 2001.

—— *Journal des Faux-Monnayeurs*, Paris: Gallimard, 1967.

—— *Les Nourritures terrestres*, Paris: Gallimard, 1935.

—— *Souvenirs et voyages*, ed. Pierre Masson, with Daniel Durosay and Martine Sagaert, Paris: NRF, Bibliothèque de la Pléiade, Gallimard, 2001.

—— 'Voyage au Congo', *La Nouvelle Revue Française*, 28: 162, January-June 1927, 320-361.

Gide, André, and Élie Allégret, *L'Enfance de l'Art: Correspondance avec Élie Allégret (1886-1896), Lettres d'André Gide, Juliette Gide, Madeleine Rondeaux et Élie Allégret*, ed. Daniel Durosay, Paris: NRF, Gallimard, 1998.

Gide, André, and Marc Allégret, *Correspondance avec Marc Allégret 1917-1949: Cahiers André Gide 19*, ed. Claude Martin and Pierre Masson, Paris: NRF, Gallimard, 2005.

Gide, André, and Roger Martin du Gard, *Correspondance: I*, Paris: NRF, Gallimard, 1968

Girardet, Raoul, *L'Idée coloniale en France de 1871-1962*, Paris: La Table ronde, 1972.

Girodet-Trioson, Anne-Louis, 'Le Peintre, poème', in *Œuvres posthumes de Girodet-Trioson, peintre d'histoire; suivi de sa correspondance; précédés d'une notice historique, I*, ed. P. A. Coupin, Paris: Librairie Jules Renouard, 1829, 1-199.

Gouges, Olympe de, *Œuvres*, Paris: Mercure de France, 1986.

Gramsci, Antonio, *Prison Notebooks*, *I* and *II*, trans. by Joseph A. Buttigieg and Antonio Callari, New York: Columbia University Press, 1992 and 1996.

Green, David, 'Photography and Anthropology: The Technology of Power', *Ten: 8*, 14, 1984, 30–37.

Guy, Camille, 'La France au Cameroun', *Bulletin de la Comité de l'Afrique Française*, 23: 6, June 1923, 325–330.

Habermas, Jürgen, *The Structural Transformation of the Public Sphere: An Enquiry into a Category of Bourgeois Society*, trans. by Thomas Burger, Cambridge: Polity, 1989.

Haney, Erin, *Photography and Africa*, London: Reaktion, 2010.

Harter, Pierre, *Arts anciens du Cameroun*, Arnouville: Arts d'Afrique Noire, 1986.

Haworth-Booth, Mark, Anne McCauley and Heidi Humphrey, *The Museum and the Photograph: Collecting Photography at the Victoria & Albert Museum, 1853–1900*, Williamstown, Mass. Sterling and Francine Clark Art Institute, 1998.

Hazoumé, Paul, 'Amélioration des conditions familiales et sociales en Afrique-Occidentale Française', in *Congrès International et Intercolonial de la Société Indigène: I*, Paris: École coloniale, 1931, 305–314.

Hegel, Georg Wilhelm Friedrich, *Aesthetics: Lectures on Fine Art, I*, trans. by T. M. Knox, Oxford: Clarendon Press, 2010.

—— *Lectures on the Philosophy of World History: Introduction: Reason in History*, trans. by H. B. Nisbet, Cambridge: Cambridge University Press, 1975.

—— *Phenomenology of Spirit*, trans. by A. V. Miller, Oxford: Clarendon Press, 1977.

Hight, Eleanor M. and Gary D. Sampson ed. *Colonialist Photography: Imag(in)ing race and place*, London and New York: Routledge, 2002.

Hirschberg, Walter, *Die Künstlerstrasse: Auf Studienreise durch Kamerun*, Vienna: Wollzeilen Verlag, 1962.

Hodeir, Catherine, and Michel Pierre, *L'Exposition coloniale de 1931*, Brussels: André Versaille, 2011.

Houseman, Michael, 'La chair est image: Europe occidentale', in *Qu'est-ce qu'un corps?*, ed. Stéphane Breton, Paris: Flammarion, 2006, 59–80.

Huguenin, E. 'Cameroun: fin d'année à Foumban', *L'Ami des Missions*, March 1930, in *Njoya et le royaume bamoum: Les archives de la Société des Missions Évangéliques de Paris, 1917–1937*, ed. Alexandra Loumpet-Galitzine, Paris: Karthala, 2006, 328–330.

Hurault, Jean, 'Une Phase de la conquête allemande du Cameroun: l'occupation de Banyo (1902)', *Revue française d'histoire d'Outre-Mer*, 61: 225, Winter 1974, 579–593.

Jay, Martin, and Sumathi Ramaswamy, ed. *Empires of Vision: A Reader*, Durham and London: Duke University Press. 2014.

Jeffrey, Ian, *ReVisions: An Alternative History of Photography*, Bradford: National Museum of Photography, Film and Television, 1999.

Jolles, Adam, *The Curatorial Avant-Garde: Surrealism and Exhibition Practice in France, 1925–1941*, University Park: The Pennsylvania State University Press, 2013.

Juillard, Jacques, 'Le Peuple', in *Les Lieux de mémoire, III*, ed. Pierre Nora, Paris: Gallimard, 1992, 184–229.

Kane, Cheikh Hamidou, *L'Aventure ambiguë*, Paris: René Juillard, 1962.

Konrad, Dagmar, 'The Mission Station', in *Mission Possible? The Basel Mission Collection — Reflecting Cultural Encounters*, ed. Anna Schmid, Kathrin Fischer, Basel: Christoph Merian Verlag and Museum der Kulturen Basel, 2015, 69–75.

Labouret, Henri, 'Avant Propos', *Togo-Cameroun*, April-July 1935, 87.

Laburthe-Tolra, Philippe, 'Charles Atangana (c. 1881-1943): Un chef camerounais entre deux colonisations', in *Les Africains: V*, ed. Charles-André Julien, Magali Morsy, Catherine Coquery-Vidrovitch and Yves Person, Paris: Éditions J. A., 1977, 107-141.

Lacan, Jacques, 'The Youth of Gide, or the Letter and Desire', in *Écrits*, trans. by Bruce Fink, New York and London: W.W. Norton & Company, 2006.

Landau, Paul S. and Deborah D. Kaspin, ed. *Images and Empires: Visuality in Colonial and Postcolonial Africa*, Berkeley, Los Angeles and London: University of California Press, 2002.

Las Casas, Bartolomé de, *In Defense of the Indians*, trans. by Stafford Poole, DeKalb: Northern Illinois University Press, 1992.

Lebovics, Hermann, *True France: The Wars over Cultural Identity, 1900-1945*, Ithaca and London: Cornell University Press, 1992.

Leenhardt, Maurice, 'Rapport général sur l'action coloniale et les mentalités indigènes', in *Congrès International et Intercolonial de la Société Indigène: II*, Paris: École coloniale, 1931, 205-209.

Leistle, Bernhard, 'Introduction', in *Anthropology and Alterity: Responding to the Other*, ed. Bernhard Leistle, New York and London: Routledge, 2017, 1-24.

Lenôtre, G. 'Courrier de l'exposition', *Le Monde illustré*, 1687, 27 July 1889, 51.

L'Estoile, Benoît de, *Le Gout des Autres: De l'Exposition coloniale aux Arts premiers*, Paris: Flammarion, 2007.

Levinas, Emmanuel, *Totality and Infinity: An Essay on Exteriority*, trans. by Alphonso Lingis, Pittsburgh: Duquesne University Press, 1969.

Ligue des Droits de l'Homme, *Le Congrès national de 1931: Compte-rendu sténographique (23-25 mai 1931)*, Paris: Ligue des Droits de l'Homme, 1931.

Loumpet-Galitzine, Alexandra, 'Dieu et le roi: les Bamoun et le protestantisme', in *Njoya et le royaume bamoum: Les archives de la Société des Missions Évangéliques de Paris, 1917-1937*, Paris: Karthala, 2006, 16-33.

—— ed. *Njoya et le royaume bamoum: Les archives de la Société des Missions Évangéliques de Paris, 1917-1937*, Paris: Karthala, 2006.

Lucey, Michael, *Gide's Bent: Sexuality, Politics, Writing*, New York and Oxford: Oxford University Press, 1995.

Lyautey, Hubert, 'Discours', in *Congrès International et Intercolonial de la Société Indigène: II*, Paris: École coloniale, 1931, 15-18.

—— 'Discours de l'ouverture', in *Exposition coloniale internationale et de pays d'outre-mer: Rapport général présenté par le gouverneur général Olivier, délégué général: Tome IV: Vie d'exposition*, Marcel Oliivier, Paris: Imprimerie nationale, 1934, 374-377.

Maclean, Eva, 'Kunst in Kamerun', *Deutsche Kolonialzeitung*, 52/11, 1940: 209-212.

MacPherson, C. B. *The Political Theory of Possessive Individualism: Hobbes to Locke*, Oxford: Clarendon Press, 1962.

Marchand, Théodore Paul, 'Arrêté créant une école d'artisanat à Foumban', *Journal officiel des territoires occupés de l'ancien Cameroun*, 163: 1, 1 March 1927, 133.

—— 'Arrêté portant attribution d'allocation à des chefs indigènes', *Journal officiel des territoires occupés de l'ancien Cameroun*, 332, 15 March 1934, 168-169.

Marc-Vincent, P. 'Cinquante ans d'efforts français en Tunisie', in *Le Livre d'or de l'exposition coloniale internationale de 1931*, Fédération Française des Anciens Coloniaux, Paris: Librairie ancienne Honoré Campion, 1931, 44-45.

Marseille, Musée d'Arts Africains, Océaniens, Amérindiens, *Les dessins bamum*, Marseille and Milan: Skira, 1997.

Martin, Henri, letter to the Directeur de la Société des Missions Évangéliques de Paris, 3 July 1933, extracts in *Njoya et le royaume bamoum: Les archives de la Société des Missions Évangéliques de Paris, 1917-1937*, ed. Alexandra Loumpet-Galitzine, Paris: Karthala, 2006, 340-341.

Marty, Éric, 'Notice' in André Gide, *Journal: I: 1887-1925*, ed. Éric Marty, Paris: NRF, Bibliothèque de la Pléiade, Gallimard, 1996, 1297-1317.

Marx, Karl, *Capital: A Critique of Political Economy*, trans. by Ben Fowkes, Harmondsworth: Penguin Books, 1990.

Marx, Karl, 'The Civil War in France', in *The First International and After: Political Writings, III*, Harmondsworth: Penguin Books, 1992, 143-249.

Marx, Karl, 'The Class Struggles in France: 1848-1850', in *Surveys from Exile: Political Writings, II*, trans. by Paul Jackson, Harmondsworth: Penguin Books, 1992, 35-142.

Marx, Karl, 'The Eighteenth Brumaire of Louis Bonaparte', in *Surveys from Exile: Political Writings, II*, trans. by Paul Jackson, Harmondsworth: Penguin Books, 1992, 143-249.

Masson, Pierre, 'Introduction' in André Gide, André, *Souvenirs et voyages*, ed. Pierre Masson, with Daniel Durosay and Martine Sagaert, Paris: NRF, Bibliothèque de la Pléiade, Gallimard, 2001, xi-xxxv.

Maxwell, Anne, *Colonial Photography and Exhibitions: Representations of the 'Native' and the Making of European Identities*, London and New York: Leicester University Press, 1999.

McEvilley, Thomas, 'Doctor, Lawyer, Indian Chief', *Artforum*, 23, November 1984, 54-60.

Mekouar, Mouna, et al. *Roger Parry: Photographies, dessins, mises en pages*, Paris: Gallimard, 2007.

Moneta, Jacob, *La Politique du Parti communiste français dans la question coloniale, 1920-1963*, Paris: François Maspero, 1971.

Morin, Floriane, 'Mosé Yeyap (1895-1941), cet «eminent révolutionnaire»...', *Totem*, 63, 2013, 6-9.

Morton, Patricia A. *Hybrid Modernities: Architecture and Representation at the 1931 Colonial Exhibition, Paris*, Cambridge, Mass. and London: MIT Press, 2000.

Mouchili, Ismaïla, 'Introduction de la religion musulmane dans la region bamoum', in *Le Royaume Bamoum*, Claude Tardits, Paris: Librairie Armand Colin, 1980, 976.

Naville, Arnold, *Bibliographie des écrits de André Gide*, Paris: Guy Le Prat, 1952.

Nelson, Steven, *From Cameroon to Paris: Mousgoum Architecture in and out of Africa*, Chicago and London: University of Chicago Press, 2007.

New York, Solomon R. Guggenheim Museum, *In/sight: African Photographers, 1940 to the Present*, New York: Abrams, 1996.

Nicod, Henri, *Sur les sentiers de l'Afrique Équatoriale*, Paris: Société des Missions Évangéliques, 1931.

Njimonya, Jean, 'Moïse Yeyap', manuscript in *Njoya et le royaume bamoum: Les archives de la Société des Missions Évangéliques de Paris, 1917-1937*, ed. Alexandra Loumpet-Galitzine, Paris: Karthala, 2006, 161-164.

Njoya, Abraham and Paulo Pepuere, 'Histoire de l'Église bamoun depuis 1905 par les mission-aires de Balle', manuscript in *Njoya et le royaume bamoum: Les archives de la Société des Missions Évangéliques de Paris, 1917-1937*, ed. Alexandra Loumpet-Galitzine, Paris: Karthala, 2006, 138-152.

Njoya, Adamou Ndam, *Le Palais de Foumban: Chef d'oeuvre d'art et d'architecture*, Yaoundé: Éditions Ndam et Raynier, 1975.

Njoya, Ibrahim, *Histoire et coutumes des Bamoum*, trans. by Henri Martin, Paris: Mémoires de l'Insti-tut Français d'Afrique Noire, Centre du Cameroun, 1952.

Oeschner de Coninck, Edouard, 'Lettre addressée au Directeur des Missions de Paris, 5 septembre 1934', manuscript in *Njoya et le royaume bamoum: Les archives de la Société des Missions Évangéliques de Paris, 1917-1937*, ed. Alexandra Loumpet-Galitzine, Paris: Karthala, 2006, 346.

Olivier, Marcel, 'Avant-propos', in *Le Livre d'or de l'exposition coloniale internationale de 1931*, Fédération Française des Anciens Coloniaux, Paris: Librairie ancienne Honoré Campion, 1931, 11.

—— *Exposition coloniale internationale et de pays d'outre-mer: Rapport général présenté par le gouverneur général Olivier, délégué général: Tome I: Conception and organisation*, Paris: Imprimerie nationale, 1933.

—— *Exposition coloniale internationale et de pays d'outre-mer: Rapport général présenté par le gouverneur général Olivier, délégué général: Tome IV: Vie d'exposition*, Paris: Imprimerie nationale, 1934.

—— *Exposition coloniale internationale et de pays d'outre-mer: Rapport général présenté par le gouverneur général Olivier, délégué général: Tome V: Les sections coloniales*, Paris: Imprimerie nationale, 1933.

Paris, Musée du Trocadéro, *Catalogue de l'exposition de la mission au Cameroun de M. H. Labouret*, Paris: Musée du Trocadéro, 1935.

Paudrat, Jean-Louis, 'From Africa', in *"Primitivism" in 20th Century Art: Affinity of the Tribal and Modern*, ed. William Rubin, New York: Museum of Modern Art 1984, 125-175.

Peffer, John, and Elisabeth L. Cameron, ed. *Portraiture and Photography in Africa*, Bloomington: Indiana University Press, 2013.

Peltier, Philippe, 'From Oceania', in *"Primitivism" in 20th Century Art: Affinity of the Tribal and Modern*, ed. William Rubin, New York: Museum of Modern Art, 1984, 99-123.

Perrier, Louis, *Enquête sur les Indigènes*, Montauban: Société des amis des Missions et des indigènes 1909.

Peyrouton, Marcel, 'L'Algérie métropole second', in *Le Livre d'or de l'exposition coloniale international-ale de 1931*, Fédération Française des Anciens Coloniaux, Paris: Librairie ancienne Honoré Campion, 1931, 36-38

Picard, Alfred, *Exposition universelle internationale de 1889 à Paris: Rapport général: II: Travaux de l'Exposition universelle de 1889*, Paris: Imprimerie nationale, 1891

—— *Exposition universelle internationale de 1889 à Paris: Rapport général: IV: Les beaux-arts, l'éducation, l'enseignement, les arts libéraux*, Paris: Imprimerie nationale, 1891.

Podro, Michael, *Depiction*, New Haven and London: Yale University Press, 1998.

Power, Thomas F. Jr. *Jules Ferry and the Renaissance of French Imperialism*, New York: Octagon Books, 1966.

Pratt, Mary Louise, *Imperial Eyes: Travel Writing and Transculturation*, London and New York: Routledge, 1992.

Ranger, Terence, 'The Invention of Tradition in Colonial Africa', in *The Invention of Tradition*, ed. Eric Hobsbawm and Terence Ranger, Cambridge: Cambridge University Press, 1992, 211-262.

Ravenhill, Philip L. 'The Passive Object and the Tribal Paradigm: Colonial Museography in French West Africa', in *African Material Culture*, es. Mary Jo Arnoldi, Christraud M. Geary and Kris L. Hardin, Bloomington and Indianapolis: Indiana University Press, 1996, 265-282.

Rein-Wuhrmann, Anna, *Fumban, die Stadt auf dem Schutte: Arbeit und Ernte im Missionsdienst in Kamerun*, Basel: Basler Missionsbuchhandlung, 1948.

—— *Mein Bamumvolk im Grasland von Kamerun*, Basel: Basler Missionsbuchhandlung, 1925.

Reynaud, Paul, 'Introduction', in *Le Livre d'or de l'exposition coloniale internationale de 1931*, Fédération Française des Anciens Coloniaux, Paris: Librairie ancienne Honoré Campion, 1931, 9.

—— 'Discours de l'ouverture', in *Exposition coloniale internationale et de pays d'outre-mer: Rapport général présenté par le gouverneur général Olivier, délégué général: Tome IV: Vie d'exposition*, Marcel Olivier, Paris: Imprimerie nationale, 1934, 380-385

Richmond, Diane, 'Le quartier réservé de Casablanca', *Nos Regards*, 1, May 1928, n.p.

Roberts, Stephen Henry, *The History of French Colonial Policy: 1870-1925*, London: Cass, 1963.

Ripert, Gaston, 'Une appréciation sur le sultan Njoya', typescript in *Le Royaume Bamoum*, Claude Tardits, Paris: Librairie Armand Colin, 1980, 997-1003.

—— 'Lettre de l'Administrateur des Colonies Ripert de la Circonscription de Dschang à Monsieur le Commissaire de la République, 3 juin 1924', typescript in *Le Royaume Bamoum*, Claude Tardits, Paris: Librairie Armand Colin, 1980, 1004-16.

—— 'Lettre de l'Administrateur Ripert au Sultan Njoya, Foumban, 26 mai 1924', in *Njoya et le royaume bamoum: Les archives de la Société des Missions Évangéliques de Paris, 1917-1937*, ed. Alexandra Loumpet-Galitzine, Paris: Karthala, 2006, 461-464.

Rouillé, André, ed. *La Photographie en France: Textes et controversies, une anthologie 1816-1871*, Paris: Macula, 1989.

Rowlands, Michael, 'Of substances, palaces, and museums: The visible and the invisible in the constitution of Cameroon', *Journal of the Royal Anthropological Institute*, 17, s1 May 2011, 23-38.

Rysselberghe, Maria van, *Les Cahiers de la Petite Dame: Notes pour l'historique authentique d'André Gide, 1918-1929: Cahiers André Gide 4*, Paris: NRF, Gallimard, 1973.

Saint Léon, Pascal Martin, and N'Goné Fall, ed. *Anthology of African and Indian Ocean Photography*, Paris: Revue noire, 1999.

Sarraut, Albert, *Grandeur et servitude coloniales*, Paris: Éditions du sagittaire, Anciennes Éditions Kra, 1931.

—— *La Mise en valeur des colonies françaises*, Paris: Payot, 1923.

—— *Projet de loi portant fixation d'un programme général de mise en valeur des colonies françaises*, No. 2449, Paris: Imprimerie de la Chambre des Députés, 1921.

Sartre, Jean-Paul, *Being and Nothingness: An essay on phenomenological ontology*, trans. by Hazel E. Barnes, London and New York: Routledge, 2003.

—— *Critique of Dialectical Reason*, I, trans. by Alan Sheridan-Smith, London: New Left Books, 1976.

Sekula, Allan, 'The Traffic in Photographs', *Art Journal*, 41: 1, Spring 1981, 15-25.

Segal, Naomi, *André Gide: Pedarasty and Pedagogy*, Oxford: Clarendon 1998.

Sheridan, Alan, *André Gide: A Life in the Present*, London: Hamish Hamilton, 1998.

Sicard, Marie-Louise, 'Écrivains coloniaux... et d'ailleurs', *Les Annales Coloniales*, 2 May 1928, 1.

Snyder, Joel, 'Picturing Vision', *Critical Inquiry*, 6: 3, 1980, 499-526.

Sonnenfeld, Albert, 'André Gide's Congo Journals: A Reappraisal', *L'Esprit créateur*, 1: 1, Spring 1961, 21-28.

Summers, David, *The Judgement of Sense: Renaissance Naturalism and the Rise of Aesthetics*, Cambridge: Cambridge University Press, 1987.

—— *Real Spaces: World Art History and the Rise of Western Modernism*, London: Phaidon Press, 2003.

—— *Vision, Reflection, and Desire in Western Painting*, Chapel Hill: The University of North Carolina Press, 2007.

Taffin, Dominique, 'Le Musée des colonies et l'imaginaire colonial', in *Images et colonies: Iconographie et propagande colonial sur l'Afrique française de 1880 à 1962*, ed. Nicolas Bancel, Pascal Blanchard and Laurent Gervereau, Nanterre and Paris: Bibliothèque de documentation internationale contemporaine and Association Connaissance de l'histoire de l'Afrique contemporaine, 1993, 140-144.

Tagg, John, *The Disciplinary Frame: Photographic Truths and the Capture of Meaning*, Minneapolis: The University of Minnesota Press, 2009.

Tahiti, Musée de Tahiti et des îles, *Roger Parry, 1931: Au-delà du mythe tahitien*, Pirae: Au vent des îles 2006.

Tardits, Claude, 'Un grand dessinateur: Ibrahim Njoya', Marseille, Musée d'Arts Africains, Océaniens, Amérindiens, *Les dessins bamum*, Marseille and Milan: Skira, 1997, 55-57.

—— *L'Histoire singulière de l'art Bamoum, Cameroun*, Paris: Maisonneuve & Larose, 2004.

—— *Le Royaume Bamoum*, Paris: Librairie Armand Colin, 1980.

Taylor, Charles, *Hegel*, Cambridge: Cambridge University Press, 1975.

Taylor, Lucien, ed. *Visualizing Theory: Selected Essays from V.A.R., 1990-1994*, New York and London: Routledge, 1994.

Thieme, Ulrich, and Curtis Becker, ed. *Allgemeines Lexikon der Bildenden Künstler*, 33, Leipzig: Veb E. A. Seemann, no date.

Thirion, André, *Revolutionaries Without Revolution*, trans. by Joachim Neugroschel, London: Cassell, 1975.

Todorov, Tzvetan, *On Human Diversity: Nationalism, Racism, and Exoticism in French Thought*, trans. by Catherine Porter, Cambridge, Mass. and London: Harvard University Press, 1993.

Tolton, C. D. E. *André Gide and the Art of Autobiography: A Study of* Si le Grain ne meurt, Toronto: The Macmillan Company of Canada Ltd., 1975.

Violette, Maurice, 'Discours de M. Violette', in *Le Congrès national de 1931: Compte-rendu sténographique (23-25 mai 1931)*, Ligue des Droits de l'Homme, Paris: Ligue des Droits de l'Homme, 1931, 309-324.

Warehime, Marja, 'Exploring Connections and Rediscovering Difference: Gide *au Congo*', *The French Review*, 68: 3, February 1995, 457-465.

Werth, Léon, 'Croquis d'exposition: Un vieux noir dansait', *Monde*, 169, 29 August 1931, Special number, 3.

—— 'Sur la terre d'Annam', *Monde*, 169, 29 August 1931, Special number, 14.

West, Shearer, *Portraiture*, Oxford and New York: Oxford University Press, 2004.

Woodall, Joanna, ed. *Portraiture: Facing the Subject*, Manchester and New York: Manchester University Press, 1997.

Yeyap, Mosé, 'Histoire des Bamouns', in *Njoya et le royaume bamoum: Les archives de la Société des Missions Évangéliques de Paris, 1917-1937*, ed. Alexandra Loumpet-Galitzine, Paris: Karthala, 2006, 101-128.

Young, Robert J. C. 'Bayart's Broken Kettle', *Public Culture*, 23:1, 2011, 167-175.

Illustration Credits

Index

Numbers in **bold** refer to illustrations